MOONSHOT

aim high, dive deep
live an extraordinary life

Aloha Favorita
I love your
rock-n-roll
spiritual Self.
Keep living your
Moonshot &
allow Magic
always.
My best gift to
you,
♡

Amy Elizabeth Gordon

Amy Elizabeth Gordon MA

BALBOA.
PRESS
A DIVISION OF HAY HOUSE

Balboa Press books may be ordered through booksellers or by contacting:

Balboa Press
A Division of Hay House
1663 Liberty Drive
Bloomington, IN 47403
www.balboapress.com
1 (877) 407-4847

Because of the dynamic nature of the Internet, any web addresses or links contained in this book may have changed since publication and may no longer be valid. The views expressed in this work are solely those of the author and do not necessarily reflect the views of the publisher, and the publisher hereby disclaims any responsibility for them.

The author of this book does not dispense medical advice or prescribe the use of any technique as a form of treatment for physical, emotional, or medical problems without the advice of a physician, either directly or indirectly. The intent of the author is only to offer information of a general nature to help you in your quest for emotional and spiritual well-being. In the event you use any of the information in this book for yourself, which is your constitutional right, the author and the publisher assume no responsibility for your actions.

Print information available on the last page.

ISBN: 978-1-9822-2852-1 (sc)
ISBN: 978-1-9822-2853-8 (e)

Library of Congress Control Number: 2019906930

Balboa Press rev. date: 06/18/2019

Endorsements

Equal parts lyrical, confessional, & practical, Amy Elizabeth vulnerably uses her own journey through addiction and trauma to inspire readers to move beyond limiting beliefs and heal from the past. She offers creative and accessible tools to help cultivate forgiveness, release blame, and connect with something beyond the default us/them binary perspective so often stoked in our polarizing North American culture. If there are aspects of your own past you've felt ashamed of or tried to bury and are looking for a book that's raw enough and real enough to help you integrate more of who you are, explore *Moonshot*. It's full of unexpected gems.

Alicia Muñoz
Author of *No More Fighting: 20 Minutes a Week to a Stronger Relationship*

Moonshot is an elegant and visceral memoir that dares one to question one's own resilience and courage. Indeed, Amy Elizabeth is as transparent as she appears in these pages. Love the interactive curriculum & its usefulness.

Kekuhi Keali'ikanaka'oleohaililani, Trainer
Hālau 'Ōhi'a

Moonshot is music to my 'Best Self' accountability ears. It is a call to action: To stop blaming others, ourselves, life circumstances and to show up better in the world. This is not a fluffy, self-help book filled with rainbows and unicorns — but rather, a transformative heart-opening, teaching memoir wrapped in sage wisdom and a bow of gorgeous prose. Amy Elizabeth Gordon invites us to bear witness to the depths and darkness of her own life journey through addiction and trauma to stand in what's possible — fierce tenderness. Her work is the bridge between despair and repair. It is an invitation for women to 'tenderize' our own hearts and to craft a new heart-centric story, the true story of who we are at our core.

Kristen Noel, Editor-in-Chief, *Best Self Magazine*

Nature did not design us to be alone. Evidence shows that people who enjoy close, fulfilling relationships with others are happier, healthier, and more creative. Moreover, they live longer on average and have a lower incidence of major illnesses such as heart disease and cancer. If this does not prompt you to read Amy Elizabeth Gordon's wonderful *Moonshot*, please reconsider. Highly recommended!

~ Larry Dossey, MD
Author: *One Mind: How Our Individual Mind Is Part of a Greater Consciousness and Why It Matters. Executive Editor: Explore: The Journal of Science and Healing*

What an enchanting, captivating, beautiful, practical (I'm running out of adjectives) book! Based in personal experience and penetrating prose, *Moonshot* lays out a magnificent program for closer, more nourishing relationships. This book is meant for anyone who needs more love, empathy, and compassion in their life -- and who doesn't? Let Amy Elizabeth Gordon be your guide to a richer, deeper commitment -- not just to others, but to the world.

~ Barbara Montgomery Dossey, RN, PhD, FAAN
Author: *Florence Nightingale: Mystic, Visionary, Healer; Holistic Nursing: A Handbook for Practice; Nurse Coaching, Integrative Approaches for Health and Wellbeing.*

Dedication

This book is dedicated to my Dad, lover of birds and sunrise and poetry. He taught me to prepare for a slight change in temperature or a sudden rain storm, and how to test the brakes on a car. He advised me to quit looking busy for busyness sake, slow down, and smell the roses.

Grateful for the warmth of his heart and the poetry of his soul, I also felt his anguish. Life being both beautiful and terrifying, he introduced me to both the magic of sunrise as well as the dark night of the soul. He suffered from heart disease and regrets. I pushed at the stickiness of his torment gingerly with my small hands, and for a time, I was stuck.

To me, his youngest child and only daughter, he embodied the Albert Camus quote, "In the midst of winter, I found there was, within me, an invincible summer. And that makes me happy. For it says that no matter how hard the world pushes against me, within me, there's something stronger – something better, pushing right back."

If it is true that the unlived lives of the parents have the greatest influence on the child, as Carl Jung once stated, then my Dad's unmet desires, for big love, beauty in nature, thriving health, connected families, published books, and world travel, these all influence me greatly.

My father died of heart disease. I dedicate this book to him. I vow to heal broken heartedness, heart dis-ease, in our American culture, in the world at large. My come from is holistic—healing relationships by igniting compassion, generosity, and transformation for a united world. Heart-centric awareness propels me on my moonshot to be source for transformation. I do this with generosity and grace, as I have learned to slow down, enjoy beauty, and live an extraordinary life. Thank you, Dad.

I know the deep peace of the beauty of the present moment. So, Dear Reader, do you.

Acknowledgments

Thank you to those who generate awareness and truly live a heart-centric life.

Thank you to my many mentors and teachers over the years, my sponsors and sponsees, and my clients, for inspiring me to be my best and walk my talk.

Thank you to Kekuhi, my *kumu*, my teacher of Hawai'i lifeways. You rock my world into another dimension entirely. *Mahalo nui loa*, great big thanks.

Thank you to Sam Cudney, my editor, for your patience, humor, and encouragement. Thank you to my coaches and guides along the way: Laura Burkhart, Nikki Van De Car at kn literary arts, Sage Adderley -Knox at Sage's Blog Tours, and all the beta readers and supporters of this mighty endeavor. I have the utmost respect for anyone who completes a book, particularly a memoir; the story never ends.

Thank you to my extended family and friends circling the world. I would not be who I am without you in my life. Yes, you.

Thank you to Kath & Jim, Mima & Pop Pop, for being an active part of our family. Your generosity, participation, and kindness provide us the perfect environment in this peaceful tropical paradise to grow our wholesome family. Really, what could be better for our boys than having adoring grandparents living under the same roof?

Thank you, Mom. Words cannot express my devotion to you. Your strength and tenderness combined with your smarts and creativity fill me to over-flowing.

Thank you to TEAM. My deepest and most profound gratitude to Toby, Everett, Amy (yes, that's me) and Marc. Goodness me, my beloved family, what would I do, who would I be without you? I'm glad I don't have to entertain that thought another second. When I asked you recently what would make our relationship a 10 on the extraordinary scale, you said, "show up more." I am committed to moving the needle from an 8, which is pretty darn good, to a 10, with my presence and my state of being.

Thank you, Marc, especially for sharing the food you lovingly prepare, the books you read to me, the pleasure you bring to me, the healing you patiently afford me, and the stellar commitment of a being a Renaissance Man. You are the King to my Queendom. From paternity leave to household mastery, your creative spirit shines brightly as the seed bed of our success. My best quality of love to you always.

Thank you, Great Spirit of the Universe, the source of sweet, succulent sustenance, for guiding me, always, back to love. Source sources me.

Table of Contents

Acknowledgments...ix
Introduction xiii

Part I: What it was like

Realm of Resilience.. 1

Chapter One: Trust..7
Chapter Two: Focus 21
Chapter Three: Repair 29
Chapter Four: Faith 39

Part II: What happened

Realm of Core Compassion 61

Chapter Five: Clarity.. 65
Chapter Six: Openness 79
Chapter Seven: Reactivation...99
Chapter Eight: Energy 117

Part III: What it's like now

Realm of Service 137

Chapter Nine: Interdependence 141
Chapter Ten: Responsibility 161
Chapter Eleven: Generosity...191
Chapter Twelve: Consciousness 233

Appendix I: Resistance 261
Appendix II: Daily Tender Job Description...................263
Appendix III: 'olelo Hawai'i-The Hawaiian Language... 265
Appendix IV: The Do's & Don'ts of Evolution............... 267
Appendix V: Cultivate C.O.R.E. Compassion.............. 269
Appendix VI: Portals of Deep Connection 271

Introduction

We aim for the moon.

We dive to the bottom of the ocean.

We integrate the unconscious with the conscious, and in this process, we become whole.

If you've been through hell and don't want to go back, if you're tired of questioning your belonging and worthiness and are ready to surrender to success, or if you're a social pioneer on the leading edge of evolutionary consciousness, welcome.

This is my promise: if you open your heart, drop the stones of resentment from your heart, and cover your heart with love, you will receive benefit.

This transformational memoir is a guide to do that. It is the real, raw, and vulnerable me, inviting you to cross the bridge to the neighborhood of my mind --some places horrifying and dark, and others electrifying and bright.

I invite you into my story, my world, the truth as I know it today, as a way to inspire you to look at your own story, to enter your own world more fully in order to integrate into your wholeness, as a heart-centric and conscious person.

This is a benefit-oriented book. My declaration is that we claim our moonshot for an extraordinary life by super-charging our life with twelve core distinctions and cultivating resilience, compassion and service.

The world needs us, basically, to get over ourselves, heal the heart hurts, and live tenderly, powerfully, and generously.

Why we are doing this is because when we thrive, our families thrive. My husband and I provide fertile soil of love, presence, tenderness to those beloveds who live with us, our boys and his parents. When we tend to this landscape, this space between, these relationships in our lives, we are indeed healing the planet. Our landscapes thrive when we eliminate indoor pollution of negativity and embody fierce tenderness.

We can thrive as humans and rebuild healthy ecosystems around us, and we cannot evolve alone. We cannot know love in our minds, rather, we feel it in our hearts, and see it in our actions.

Everything is connected.

I'm enjoying more than 24 years as a sober woman of integrity, in active recovery from alcoholism and other things that leak my energy and rob me of the beauty of the present moment. My husband and I blazed nearly two decades together thus far; living, loving and learning daily. For more than 30 years I have practiced yoga and meditation as touchstones to guide me to the glory of the present moment.

I engage in revolutionary relationships and an extraordinary life. I have the great good fortune of helping others dwell in the space of aloha, deep love and compassion, as I coach them how to cultivate core compassion and enjoy holistic heart health. Living in Hawai'i is incredibly conducive to living in the heart by the very nature of aloha.

We are all wounded in relationships, and it is in relationships that we heal. The wake-up call of our times, what I refer to as the SOS of our times, is putting love into action and healing the relationships with Self, Other, and Spirit. This is aloha for me.

My offering here is to help solve the growing epidemic of heart dis-ease. This is a contemplative journey, not a medical exploration. By holding ourselves accountable, without being too tight that we carry the weight of the world on our shoulders, or being too loose that we become disheartened and apathetic, we can look at heart health from a relational perspective. I have altered minor details of my life narrative in the interest of preserving anonymity, but the substance remains.

The results for you, Dear Reader, should you engage with the material, include clarity of mind, openness of heart, rekindling of spirit, and energizing of life force.

No longer willing to manufacture my own suffering, I'm compelled to show you, how to do the same.

The stories and suggestions that follow are the fat quarters of my life quilted together with the stitches of aloha and addictions recovery, relationship healing, and contemplative practices. May this book inspire you with warmth and comfort, as my mother's handmade quilt, complete with a traditional Hawaiian echo stitch, provides me.

Here's what we do: we explore the 12 distinctions of extraordinary living: trust, focus, repair, faith, clarity, openness, reactivation, energy, interdependence, responsibility, generosity, and consciousness. The spine of each chapter consists of six sentence stems which serve as an invitation for you to write your own life story.

Where I'm from...

As I'm sitting here, I'm experiencing...

Where I'd like to be...

What matters most...

One thing I can do to get me there...

One thing I appreciate...

The first four distinctions have to do with recognizing our resilience: trust, focus, repair, and faith. What is was like for me was tough and tender: parents' divorce, trauma, drunkenness; I now see how resilience, the ability to thrive despite negative circumstances, is vital. It is the foundation for a quality of connection with others. It allows compassion to grow.

In the next four distinctions, we move into the realm

of compassion and the core concepts of clearing your mind, opening your heart, reactivating your spirit and energizing your life. We are compassionate beings who long to be of service. Developing compassion for self is crucially important. When we can fully and completely love and accept ourselves on a deep level all things are possible. We can then upgrade the quality of love in all of our relationships. With our spouse, our children, our vocation, our money, our landscape, our communities. All relationships can be a 10 on a scale of 0-10, from nothing to extraordinary.

We live an extraordinary life in order to be happy, sure, but also to be of service. To be Source for a transformed world. When I reach my hand out to a young woman struggling to stay sober, I am helping not only her, but her daughter, her mother, her dog she neglects, her neighbors that she drives by while drunk or sober, her garden that she forgets to water when she is hungover. I am also helping me to stay sober, to remember what it was like. We have to give it away to keep it. We cannot transmit something we haven't got. These recovery sayings keep my recovery alive. It is not something I graduate from and in fact I still go to meetings after over 8,888 days of sobriety.

Choosing responsibility over reactivity is high level functioning and it feels better than any drunk or high I ever experienced. After all, I drank to calm the tension, to quell the feeling of being out of control by truly losing control and absolving myself of responsibility. I am responsible. For being a sober woman of integrity. For choosing aloha over fear and trouble of any kind. For stepping into my contract with myself as a tender, powerful, generous woman.

From this place, I feel very full, satiated, resourced. And I have so much to give. In the past, I waited until I felt good to be of service to others. Now I know that serving others is the ticket to feeling good. I had the equation backwards. I was waiting for time to show me some better thoughts. I was waiting to feel motivated to move toward my vision. I was waiting to feel better before serving.

Dear Reader, join me as we traverse the longest journey of them all—from the dark neighborhoods of the contracted egoic mind to the stunning expansive vistas of the open and tender heart.

Let us begin.

Soulmate Prayer

God, Guide me closer to you,
Strengthen my intuitive knowledge of your presence
within me.
Let this knowledge fill me with everlasting love and joy.
Remove from me confusion and doubt,
and Allow me to be at Deep Peace with what Is.
God, you are my Soulmate,
I need not look beyond you
for my Salvation.
Source, source me.

~Amy Elizabeth Gordon, Denver, 1994

Part I: What it was like

Realm of Resilience

resilience-ordinary definition:
the capacity to recover quickly from difficulties; toughness

resilience-extraordinary definition:
the capacity to transform hurt into opportunity; tenderness

Grief and resilience live together.
~Michelle Obama, Becoming

Picture the meat tenderizer mallet in my mom's hands. Hear the thud of the mallet on the steaks on the counter. Again. The swinging and pounding of the mallet repeats, tenderizing the meat. The mallet penetrates deeply. It looks dangerous, but its purpose is to tenderize, to penetrate deeply, to make the tough meat palatable. As so it is with memoir. Thoroughly overcooked, my story sits, dried and tough. My past is marbled with drama and trauma; unappetizing yet intricately laced in the meat of the story.

Believe me, I tried to digest it all; I chewed and chewed, yet the blob stayed in my mouth, gag-reflex triggered. The undigested, flavorless meat, grey and unappetizing, bothersome at best.

I spit it into a paper napkin and throw it away; yet there is no away. Not with our life stories. They can clog our arteries and hurt us, or they give us the choice to tenderize our hearts and fertilize the space between.

"Tell me about despair, yours, and I will tell you mine," Mary Oliver reminds us.

It all started as a moonshot.

Summers in Florida are hot. Period.

July of 1969, no exception. The forecast called for humidity, but no thunderstorms, a crucial piece of data for determining the moonshot. JFK's imperative that man gets to the moon by the end of the decade generated internal heat for beings around the world. This heat, for many, had the flavor of mind-blowing, exhilarating optimism, and infinite potentialities. For others, the heat took on a more negative charge; resentment that funds went upward toward visionary aims instead of dealing with domestic issues down on Earth like poverty and crime, down here in America.

Thankfully, my parents, gathered with family and friends on the coast of Florida, celebrated the moonshot. They were in the exhilarated camp. This was indeed extraordinary.

Dad got the coals ready on the Coleman BBQ while mom

pounded the meat tenderizer on the steaks. Steaks meant celebration. The neighbor, Susan, shucked the ears of fresh picked Zellwood corn. Always around, always helpful, Susan prepared the sides and desserts. More butter needed, always more butter needed, Susan and butter were hand in hand. My mom prepared the main dish. Everyone brought the booze.

My parents had, at this time, four children, ages 10 and under, who ran down the beach, lighting fireworks and getting high off the energetic buzz of excitement that historic night of the first lunar landing. The moon, symbolic of the unconscious, loomed high in the sky, no longer a hope and a wish.

We were, collectively, bridging the conscious with the unconscious. This took place at a pivotal time. The moonshot, the Apollo mission, was "the result of thorough research carried out by a successful team, whose strength rises from a common thought made up of simple ideas, growing and coming together in one dream, yours and ours." I came across this description on an ordinary clothing tag recently, but it sums up most worthwhile endeavors in life.

It takes more than me. Simple ideas, common thought.

The late 60s in American history, full of swirling energies of change and possibilities, the fertile ground for greater consciousness, was the birthplace of the moonshot, both for Neil Armstrong and for my conception. Suspended in a moment pregnant with possibilities, my parents consummated this joy. The backdrop of the American culture, so promising and inspiring, had a moment to shine. Those in power advocated overcoming scarcity, fear, and negativity, and finding common ground. This climate of greater consciousness, of human advancement, bathed my parents as they made love.

The backdrop of my conception is creative non-fiction. I don't know if they ate steaks the night man landed on the moon, but it certainly goes with the meat tenderizer concept. And you know what? It doesn't matter. It works. It works because tenderizing my heart makes for a more palatable offering.

3

Where I'd like to be is offering you a tender, juicy, tasty offering of a life worth living, in order to inspire you to see, in case you haven't already, that your life is worth living, extraordinarily so. I do not have to keep chewing the bland steak, the old overcooked story.

Where I'm from, I tethered myself back to the reality and power of love.

As I'm sitting here, a tender, powerful, generous woman, my history, my story, sits before me. My heart opens wider to a heart-centric life. I consciously choose to tenderize my heart on a daily basis, to cover it with love, and let that love spill out and make a mess. Tears come with tenderizing, and usually a good bit of snot, and sometimes an imploding headache. I take a deep breath and remember the wisdom of my body. The body speaks my mind, releases the pinch of constriction, lets the blood flow freely to the sore spots, feels it to heal it, and releases any issues stored in my tissues. I thank my body by taking another deep breath.

What matters most is embracing the magic of choosing love over drama, or as we say in Hawai'i, choosing *aloha* over *pilikia*, trouble of any kind. In the past, the troubles dominated my mental real estate, taking up the scenic landscape with high-rise pillars of doom. I lost sight of the clouds, the birds, the beautiful sunrise that happens every day without fail. In the past, what it was like was I was adrift, spinning out of control at times while exerting control in a grasping, constricting way. I trusted everything and then nothing. Trust bled to mistrust and I landed in a psychological hell realm.

One thing I can do is recognize I am 100% responsible for my life's story, and as such, be source for a transformed world. I can integrate what happened in my life and see how my experience does not define me.

One thing I appreciate is that I'm on this incredible journey, this opportunity to live an extraordinary life of love, connection and commitment. I can get out of those scary places in my mind more quickly and with more grace than ever before. And truthfully, I don't enter them as often as I used to.

This is what it was like. Losing trust in myself, unable to focus on what mattered most, creating wreckage and losing faith in the carefree feeling of youth. My adolescence fostered resilience in me. Resilience of staying alive, strengthening my soul and returning to love, despite trying experiences that tested my trust.

Chapter One: **Trust**

---

trust-ordinary definition:
firm belief in the ability or strength of someone or something

trust-extraordinary definition:
undeniable belief in the inherent worth and dignity within
each of us

Darkness cannot drive out darkness:
only light can do that.
Hate cannot drive out hate:
only love can do that.
~Martin Luther King, Jr.

Racism is a heart disease, and it's curable.
~Ruth King

Mustard Yellow Sweater

My husband wakes me this morning, with a gentle nudge, a whisper, and a wooden tray plated with hot breakfast, his renewed love affair with an immortal 100- year-old sourdough starter made into pan-a-cakes, as our younger son calls them. Breakfast in bed is a beloved statement in the language of our marriage, definitely overshadowing the oft-forbidden act of waking me up. My pillow over my head past sunrise tells him that this is an unusual day.

Normally on a Monday, I would be returning from a sunrise paddle with an outrigger canoe on the mighty Pacific. Today, I sleep in. It is January 30th, a date etched in memory, and my husband knows this, too, and he wants to show his loving presence to me on this day. His being here, his very presence in my life, helps bring light to my mind's neighborhood of dark trauma memories.

Some years I think about this particular date well in advance; some years I completely forget. Current events, both near and far, certainly provide fertilizer for this memory to blossom annually, or not.

As I'm sitting here I'm experiencing wild winds whipping across the land, wrathful men wielding power in the White House, and fear is flooding my homeland. All of these conditions, independently and most certainly collectively, spike my nervous system radar to high alert. I notice the caution in my inhale, the creeping dread in my exhale. I notice life events wrestling with my serenity.

The sun rises, once again, and, so too, do I.

I rise to the memory of this day: January 30th, many moons ago, back in 1986. Even though it's been over thirty years, I still remember what I was wearing the night I was raped, the night I lost my virginity.

Where I'm from is that this night, January 30th, is the night in which I, the 15-year-old adventuresome girl, fell directly into the pit of guilt. Perhaps I inherited this guilt from my ancestors. The story I make up about the legacy of guilt around sexuality is that it hurts and haunts me. Sinning feels like shit. Feeling guilty about sinning feels like hell.

This guilt is what I imagine my mother experienced because she got pregnant with me while on the pill. The guilt is what I imagine my grandmother experienced after abusive interactions with her husband, which she drank to excess in order to escape. The guilt is what I imagine my great-grandmother experienced while she struggled with finding her voice, owning her passion, and settling her boundaries. These powerful women felt the pinch of dominant culture: *Women, look good, be quiet, and serve men.*

On this night, I felt the pinch, the cramping, the blood.

How many times had I obliged to the rhythm of the weekly religious rituals and recited the difficult sentiment, "I am not worthy, but only say the word and I shall be healed." The unworthiness which I had previously recited by rote memory, before I really even understood what I was saying, now actually made some sense. *I am not worthy...*

The physiological dread, deep in the pit of my belly, of feeling less-than worthy and living in a daily hell as a dreadful sinner haunted me for decades into my adulthood. This guilt, that feeling that I had done something wrong, festered into toxic shame, the feeling I was something wrong. This guilt, coupled with my insatiable quest for healing, thus formed the foundation of my experience of reality during many chapters of my early life: I thought I was broken; that I needed to be fixed.

Just as all four my brothers were ready to launch into school regularly, and my mom could get back to work, I arrived on the scene. I wasn't truly abandoned, but some part of me felt unwanted, though I know my family would never admit to that, that was the story I made up about why I spent so much time alone. I've spent decades worrying and tried so hard to change or fix myself, to be seen, to be gotten, to not be alone.

Moonshot

Work and loyalty to work ate up lots of my parents' time and energy. My brothers were much older and mostly out of the house, not hanging at home with a young sister. The oldest brother had been in the military, next brother off to college, next brother disappeared, and then reappeared with consistent irregularity, and the youngest brother was busy with sports and friends.

My parents were divorced and really had no idea what was going on with me. On the outside, I looked good. Prior to my rape, I was a beach loving surfer girl. I got good grades. I smiled. After, the darkness crept into my life and my bowl of light spilled, I didn't smile as much. And as the blackouts from drinking blotted out space on the calendar, I dressed in black, dyed my hair, wore white face makeup, and black lipstick. I vividly recall getting my school photos taken in high school and the photographer saying I was too pale to show up on the photograph. I was a ghost to myself. I still got good grades, yet I was hurting. My soul suffered. No one saw me. I felt invisible. I didn't let people take photos of me, unless mandatory, as above story denotes. I didn't tell them what was going on; I didn't want (to cause) trouble.

In my silence, I was abandoned by innocence, and Self, and wedded to guilt, shame, bewilderment, and despair. Lent, came soon after my rape. Even that couldn't save my soul. I gave up alcohol. I gave up drugs. I gave up fooling around in general. For thirty-nine days, I repented. Yet in my core, I didn't believe it was enough to save me from going to Hell. On the fortieth night, the night before Easter, I got drunk again. I was raped, again, that night, by another guy from the punk rock scene.

As I look back on these major life events with wrinkles of wisdom wrapping around my eyes to give me a greater perspective, I don't think I really believed, in my soul, that I was a sinner. Rather, I was a confused, lost, young girl who had definitely severed contact with her inner guidance system, who didn't open up to others to get help, who blamed and shamed and critized others, and who subsequently compromised her morals. Doing things drunk I wouldn't have done sober, I was a ghost of my true self. Period.

I don't remember the exact temperature this night in Florida, but it must have been one of those rare chilly evenings because I was wearing a sweater, an itchy sweater. A mustard yellow sweater. I don't remember seeing the waning crescent moon or the myriad of stars above me that night in the downtown alley. But I imagine now that they were there, as they consistently are, just like my spirit guards, my angels, whether I see them or not. Sometimes I wonder if they were off-duty that night, yet **where I'd like to be** is with a deep faith that they really are always present; I just occasionally lose conscious contact with them. These spirit guards are the angels of my ancestors, known and unknown, my intrinsic connection to the web of life.

I don't remember if my eyes were open or not, I was in an alcohol and drug induced blackout, not yet passed out — blacked out, experiencing life but not consciously partaking in it or remembering it. Afterwards, I went through the motions of my life, but my memory couldn't log it and my psyche pulled my soul away— in some ways it is almost like it never happened to me.

It did happen.

I remember what I was wearing the night I was raped. A mustard yellow sweater. The black and white tight pants, a find from the Salvation Army thrift shop. A black lacy babushka scarf covering my hair. Steel-toed shoes, Doc Martens, and the Goodwill mustard yellow sweater. Funny, that goodwill and salvation covered me, in this moment of despair.

I do remember at the beginning of this fateful night, I partied with a girlfriend, raiding her mother's booze pantry. She lived on a dirt road in the undeveloped land between where my mother and my father lived. Land that today is full of pavement and structures and fenced-in retention ponds serving as reservations for the displaced natives. These woefully inadequate and sad pockets of nature—home to birds, turtles and 'gators—are miniatures of the wild swamps that once dominated the landscape.

This is yet another manifestation of the dominant culture's notion of us and them.

She was older, crazier, and determined to push life to the edge. She brought me along and we careened right up to it on more than one occasion. We sped through burgeoning suburbia on our way to downtown.

I remember the hard liquor, Seagram's Seven (or was it Southern Comfort), cheap beer, Coors, illegal drugs, cocaine and marijuana, and loud music, Peter Gabriel's *Sledgehammer.*

My brothers didn't notice I wasn't home on a school night, they were probably out themselves. My parents didn't notice my drinking over the last year; they were working. Mom once asked why I had so many liquor bottles on my window sill. I lied by telling the partial truth and told her they were there for holding candles and incense. I did have candles in them, and I drank them first. I didn't tell her that.

Did she believe me? Did she believe the middle school pledge we both signed about staying away from alcohol? I don't know. What I know is that alcohol was omnipresent in my life. And my family didn't seem to know.

She drank.

He drank.

They drank.

It was a way of life, our way of life.

Why wouldn't I?

Southern Comfort provided the anesthetizing effects for living in the South, but not comfort. Coors beer provided the ritual of fitting in, holding a can like everyone else did—an ersatz sense of belonging. I hated beer. I also hated fitting in. Yet the feeling I hated even more was loneliness.

Social lubrication of mind-altering substances temporarily evaporated my loneliness.

The lines of cocaine provided an exponential high followed by a plummeting low. The dangerous thrills of this behavior took the normal roller coaster of teenage life to precarious levels. Coke numbed my mouth and raced my heart. I could have died doing drugs. I was living so high the few times I did coke I didn't care about danger. Death seems impossible when you feel invincible.

Pot, silly, stupid, stinking marijuana, attempted to calm my belly and convince me chips and hand-pumped cheese stuff from a convenience store tasted good. My friends tried to dry their wet weed in the microwave in the 7/11.

It didn't work.

And the drugs and booze didn't work. They didn't get me where I wanted to go. Where I wanted to go was away from the chaos of my mind. The substances worked momentarily, temporarily casting the illusion of escape. But the next day inevitably brought more chaos. As I chased the next high or drunk, I was like a snake eating its own tail. But I kept trying them. The insanity of doing the same thing over and over again, expecting different results.

I was a smart kid doing stupid things, like many kids. We partied in a vacuous culture void of substance yet full of material goods. On January 30th of that year I was a punk. An anarchist. The years prior I was the innocent surfer girl, I wanted to party and feel good. That didn't work out too well, and as the trauma stockpiled, so did the white cake powder on my face, the dark eye make-up and lipstick as well as the black clothes on my skin.

My body spoke my mind. It ached and screamed and pushed and pulled.

Anxiety coursed through me from head to toe, even under the fog of booze dampening it down. Adolescent hormones hijacked my brain and then succumbed to the onslaught of the stimulants and depressants. The drugs and booze silenced the still small and powerfully innocent voice which screamed in protest.

"No."

"Stop."

"That hurts."

"I don't want to."

No one heard.

Earlier in the evening of that January 30th, the pumping music of the latest hit rattled my bones as we danced. We were out on a school night, at a nightclub. We danced, our bodies moving wildly, unabashedly, and free. We laughed, wildly, unabashedly, and freely.

The glaze of the mid-life malaise I had witnessed in my parents, and desperately wanted to avoid in my own life, had yet to descend. I felt omnipotent. I felt invincible. I thought I could see clearly what was wrong with the world and therefore could and should solve the world's problems.

I've always wanted to save the world. Even at 15, at a dance club, I could barely save myself. So what did I do after I wrote the scholarship winning essays about how I would bring about world peace? I danced. I partied. I got fucked. I became powerless.

The bouncer smiled at me. He always did. His eyes looked me up and down and up again. He knew before I did that my body was currency. How I looked brought with it a false sense of command. He didn't seem to notice that I had walked in and then stumbled out, he was busy flirting with someone else, trying to put her hoop earring in his ear. What self-control and power I had in that moment turned off when the booze and drugs coursed through my veins, deluded my mind and weakened my volition. I was powerless.

The powerful effects produced by these substances was still a fairly new experience for me, one that I found wildly exciting. I gave myself to them. I got on the wild ride of intoxication. I didn't give myself willingly to the events that followed, yet I was locked in on the ride, the invisible safety bar tightening in my lap like a rollercoaster, preventing me from getting off.

Friends spilled out of the club. I walked down an alley, downtown. The punk rockers and skinheads were there, partying. Here, I wasn't invisible. I was wanted. Or so it seemed.

Invisibility faded. That night my mom did notice me. She saw how my friends carried me into the kitchen, for I was unable to walk. The vomit was caked in my babushka and hair as well as my mustard sweater. I was there, but not really there. In a blackout, the details fuzzy, the buffer enormous.

The surrender to intoxicants was sweet. That first taste of oblivion hooked me. I could not be responsible for what happened to me. The pressure valve popped in a fleeting moment of release. My sense of self, a veritable pent-up cooker of deep-seated love, confusing sticky emotions and intensely wild experiences disintegrated into the soup of inherited guilt and cultural dysfunction. The floaty feeling of watching my life from a safe distance during the first few drinks is what I have now come to call disembodied drunkenness. For the next decade of debauchery, it became home.

The hangover was another story; it was hell—head imploding, gut exploding. I awoke January 31st to splayed phone wires in my bedroom from where my mother had ripped it out of the wall in her fit of anger when she discovered the state I was in when I got home. The note from my Mom said I was grounded for the first time, ever. I didn't tell my mom I was raped. We didn't talk about what happened that evening. Decades would pass before we finally did.

On January 31st, I called him from the phone in the family room with the super long cord that reached into my room and asked him what happened. He laughed. I ached. He said, "You don't remember?" Not only was he a dick that night, he was a morning-after dick. He was also a skinhead. A bald, tattooed, burley-assed white-supremacist who happened to be out of jail that weekend and not performing with his band. He took my purity. Without my permission.

The blood caked between my legs hurt to scrub away. My pussy ached. I knew the guy; therefore, I didn't call it rape. Didn't it have to be unwanted sex with a stranger to be called rape? For years I thought of this night as *the night I lost my virginity*. It wasn't until working with my third psychotherapist, a somatic specialist, the one that helped me focus on my body and its inherent wisdom, that I named it for what it was. Rape.

What did my mind do with that? It told me *I loved him* and attempted to make the irrational somehow rational. In its ever-present effervescence, my heart convinced me *he loved me*. His penetration kidnapped part of my soul. How would I get my soul back?

The answer for me has always been love, originating at the most center of my innocence, the birthplace of my integrity, and the heart home of my soul. This formed a pattern of coping, woven with the notion that loving you is hurting me, but I over-rode the hurt. I thought I deserved it the punishment and perhaps I could love my way out of the abuse.

Love can heal the hurt.

Even when the sexual abuse happened again, this time with a Polaroid photo capturing naked shots of my chest in front of his gang, as he held my arms pinned back and ignored my protestations, the obscurations of my mind told me it was love.

I was tied to him. Tethered. Caught.

Perhaps because he had taken a part of me, and taken part of me apart, and I wanted it back and I wanted to be whole again. Over the years I worked with shamans to retrieve my soul, somatic therapists to heal my body, mind, and spirit, massage therapists to release muscle tension, and deeply spiritual work reclaiming the body erotic, to regain my innate capacity for sexual pleasure.

One thing I can do to heal resentment and drop the stones from my heart, those heavy and hard knots of confusion and pain, is to no longer rationalize relationships with men who hurt me or who hold opposing values. Not going contort myself to take it. I see, in the global perspective, that evil men have taken purity. Violent men have taken peace. Disturbed men have taken harmony. And I wanted it back. I did. I do. I can. I have. So can others whose heart longs to heal, to be whole, to love all. I no longer engage in the energetic exchange of abuse, when loving you is hurting me.

What matters most is forgiveness. I could never bring myself to hate him. I turned this hateful and violent act against myself and drank alcoholically for a decade. This violent overthrow of my power merged maliciously with my powerlessness over alcohol. I spent ten years blaming myself, before I got to forgiveness. I had always known, from the depths of my heart and the from the essence of my childhood religion, that hate breeds more hate and I didn't want to breed hate, even though I was raped by a hater. I just didn't recognize how cunning and powerful my self-hate disguised itself in my drinking behavior.

One thing I appreciate is that anger had become one of my teachers. This natural and powerful energy deserves my respect and guides me to set boundaries. And always return to love. We work together to do what needs to be done, namely, for me, that's staying sober, setting boundaries, and helping others.

It's still January 30th, now over thirty years later. I'm still in bed. I finish the pan-a-cakes and coffee that my beloved brought to me. All day I smell maple syrup in the house. The sweetness around me is real. I savor it. I cherish the fidelity I share with my devoted husband. I relish the absence of hate. I honor the commitment I have made to recovery from alcoholism. I heal my body, my mind, and my spirit each time I release the grip, forgive myself for my past, learn from my experiences, and grow my understanding of grace.

Where I'm from, we watched the TV screen fade to static after the late-night news, bright transmission segued to dark with a fuzzy mass of black and white dots racing all over the screen. I was rarely awake at this late hour, but when I was, I heard the chiding comments of my brothers, "Who do you think is gonna win?" At an early age I learned about competition, about us and them, about black and white, and to some people, it was funny. I grew up in the south. Not overtly taught to hate; rather, I was brought up in the culture of "us and them." Notice the differences; judge.

Yet my innocent little girl noticed the other kids in my class with the same last name, the same laughter, the same hula-hooping. I felt their hearts beat like mine.

We have the same last name, *aren't we family?* I mused, but could never utter the words.

As I'm sitting here, I'm experiencing deep acceptance for what happened, a lack of negativity such as outrage or regret, and a genuine desire to see how my experience can benefit others.

Where I'd like to be is living in a cultural understanding that we are them. Or, to put it simply, to let go of the notion of "us and them." There is no "out there" out there.

What matters most is the ability to trust. In the most extraordinary sense of the word, I trust the inherent worth and dignity in each and every human being. Some call this brilliant sanity or basic goodness. It is there and it's my job to see it and reflect it back to whomever I'm interacting with at the moment.

One thing I can do to get there is to come home to myself with trust. I can do this when I'm tethered back to myself with love, and by not abandoning myself. Simply taking a deep breath and putting my hand on my heart returns me home to myself.

One thing I appreciate is the inherent power in trust. This power comes from a core of tenderness and emptiness. Emptiness has no room for judgment or hate. What it does have is vast potential for transformation, healing heart hurt, and holding the love inside all of us to become more conscious.

The first distinction of an extraordinary life is trust. In the past, I didn't trust others and I didn't trust myself. Now I can say with conviction, I trust myself not to abandon myself. I won't give up, I won't back down. I'm going all in for the mind-blowing capacity of love to heal heart dis-ease and transform the world.

I trust you to not abandon yourself.

A Blessing to Come Home to Yourself

May all that is unforgiven in you
Be released.
May your fears yield
Their deepest tranquilities.
May all that is unlived in you
Blossom into a future
Graced with love.

~John O'Donohue, To Bless the Space Between Us

Chapter Two: Focus

focus-ordinary definition:
the center of interest or activity

focus-extraordinary definition:
laser love on the center of interest

We seldom realize, for example, that our most private thoughts and emotions are not actually our own. For we think in terms of languages and images which we did not invent, but which were given to us by our society.
~Alan Watts

Psychic Violence

In the past, I drank too many tequila shots and walked, or rather stumbled, into a dark neighborhood, an upscale neighborhood we called the Duck Pond Area. Stumbling by myself, on the way to a punk rock show at the community hall, I was 16, just over a year past my mustard yellow sweater alley trauma. My other girlfriends who were with me had already passed out from too much booze, and so I was alone, for the moment.

The bands Psychic Violence, Agnostic Front, and Corrosion of Conformity filled out the line-up. The rapist, the one whose collect calls I accepted from jail, the one for whom I bought Christmas presents, the one I thought I loved, was already at the show with my other skinhead "friends."

Where I'm from, I was looking for love and longing for belonging, I tried to fit into the *scene*, as we called it then. I struggled because I didn't quite *hate* the way they did, the way they sang about their hate made my skin crawl, the way they treated others made my blood boil. To put it mildly, they behaved badly. It's likely I drank even more to blur out my intolerance of their intolerance. The tequila shots numbered in the teens, I lost count. *Tequila, to kill ya*, we laughed as we got wasted.

Secretly, I hoped none of them noticed my lack of hate.

Drunk. Confused. Alone. This was a popular refrain in the teenage anthem of my mind. Fast-fury of blurry activity. Slow-motion of frozen fear. Back and forth, I floated. That night, on the way to a punk rock show featuring Psychic Violence, I endured it. A black Camaro swerved over, parked, and five young black men jumped out and rushed me. The space filled with hate. The skinhead's hate up the street where I was headed, collided with the dark hate in the park and I was the intersection of it all. Despite extreme drunkenness, the will to live propelled me forth as I careened across the park, toward the street lamps.

I couldn't escape.

Random act of violence ensued.

The fear coursed through my veins in a lightning bolt of sober and clear thinking. I saw the lead pipe as it headed for my eyes. I feared this.

A mile away, the skinheads screamed at passers-by, uttered random threats, perpetuated hate. I feared that.

The lead pipe, swung like a baseball bat, crashed into the top of my head, for I ducked. Thankfully, I ducked.

Blood. Iron taste in my mouth. Blurry eyes.

I don't know what happened next, but I stayed upright. I made it to the corner, to the show, on to the hospital (observed overnight for possible concussion), and eventually the next day, to the police station.

I couldn't press charges.

They did a police line-up to get me to choose the aggressor. I couldn't tell.

I was very drunk.

I said, "they all look the same."

As I'm sitting here, I realize, that, Dear Reader, was racism; rooted in fear.

Carrying internalized shame about being a white woman of privilege for far too long, I now willingly drop this old story which no longer serves me. Dropping the stones of resentment from me, I tenderize my heart, daily. Dominant culture, at least the soup I grew up in, was/is racist; it instills the notion of "us and them" in subtle and not so subtle ways. This inherently begs the question, do I fit in? Am I part of us? Do I belong?

I didn't feel I fit in with mainstream culture, I didn't feel comfortable with the us and them mentality, it was the breeding ground for hate. It seemed like them and them, those who hate and those who hate only certain people. I only hated those who hated. Ah-ha! There's my us and them. I knew it was in there somewhere. If I spot it in someone else, I've got it in me. This line immediately cuts through my judgment of other. If I spot it, I got it. You spot it, you got it.

Where I'd like to be is knowing that I we are them, and communing with others who get this mindset of responsibility also. Like really get it, not just give lip service. This higher consciousness, this higher level of awareness is socially pioneering.

I didn't fit in with that group of skinheads because I didn't hate. I felt shitty when I judged others, and yet it happened by default. I felt guilty when I saw people less fortunate than me or who I perceived as less fortunate than me. In the past, I rarely felt right-sized. I was a megalomaniac with an inferiority complex. I puffed up or shrank back in attempts to manage my anxiety. I didn't feel comfortable in my skin.

Social injustice churned me up inside and I asked a lot of questions growing up and into young adulthood. It seemed I got very few answers. During the Los Angeles Riots of 1992, the old footage of the Watts Riots from the 60s aired and I vividly recall standing at the TV, mouth agape, witnessing hate.

The others near me witnessed my upset and said, simply, "Oh, Amy, change the channel, don't get so upset."

"Changing the channel doesn't change the world," I retorted.

Silence. Loneliness. No "us" emerged. No sense of belonging as social pioneers, change agents standing for love. Instead, I internalized the oppression and blamed myself. This cycle of lack of control building tension and self-aggression fueled my alcoholism. Or alcoholism fueled my perceived lack of control, mounting tension and a judgment of self that felt toxic. I don't know which came first, I just know I suffered. I blamed others and saw the futility of that.

Then I blamed myself. For a decade. I drank destructively and lost focus on what mattered most: Loving. Being outside in nature. Feeling joy in my body. The pink cloud of childhood faded to a bruised purple hue that colored how I began seeing the world. I recall vividly even trying to wear rose colored glasses to boost my mood. They were woefully inadequate to coax spirit back home to my body. Oftentimes, I felt dissociated from my body, floating above and away. Yet this did not feel like I was free or safe, rather I felt scared and untethered. The orbit out of whack, I drifted farther into the bleak black galaxy of depression.

Over time, I learned to quit blaming anything or anyone, including myself. But for nearly a decade, from the age of 14 to 24, I lived in an icy hell with heated negativity to propel me into action. I looked good. I got scholarships. I graduated.

Inside I dissolved. Depression caused drunkenness. Drunkenness caused depression. I know not which.

What matters most was that I was resilient and I learned, eventually, to quit manufacturing my own misery. The order of this pivot in my life is crystal clear to me, no confusion at all. My suffering ceased when I quit drinking, not before. My life started over with sobriety and I began anew with a different Moonshot towards an understanding at a deeper level what makes me tick, rather than trying to numb out my super-sensitive superpowers. Life events got better, but more significantly; my internal factory of woe-is-me shut down as I woke up.

I still have the silver necklace I wore that night of the lead pipe assault, it was the gender symbol for a woman. Now, it is no longer caked with my blood as it was for years. It journeys with me on the road of resilience, symbolic of the powerful compassion of the sacred feminine.

One thing I can do is to focus my present moment awareness right here, right now. I can continue to change the channel on my own discursive thoughts. Focus on what matters most in the moment. Yes, hard times fall on us all, I get that. Digesting, assimilating, and eliminating what is no longer needed makes all the difference in the world.

I learned how to cease fighting anyone or anything, including myself. And this has made all the difference in the world. I can choose what to focus on. I've learned there are two types of business. There's my business, or none of my business. If my work really is about taking care of myself, creating the best experience for myself, and feeling resourced enough to be a powerful presence in the world, then this manifesto from

Bruce Lipton, Because You Are an Energy Field, is a good reminder that I am part of this new evolution. (See Appendix IV for a more detailed description.)

We have this posted on our bathroom wall to read regularly. This reminder saves my ass, repeatedly.

I see many Americans caught in judgement, rooted in fear, disguised as hate. It is either outwardly expressed, wanting to build walls to keep "them" out, surfacing as random acts of racial violence. Or it is inwardly expressed, believing something is wrong internally that needs to change in order for you to fit in, to find belonging, to experience worthiness.

Both external and internal judgement are toxic. Hate begets hate, inside and out.

I blamed myself for what happened and the subsequent random acts of racial violence. My rape. In the past, I didn't call it rape. *I lost my virginity*, to a skinhead. The assault, I didn't call it assault. *It was my karma* for hanging out with skinheads.

It must be my fault, the mantra of the self-aggressive woman. Ouch.

One thing I appreciate is that I now tell myself a different story about these hard-core experiences. I can see how my experience can benefit others.

One thing I can forgive myself for is that I used to abandon myself. Today, I don't. Not a day goes by that I don't touch my own heart and recognize my resiliency.

The second distinction of an extraordinary life is focus. In the past, I focused on others and their happiness and made everything my business. It didn't really generate happiness around me. I didn't focus solely on what I could truly change; myself. Now I can say with conviction, there is my business and none of my business. I'm going all in for the loving myself up, forgiving everyone for everything, and minding my own business (which truly has a ripple effect on the whole world).

I invite you to focus on yourself.

Clinging

Yesterday's funk clinging to my clothes,
wheezing and sneezing, I sigh.
Clouds of noxious insecurity linger around me,
conspiring in malevolent plots,
clinging to my fighting-at-all-cost-ego,
keeping my head down, shoulders slumped, spine limp.

Tomorrow's worry clinging to my dreams,
questioning my decisions.
Tenacious termites of doubt doing double time,
secretly and silently robbing my serenity,
rotting the foundation of my peace,
niggling within crevices of carefree coexistence, eroding
certainty.

Now's to-do list clinging to my mind,
rehearsing and reviewing on a daily basis.
Mundane dalliances dance in my life,
filling the calendar with minute particulars,
stepping on the toes of inner wellbeing,
invading the white space with dots, dings, reminders.

Childhood's regrets clinging to my own motherhood,
pumping me up to do it differently than THEY did!
Caustic judgement of previous generations swarm,
stoking my ego into hot righteousness,
whispering sweet nothings to my decisions,
amplifying moments that matter into REALLY BIG DEALS.

Sex's scents clinging to my skin,
sending shivers of release down and out.
Molecules of him swirling in my cells,
blurring lines between we, me and he,

mingling moments of unified pleasure,
smoothing the waters in the space between.

Sleep's memories clinging to my wakefulness,
digesting dreams of un-lived lives.
Moments of chaos cloud the calm of clarity,
swirling realities of who, what, where, when,
filing events into hippocampal camps,
writing the story of my life with emotional undercurrents.

Spirit's resilience clinging to my heart,
squeezing reassurance with each beat.
Deeper knowing precludes cognitive knowing,
inviting the exhale to release what is no longer needed,
inspiring the inhale to take in the beauty of the eternal now,
breathing the breath, "all is well…"

~Amy Elizabeth Gordon
Waimea, 2015

Chapter Three: Repair

repair-ordinary definition:
fix or mend (a thing suffering from damage or a fault)

repair-extraordinary definition:
acknowledge (and then mend) your part in the suffering or breakdown

If you want to be free, you must first accept that there is pain in your heart. You have stored it there. And you've done everything you can think of to keep it there, deep inside, so that you never have to feel it.
~Michael A. Singer, the untethered soul

He Told Me to Take It

My father is talking at me. It's one of his well-meaning mini-lectures about his understanding of life. He was born on the Chesapeake Coast of Virginia, raised in the militaristic backdrop of "buck up -- be strong -- do as you're told."

This message didn't sit well with my father, a poetic and passionate man who loved birds and beaches. He had feelings he couldn't name, couldn't talk about, and certainly couldn't own. Yet, his dutiful self carried out the duty of the generations that went before him; and so it was, he introjected into me the notion to work hard, think hard, philosophize about a better life, and ultimately, numb out.

Dad, "You're too sensitive, Amy."

What I heard, *"You let yourself get washed away in the feelings world."*

Dad, "You worry too much, Amy."

What I heard, *"Simply take it for what it is and ignore what bothers you."*

Dad, "Learn a sport."

What I heard, *"Be a sport. Don't rock the boat. Be a good girl."*

Dad, "Walk with an encyclopedia on your head so that you have good posture when you are on stage for Miss America."

What I heard, *"People are watching you, judging you, and you must be upright to perform and be on stage at all times. Be prepared."*

Dad, "Talk clearly."

What I heard, *"Don't make the same mistakes I did."*

The unlived lives of my parents influence me. Granted, I'm aware what I heard and what I interpreted it to mean might not have always matched up with their intentions. I get it. It still hurt. The implications of these lectures: *"Your feelings make you weak, your vulnerability is a liability. Just take it."*

The surfer, I forget his name, is dropping his swim trunks to his ankles, pointing to his crotch. A strapping young man, born in an Atlantic beach town, raised in the, "look good, feel good, cover your ass," climate of mistrust.

Many Americans, who in the 1980s, were caught up in mis-trusting the system and mis-trusting the world, were therefore unable to trust themselves. Or maybe it simply started with a lack of trust in oneself. I don't honestly know. Regardless of where it started, the contagion of mistrust infected the space between people. I caught it.

Perfect sized waves, perky breasts, and parties with packed bongs, these were the only things that mattered, especially for this surfer.

A teenager's sexual exploration, mine, exploded there and then. He told me to take it, but in taking, I lost, temporarily, my own voice, my own body, my own pleasure. "Take it: not in your hand. In your mouth. More. Faster. Now swallow." The implications of these thrusts, *"ignore yourself and pay attention to me. Just take it."*

The psychiatrist doled out psychotropic medication. Born in the breadbasket of the Midwest, raised in the new-fangled American landscape of "take this pill and all will be well." This was also known as "better living through chemistry, take a pill for every ill."

The breadbasket of America filled to the rim with medication money; this introduced crop of pharmaceuticals in the former farmland promised the panacea and birthed the allure of the fix.

Big Pharma's taproot gripped at every Hippocratic oath taking professional caught in the Great Divide between a compassionate heart dedicated to serving others and an insatiable bank account dedicated to feeding the mouths of greed.

Masculine urges to fix this problem -- do something about this -- sullied the fertile landscape of suffering and thus gave birth to a new crop of Americans thinking a pill could do the trick.

These Americans took it, as did I. Then promptly peed it back into our landscape, giving us the privilege of the most expensive pee on the planet as well as the contamination of our waterways.

The implication of these driving forces:

"You have feelings you cannot handle? Just take it."

The repair for me in all of this mess is to acknowledge my part in the breakdown with my father, the surfer, and the psychiatrist, and all the other people in my life that I didn't have boundaries with at that time. I didn't understand the concept of self-sovereignty then. I thought if I made you happy, I'd be happier. I was sick. I now know better. I forgive myself. And in from my magnanimous heart, I forgive others for their transgressions. And now I have a bigger heart, more compassion, and intact boundaries.

Trifecta of Bliss

As I'm sitting here, I believe in the power of love to conquer all inner demons and to repair the old haunting memories like those found in, "He Told Me to Take It." Everything we experience is in part constructed from our inner dialogue. If I pause and reflect, as I often do, I have always believed in the power of love.

Where I'm from, my parents taught me about the power of love. I felt this most in my mother's strength of character and commitment to family and my father's poetic patience and ability to pause and reflect. As a young girl, I camped and hiked around the South with him in an organization called Indian Princesses. My name was Sunbeam; his Gray Fox. Our tribe was the Mandan tribe.

We were one with the trees, the lakes, the rivers. The agility of the alligators in the water and their complementary stillness while perched on logs mesmerized me. The stealthy and sly water moccasin was incredibly fast moving, matching the lightning storms, that like a snake, could come out of nowhere.

Where I'd like to be is remembering that weather is unpredictable, much like my moods. As I develop mindfulness and awareness, my own inner meteorological weather forecasting system if you will, I get to answer the questions: Is the growing cloudbank due to a lack of lunch or a lack of sleep or a daunting to-do list? How can I take ownership of the storms? How can I prepare and prevent the wreckage of a bad mood storm? The environment is reflective of the mind. It is one of my great teachers. And we can influence each other.

My father and I adored our precious times together watching sunrise over the Atlantic. A calm abiding, the peace that passes all understanding; is something I have never forgotten. Perhaps it resides within me, a pocket of warm and cuddly promise in a scratchy wool coat that life sometimes feels like. "First light," a time of infinite possibilities and wonderful hushed tones and whispers. The muted pinks and yellows shimmering and shaking on the water, refract the glimmering rising light. The continuous ebb and flow of the tide soothes our souls. Looking back, I understand more fully why I love sunrise on the beach, and why I feel the deep urge and beckoning to the shoreline: the persistent surrender and surge of awakening consciousness.

One thing I can do is to quietly enter the darkness before dawn, absorbed the ambrosial hour, look up at the fading stars and spirit guides, and hold them close to me in the darkest dark and even in the bright of day.

Dad and I logged hundreds of sunrises, and I continue this ritual with my brothers, my sons, whenever possible. Even if it hid behind a veil of clouds, playfully playing peek-a-boo, it rose. Tirelessly and without complaint. Sunrise, peppered with promises of new chances, fresh energy, and electric aliveness, a constant in our collective lives, inspires me with its tireless commitment and consistency.

The power of love fueled my desire to be of service. I found myself, at a young age, caring for animals, cleaning up after my brothers, earning badges in Indian Princesses for community service, and concerning myself with how to make the world a better place. This concern fell hard in the realm of relational field and has remained there ever since. Fascinated with how people tick, I bent over backwards trying to predict what people around me wanted or needed so that I could make them happy. I know, I know, I didn't work, but I kept trying, up until about 24 hours ago.

I heard the statement, "Oh Amy, just be happy" so many times I thought that was my purpose on the planet. Except, I misheard it. I heard, *"Make me happy."* This is not what people in my life said to me directly. That was my faulty interpretation of the "happy" commentary. My natural conclusion, if I make you happy, I will be happy. It didn't work.

Instead, I sprinted, skipped and sang outdoors. I retreated to the natural great beauty around me. The woods. The lake. The field. I would go. I still go. I heard myself think. I drank the silence and solitude. I refilled my reservoirs of giving.

What matters most is time outdoors. I am infinitely more giving and pleasant to be around when I am outside or have been outside recently. I've known this from an early age.

When indoors, the background noise of the *Today Show* on TV roused me, not birdsong. The acrid smell of Benson and Hedges cigarettes filled my lungs, not the aroma of pine. The piles of laundry screamed, the dirty dishes demanded attention, and the rake for the orange and brown shag carpet tripped me as I entered the house, as I left behind the beauty of the chaotic order of the natural world.

My heart hurt indoors. Sometimes I heard yelling behind closed doors. The story I tell myself now is this: everyone in my house was preoccupied with other things, therefore, I felt lonely.

Divorce, work, alcohol, cigarettes, talking about work, and desires to lose weight occupied more real estate in my mother's mind than contentment or ease.

Golf, food, cigars, sleeping off work, and desires to sail around the world and write a book occupied more space than grace in my father's mind.

Cars, girls, football, surfing, military, going to work, and desires for escape occupied the adolescent minds of my four brothers.

I heard my mother's heavy sigh upon my father's return from work. Routinely he slid the curtain of the newspaper in front of him. The curtain of current events parted as he emerged for dinner and *Hogan's Heroes*. The long hallway to my room carried the echoes of TV, and I found solace in my room, the only one in the family of seven with my own space.

I couldn't fix all this, this heart-ache that I felt surrounding me, though I desperately wanted to.

The white picket fence of my childhood happened to be in the judge's chamber at the local courthouse downtown. Strange conversations of alimony and custody. I didn't understand.

Now I see this chapter of my life as the doldrums, nothing moving forward, and a big dose of seasickness. Recently, I saw a National Geographic special about the Polynesian navigator Papa Mau. An incredible human being, it was noted that he didn't despair during the doldrums. Papa Mau lived "in the state of peace of a person who seemed whole." Of this I'm desirous. This is what I clamor after now. To be whole. The wholeness of me lived outdoors. Not in a courthouse or a TV-filled house.

One thing I appreciate is the steady, soothing presence of sunrise in my life to this day. The trifecta of bliss includes the iridescent hues of a silver sunrise, the healing golden glow of being outdoors, and the platinum power of infinite love to release the pinch of ache and stitch a broken soul back together again.

I look out my office window and see the sky lightening. The dark gets less dark, slowly and subtly, just as my suffering shifted from impenetrable and unmoving to tender and pink.

When I get the wave of suffering, for it still happens, I'm grateful for the moments of remembering to place my hand on my heart and tenderly think pink thoughts of compassion.

This morning, as most mornings, consists of an outdoor shower, a cold one, non-negotiable for most of the month, practice yoga, wake the boys, and engage with this gig called life, stitching the fat quarters of the quilt of my life together, using the thread of aloha to bring beauty to the masterpiece.

The sunrise always sparks the ember of resilience in my soul. It tenderizes me.

The third distinction of an extraordinary life is repair, the action of acknowledging (and then mending) your part in the suffering or breakdown. I know I played a part in the challenges of my life. I'm sorry, please forgive me, thank you, I love you, were all sentiments that came easily to me. Own your part in the suffering in your life. And only your part.

Soul in Nature

The moon mounted the clouds again.
The sun surrendered softly into the sea.
The stars pricked the sky, coyly at first, then boldly burning
in the black night.
Friends gathered together to laugh, to cry.
They say they all want the same thing.
Inner peace.
The Sea of Tranquility is a Moonshot.
She said to me, "You've been unhappy for so long.
You're homeless to yourself.
The honeymoon is over.
You're uptight."
My entire life I have heard how uptight I am.
Release the grip. Now.
There is no such thing as a low maintenance person.
Scratch the surface and we all require attention.
I require high octane.
The Power of Nature.
The Power of Community.
The reality of our interconnectedness.
To surround myself with upstanding love and deep peace
in my environment.
She encouraged me, "Wiggle your toes and smile, no
matter what you are doing."
Scratch the surface.
Take a deep breath.
We all have the same blood.
Let go of the burdened baggage of Self.
Ask the Source to Source you, to strengthen your soul.
Soul is reflected in Nature. Savor it and save it.

~Amy Elizabeth Gordon, Keokea, 2016

Amy Elizabeth Gordon MA   38

Chapter Four: Faith

faith-ordinary definition:
confidence in what we hope for and assurance about what we do not see

faith-extraordinary definition:
complete trust or confidence in everything; utter abandonment of hope and fear

Doubt everything. Find your own light.
~Buddha Siddhartha Guatama Shakyamuni

My ordinary definition of faith is lifted from Hebrews: 11. It is the notion of ordinary faith that tripped me up as I careened toward the illusive state of adulthood. I hoped for things to get better. Hope is "if only" and fear is "what if"—neither of which get me where I want to go.

Cloying Humidity (The Unusual Happens and Miracles Occur)

Escaping the cloying humidity of Florida at 36,000 feet above sea-level, I luxuriated in the first-class seat by having another mixed drink and pondering the day. A short and sassy friend from my time studying abroad, bought me a ticket to New Orleans, a first-class ticket, complete with free drinks and room for an anxious type to unwind a little, with fewer people around me. I needed a break from Florida heat and malaise so I decided to try the heat and malaise of Louisiana for a spell. A spell indeed. I landed in a blur, already drunk from the free cocktails. First things first, we went to a drive-thru booze joint. I ordered a Hurricane in a 36-ounce plastic cup with a straw. *Heaven on earth*, I thought. 151 Bacardi rum and sweetness, *oh my, heaven*. For a while, I was flying even though I'd landed.

Sweet alcoholic drinks populated my decade of debauchery from the ages of 14-24. They lorded my spare time. At 22, recently graduated from University, drunkenness still paved the main avenue through which I navigated the world. I worked at a health food store in the mall, pocketed the frozen yogurt cash in my apron instead of putting it in the till, and drank myself silly many nights a week. I passed out in my punk rock bedroom if I was lucky, or in someone else's, if I wasn't. Some would call hooking up "getting lucky." For me, it was a conquest, a Pyrrhic Victory at best. The cost of winning too high.

During that decade, with the exception of a few years

away at University, I lived with my mom and her female friend. I routinely numbed the pain in my heart, my lack of healthy, open, loving relationships, although I wasn't aware how much it bothered me at the time. I was greatly confused about my mom's relationship with this "female friend." Were they lovers? I knew they shared a home, worked together, laughed and fought together, but how do I classify this relationship? Her husband had died of a heart attack the same year my dad moved out.

My mom asked for a divorce and my dad moved out. She told me she wanted to return to work and he wanted her home. Mom was ready to work when my four older brothers finally launched into school, but this happened to be the same year she got pregnant with me. Delaying her return to work, she gave birth for a fifth time.

Mom's female friend was always there, in the photos, in my memories; she was there at my birth and at most major events in my childhood. I imagine she held my mom's hand as the anesthesia set in to "allow" the birthing to begin.

I wasn't ready to enter the world, and neither was my mom. The salty amniotic sac of shelter and safety, albeit full of some not-so-good things, alcohol, tobacco, and guilt, held me fast. Still, the forceps came in to force my body to emerge.

I wasn't ready.

The cloying humidity of Florida surrounded us back in 1970.

In New Orleans in 1992 humidity still surrounded me, cloying. My mind, overly saturated on booze, cloying in the humidity of alcohol.

Reality check points faded while in New Orleans as the booze saturated my cells. Things got bizarre, more bizarre than ever before in my wild mind. Looking back now, I think it was alcohol induced psychosis. At the time I thought I was a target for the mafia. I hallucinated that my friend's dad pointed a rifle at my head. I perceived a red beam centered on my forehead, between my eyes.

I vaguely recall having more drinks earlier that day with foreign guys in a shadowy nook somewhere in New Orleans. Later, I wondered if they drugged my drink. I know not. Or maybe it was the pot that caused the psychosis. What I do know is that I ended up a patient at Charity Hospital in downtown New Orleans. Friend called my mother when I wouldn't leave her apartment; I was uncharacteristically unresponsive and positively paranoid. She had me admitted to the hospital. She couldn't handle me. I was losing it, big time.

Charity Hospital for the poor and underprivileged, a place with the mission statement, *"The Unusual Happens and Miracles Occur,"* was one of the oldest public hospitals in the nation, second only to Bellevue by a mere month. After nearly 300 years of serving, teaching, treating patients, Charity Hospital was washed away by Hurricane Katrina in 2007. In writing this, I hopped on my computer to find images of Charity Hospital. The haunting images of this French Quarter monolith loom large in the dark recesses of my memory.

When admitted, I was convinced I loitered in purgatory. My erratic replies to the barrage of questioning confounded my admission. Was I on drugs, did I have a history of abuse, was I pregnant? I lacked the ability to differentiate true from false, I told one doctor, yes, the next, no. I was spent. Spiritually bankrupt. In need of a miracle and I got the unusual.

Most impressionable to my blurry eyes was the fact that I was also one of the only white women on the ward. August, 1992, I was 22. I wore a white rayon sundress with red flowers from The Limited, zippered in the back, and my black steel-toed Doc Martens. Doc Martens are work boots with an air-cushioned sole. They are oil- and fat resistant, and offer excellent abrasion and slip resistance; yet despite all that protection, they could not protect me from trauma. My wild and flowing curly hair formed dreadlocks at the base of my neck as I flung myself about wildly on the gurney. The staff eventually put me in five-point restraints. I recall very little from the whole ordeal.

Fast forward a decade, and I'm a staff member, a licensed mental health therapist and certified addictions counselor, at a psychiatric hospital in the Pacific Northwest, putting patients in five-point restraints. My recovery from the wild ride of mental peaks and valleys spurred my yearning for greater learning. I completed a Master's Degree in Contemplative Psychotherapy and worked in a myriad of health care settings. My life has taken me full circle, time and time again. From the poor and underprivileged to the rich and grateful. I own no house, have no doctorate behind my name, yet I feel clearer and richer than ever before in my life.

Here are some things I do remember from Charity Hospital; my period started. Blood between my legs, again, my mom arriving from Florida and rubbing dry shampoo in my hair because they wouldn't let me shower. (She has always cared more about how my hair looks than I have.) She worked her assertive magic and got me discharged from that hospital. How, I will never know. The hell she went through, I will never know. I barely understand my own hell.

After the miraculous discharge, we stayed near the Superdome which was gearing up for a huge concert, Faith No More, Guns & Roses and Metallica. The only open hotel room in the city was a penthouse. I'd never seen such a nice hotel room, spacious and haunting. My mother took out her dentures; in my delusionary state, I thought she was a vampire. She brought back Chinese food from McDonald's. I was paranoid. McDonald's only had fries and burgers and chicken nuggets, never Chinese food. I did not trust a single aspect of my experience, but faith held fast to my mom. She was a survivor. She knew how to pray. She embodied faith that everything was going to be okay no matter what. I felt it then and I've seen it countless times since. She knew how to get shit done. She could move mountains and get her delusional daughter out of purgatory. God was still within me. God was still within me. Prayers swirled around me like a sticky fog. Still, somehow, a flicker of sanity stayed lit within me, even in the shadowy darkness of this heavy energy.

The beep-beep-beep of the emergency transport careened through the airport to whisk me back home. Everyone looked like versions of people I knew and loved. Mom told me that I reported this to her. Again, I thought, *this is Purgatory, that means saying goodbye to my loved ones.* I spoke goodbye to Aunt Judy, my best friend, my brother. Chastised for my many transgressions during my drunken dis-embodied disgraces, certain I was going to Hell, I felt myself slipping away as I supposedly returned "home."

Early signs of Hurricane Andrew were whipping up in Florida when I met with my ex-boyfriend near my mother's pool, soon after returning home, pumped full of psychotropic medications. I was not yet stable. Scheduled to leave the country later that month, I planned to teach English somewhere in the former Soviet bloc, so I tried to say goodbye. It was not a good meeting with my ex.

My ex was the second most addictive substance in my life behind Bacardi. He wooed me early in high school. I finally relented. He lost his virginity to me and that burden and artifact made me special in his life. *"Amy, you are more important than time,"* he once told me. He told me that he looked at my photo before checking a clock each morning. I'm convinced if I had been a teenager in the time of cell phones, we would've been inseparable. I was finally seen, something I had been hungry for so long. He fed me.

But we needed to separate.

I had a restraining order against him for his transgression in college when he attacked me one night at a bar. Naturally, I'd been drinking, and running high on LSD for the first and only time, and flirting with my new guy. The previous night

I had grabbed my pillow and a few of my things, hopped on his motorcycle and moved in with him down the street from my ex. I'm not sure who was more upset, ex or new guy's ex-girlfriend; they both wailed on me. Ouch, it still hurt, despite the temporary drug-induced stupor.

Mom said I deteriorated again after that stormy spell by the pool. I ended up in another hospital on even more medications. The religious imagery persisted, which hinted that this was indeed a spiritual crisis, though no one named it that at the time. I was living in a culture devoid of rites of passage other than *binge and puke and spread your legs*, so naturally my heart hurt, my soul ached, and my spirit floated, lost.

Thinking I was the Virgin Mary, I walked naked down the halls with a white hospital gown tossed over one shoulder; then came even higher doses of meds, the big guns. I recall a blurry photo of my Godson in a frame by the side of my bed. This tether to my life hurt like hell, yet offered a taste of heavenly redemption at the same time.

We, mostly with my father, went to church on those Sundays when I was unsuccessful at pretending to be asleep to avoid the ordeal. Quite simply, I did not understand it, "it" being church. I never felt its support or enjoyed a sense of belonging. It certainly didn't foster a sense of worthiness in me. Shackled with the corrupt concept of original sin, it was impossible to find comfort in my own skin, to simply be okay with being me. The story I told myself was steeped in guilt. My perpetual striving for perfection didn't get me where I wanted to go. I longed for a life of unconditional love, not the life of strife.

This was a pivotal time of great transition in my life. It was the *bardo*, as the Buddhists call it. The space between. The liminal space. I had graduated with a degree in political science and an intention to save the world. My ideological intentions swallowed a serious dose of reality while at University and studying abroad.

What I hoped to fix, I discovered, was impossible because the story I created was that the foundation of our patriarchal society was based upon a corrupt political system. Wealth and power, networking and family name determined what transpired, not good intentions and common good. I grew even more despondent.

I moved home, worked at the mall, and drank even more than while in school. A lot. I was lost. Why were my efforts to ingest the spirits not waking my own spirit accordingly?

My family was relatively oblivious to my inner suffering. I had learned to lock that pain in my heart and put the lid on tight. Shut. Armored. Yet the love leaked out, and so did the hurt. The wellspring underground erupted in a stony quiet of calm. In New Orleans, I was violent, writhing, inconsolable. In Florida, my homeland, I went mute. My family noticed. My family came. My family prayed.

The priest even came, the one who baptized me as an infant, who "knew" he visited me in the mental hospital. The medical experts performed CAT scan, MRI and spinal tap— all to no avail. They, the authorities of our dominant culture, didn't know what was wrong with me and had pumped me full of psycho-pharmaceutical interventions, diagnosing me as psychotic. The result was neuroleptic malignant syndrome, the result of an adverse reaction to the administered antipsychotics.

I became mute. Catatonic.

Was I really in a catatonic psychotic episode? Or was I a young woman enduring an inadequately supported spiritual break, going through a major transition in life in a culture void of uplifting rites of passage, brought on by overconsumption of alcohol?

I was later informed that I had been a few heartbeats away from a premature reading of the Last Rites while I was hospitalized for this nervous breakdown. My mother told me they were about to introduce a feeding tube since I was unresponsive. I remember the priest there, then. Ready to usher me out in times of tragedy. Where was he during confession, during high school prom, during the death of my dignity?

My family prayed. Thank God. One brother came each morning to the hospital on his way to work. A moment of clarity flashed, and the next thing I remembered was asking him, *"Can we go work out at the gym today?"* I was back. Not fully back, and far from healed, and incredibly bewildered, but back nonetheless.

Religion, Re-Mix

We believe in many Spirits
    the Nature, the Ancestors
    creators of heaven and hell,
    of all that is, seen and unseen.
We believe in a Higher Self, within,
    the only salvation,
    eternally begotten of the Father,
    God from God, Light from Light,
    true Gods from true Gods,
    begotten, not made,
    of one Being inspired by Mind
    through God all things were made.
    For us and for our salvation
        Mind joined heaven and hell
        infused the Holy Spirits and Ideals
        and became truly human.
        For our sake, Mind was crucified under Addiction;
        she suffered, died, and was buried.
        On the third day she rose again
        in fulfillment of the legacy;
        she ascended, tethered to gravity
        and is seated in the core of the body.
        She will come again to let go of judgment,
        and her freedom will have no end.
We believe in the Guidance of Others, the Connection,
the Web of Life,
    who connects us with Father and Mother,
    who is known, felt, and glorified,
    who has spoken through the prophets.
    We believe in One Ocean, One Earth, One World,
    We acknowledge our part in taking responsibility of life.
    We look for the Brilliant Sanity within each of Us,
    and the life we will lead Today. Amen.
        ~Amy Elizabeth Gordon, Hawi, 2017

The first prayer I ever memorized was Our Father.
I loved it and felt proud to know it.
Now I offer this version of the old classic.

Our Mother
Which art in Earth
Fallowed be thy name
Thy creation came
thy Will repressed
in the Ocean as it is on Earth
You give us this day our daily bread
and patiently endure our trespasses
as we notice we blame ourselves, as we blame the elusive "other"
and lead us not into complacency and wake us up to the goodness
for thine is the only world we inhabit and our consciousness rises
now and now and now
A-ho

~Amy Elizabeth Gordon, Hawi, 2017

Where I'm from, people around me seemed either embarrassed to be American or downright staunchly American, opposite ends of the spectrum. They hid or lorded. They played small or played big; few were right-sized. People either rebelled against the greed, entitlement, violence, questionable leadership, and unsustainable lifestyles or they got swept up in them, these realities of American culture, defending them and oblivious to any alternative answers.

People numbed to the pain in their heart through addictive behaviors—drink, work, suffering—anything to keep them out of the present moment. Addiction is avoidance of direct experience. Ultimately, we don't want to feel what is deep within us or completely surrounding us, so we distract ourselves; and it's killing us. Addiction is continued use despite negative consequences. We keep blaming and shaming and judging and killing. Few recognized that they manufactured their own misery. And in my humble opinion, it's not getting us where we want to be.

As I'm sitting here, I'm noticing the lack of soul food. People are dying of starvation, it's obvious to me. In the middle of New Orleans, decades ago, I was starving for soul food. I wasn't in the present moment. This is the only place to nourish the soul.

I'm curious what it would be like if we all got a bit more present in the moment? What if Americans got a bit more right-sized about the notion of being American? And what if we all got a bit more appreciative of things that are indeed remarkable about the universal qualities of being human? The American notion of rugged individualism flies directly in the face of the collectivistic perspective I hold near and dear to my heart.

Where I'd like us to be is a place of calm abiding, with a new consciousness, a faith, a working faith of compassionate connection. From this place, we marry relational health, modern technology, and indigenous wisdom.

We all live on this planet earth. Let us seek and find the

common denominator of our existence. We must, individually and collectively, get over the past hurts and take the higher road. We can learn to harness the transformative super-power of compassionate forgiveness to turn frustrations into appreciations. We can stand as source for a transformed world. We act for social justice while we build a culture of appreciation. We plant trees and reduce single use plastic. We vote with our dollar and walk our talk. Every action reflects who we are as consciously evolving beings.

One simple, mundane example is that when I come to the kitchen sink and see the dirty dishes, I choose to see this as love notes instead of annoyances, the evidence of my family members nourishing themselves. I can choose to see this potential annoyance without the negative reactivity, and I can calmly ask for what I need from a place of appreciation. Sunday, chore day. Dishes cleaned up after each meal. An uplifted environment is different than running around cleaning up after others to titrate my anxiety (been there, done that).

What matters most is to clear up the lies I grew up telling myself. These are the lies I am naming to tame right now, as I release the pinch of dominant American culture and tenderize my heart to the truth of what it means to be human.

- The lie of "away" as a place to throw my waste (there is no "away").
- The lie of a "loser" as a result of my win.
- The lie of "failure" as a person; "experiences can be failures, not people."
- The lie of "instant gratification;" it doesn't gratify, it only makes me want more.
- The lie of "move far away from your family;" the emotional cut-off doesn't heal old wounds.
- The lie of "work your ass off and retire your fat-ass off;" this doesn't invite the sustainable, enjoyable, pace of grace and sense of purpose.

- The lie of "hustle and bustle and stay busy;" it is un-sustainable.
- The lie of "car culture freedom;" car free days are under-rated.
- The lie of "keep busy;" white space on a calendar is divine.
- The lie of the "zero-sum game;" abundance is inclusive.
- The lie of "winning the battle" in a Pyrrhic Victory, the cost of the battle is so high, it's pointless.

One thing I can do to get us there is to heal hurts by letting go of hate. Hating the haters makes no sense. Getting violent at a peace rally makes no sense. Stuffing the pain of the world into my body and mind and taking responsibility for it all doesn't work. I let go of hating myself, and I stay sober, one day at a time, and show up as a sober woman of integrity, for nearly 25 years now, nearly half my life. This is what I do as foundational work to heal the planet, one relationship at a time.

Hurt people hurt people and hate begets hate. It doesn't get me where I want to be. It doesn't get us where we belong. When I come from a place of unconditional love, my presence is 300,000 times more powerful than someone spreading fear. And this makes a difference, Dear Reader, it does indeed.

One thing I appreciate is the powerful presence my mother has had and continues to have and will always have in my life. I take ownership of the lack of intimacy we had when I was a child. I do not blame her. And I've quit blaming myself. The triangulation of her best friend's presence in my life confused me and laid some serious brain pathways for feeling left out. It is a detrimental default of mine that has deep grooves in my brain. The more I recognize moments of belonging, of the powerful presence of tenderness, the more quickly I can get myself out of that groove of hurt (which takes me right to the cul-de-sac of Woe is Me) and return to the knowing that the surrounding terrain is resilience. Resilience is the container for my hurts, my insecurities, and the realm of grace. Forgiveness of everyone, including myself, is a spiritual musle I stretch and tone daily.

The fourth distinction of an extraordinary life is creative freedom to define what my faith is today. Today I have abandoned the notions of hope/fear, us/them, sinner/savior. In this freedom of faith, I find a broad vista of acceptance, with a well-trodden path through the woods of right action and pure living, and an extraordinary life defined by my own chosen standard. I respect others to choose their own faith. The realm of resilience has the landscape of faith, the wellspring of forgiveness and repair, the mountain of focus, and the tower of trust. From here, all things are possible.

Release

I release and I let go
I let the Spirit in my life
And my heart is open wide
Yes, I'm only here for love.
No more struggle, no more strife
With my faith I see the light
I am free in the spirit, free in the spirit
I'm only here for love.

~Sang with Ecstatic Choir, Boulder, Colorado, late 1990s

In summary, the realm of Resilience is still an active part of my brain and the re-wiring that happens each day that I stay sober and open my forgiving heart to the suffering of others, including those who hoisted their suffering upon me.

Mustard Yellow Sweater and Psychic Violence are but two of the tales of my decade of despair. I internalized the negativity of these and other events more and more. The toxic shame killed part of me.

I tried carrying the weight of the world on my shoulders and it squeezed my soul in shocking electric blue boldness. The bully of my mind bruised me as much as the drama of my life. I kept on keeping on, thereby building the foundation of resiliency within me. I was strong, like my mother taught me to be. But I suffered, still. Reprieve came when I repaired the despair by finding a faith that worked. Faith that everything was going to be okay no matter what.

Trust, focus, repair and faith echo in the big heartbeat of the Earth and within the microcosm of my world with my mother. She didn't know better to not drink and smoke while pregnant; I forgive her. I trust she did her level best. The doctors were ready for me to be here, so the forceps pulled me forth.

Resilience defined me. As a wounded healer, it still does.

I focused outward and wanted everyone around me to be happy, then I focused inward and saved the only life I could save, my own. I repaired the wreckage of my past and I relaxed into a faith that works in my life in a way that is indeed miraculous.

Breathing, embodying the distinctions and writing about it help integrate this into my life. I trust myself, focus on my life, willingly repair my relationships on a daily basis, and have faith that I matter.

You matter. Your relationships matter. I invite you to own your own resiliency. Trust. Focus. Repair. Have faith. Reach out and ask for help, if needed.

Now is the perfect time to pause and breathe.

Here is a wonderful breathing suggestion that helps me balance my brain, and it can help you, too. Rewiring our brain and integrating our life story are actionable steps, not spiritual ideals.

Act now. You matter. Your relationships matter. I strongly suggest you take five minutes for this breathing exercise. Start some water boiling for your Sweet Rose Tulsi Tea ("stress-relieving and magical") and sit calmly and breathe.

Exercise—Alternate Nostril Breathing

This is a powerful technology from Kundalini Yoga traditions. It gives you greater command of the central nervous system. From this place of empowerment comes greater compassion of self. From this arises more skillful means with others. In other words, it works to transform your relationship with yourself to one that is more tender, more compassionate. From this foundation of love, you enjoy better relationships with others. This is a guarantee. The Buddha told us this, too. If you are truly loving and kind with yourself, you can never harm another human being.

- Exhale completely. Release what is no longer needed.
- Place right thumb over right nostril.
- Inhale through your left nostril. This is the calming channel in your body.
- Pause at the peak of the inhale.
- Close left nostril with right ring finger while releasing the right thumb.
- Exhale out the right nostril.
- Pause at the bottom of the exhale.
- Inhale the right nostril only. This is the energizing channel in your body.
- Pause at peak of inhalation.
- Close right nostril with right thumb while releasing the ring finger.
- Exhale out the left nostril.
- Pause at the bottom of exhalation.
- Inhale the left nostril only.
- Pause at the top of your inhale.
- And repeat.

Repeat the process for five minutes. Release both sides and inhale deeply, exhale slowly. Notice the balanced energy in your being. You may perhaps feel more awake if you were tired. You may feel calm if you were anxious. This is the state of balanced pulsation, relaxed joyfulness, calm abiding. You have energy when you need it and calm in your pocket. It is transformational. Do this while you wait for your hot water to boil in the morning. Or before bed.

Use this incredible breath tool regularly.

Next, pull out your journal and write. First thought, best thought. Set a timer for twenty minutes. Invest in yourself and your wellbeing.

Begin writing your own integrated life narrative. You can use the sentence stems as a guide to present moment awareness to build the foundation for integration.

Writing Prompts:

- Where I'm from...
- As I'm sitting here, I'm experiencing...
- Where I'd like to be...
- What matters most...
- One thing I can do to get me there...
- One thing I appreciate...

Reflect on resilience in your own life.

- One way I can trust myself to not abandon myself is...
- One way I can focus on my own business is...
- One way I can repair a broken relationship is...
- One way I can foster greater faith in my life is...

Part II: **What happened**

Realm of Core Compassion

compassion-ordinary definition:
sympathetic pity or concern for the suffering or misfortunes of others

compassion-extraordinary definition:
connecting with the tender heart of sadness buried in the layers of life

for there is nothing heavier than compassion
Not even one's own pain weighs so heavy
as the pain one feels with someone,
for someone, a pain intensified by the imagination
and prolonged by a hundred echoes.
~Milan Kundera, The Unbearable Lightness of Being

What happened is, thankfully, I got sober. This historic event changes the trajectory of not only my life, but the generations since, and in some quantum realm it changes the past. As well as the legacy of love.

At Naropa, I got more education. I chased the spiritual materialism of more self-help books, in pursuit of floating high about the drivel and despair of the doldrums on Earth, living a life of purity. In hindsight, I see that I was perpetuating the disembodied dissociative state of my years of building resilience (which is a preferable reframe than calling in, once again, all of the trauma).

Blind to the fact that I was living a spiritual bypass, blind to the reality of my rage, my outrage at what happened in my life (of which I am 100% responsible), it festered within me. Contemplative practices and sobriety didn't immediately dissolve the negativity which I internalized. Self-aggression was a more socially acceptable outfit, fashioned out of the cloth of depression, and sewn together with the thread of anxiety, versus the clownish costume of outwardly-directed vengeful victimhood.

Here's a brief list of what happened from 24-late 30s. It is inconclusive and by no means exhaustive.

- I got sober. For a good six years I used the steps of recovery to keep beating up on myself.
- I received a Master's Degree in Contemplative Psychotherapy. For a decade I identified with nearly every diagnosis in the DSM IV and feared losing my mind (again).
- I covered my Bacardi tattoo with an Egyptian scarab beetle, wanting spontaneous joy and rebirth to cover up my drinking career.
- I asked an incredible man to marry me. For a girl who never thought she would marry, this was mind-boggling. For a sober woman of integrity,

getting involved with him while he was still a married man, I naturally blamed myself when she (wifey) blamed me. The neural pathway of "it's my fault" was a fucking trench in my brain.

- I dug my way out of that.
- I had children. For a female survivor of sexual trauma with a cray cray mash up of pleasure and pain pathways crisscrossing my body and riddling my repertoire of sensuality, my birthing journeys are stories in their own right.
- I cleaned the toilet to titrate my anxiety.
- I raged when the house was unkempt.
- I vowed to better myself, to arrive at purity to wipe away the sins on the past.
- I sat in front of a light box in attempts to rid my Seasonal Affective Disorder in order to stay in our beloved Pacific Northwest community, to no avail.
- I poured myself into helping others to distance myself from my own pain.

This list, this litany, all paved the way for greater compassion, compassion for self and more skillful means with others. See Appendix V for more information on Practices for C.O.R.E. Compassion. Compassion, at its core:

- Clarity: The better I look, the more I will see.
- Openness: A heart as wide as the sky.
- Reactivation: Stimulating my soul to invite Spirit home.
- Energy: Feeling the interconnected web of all existence and the electric aliveness that comes with it.

Chapter Five: Clarity

clarity-ordinary definition:
the quality of transparency or purity

clarity-extraordinary definition:
the quality of being transparent and seeing purity in all things

Clarity comes from action, not thought.
~Marie Forleo

Cold Corpse

We buried my mom's mom when I was fifteen. I remember standing in Chemistry class on Monday, crying. I didn't know where else to cry. My teacher, with his slicked back hair and tobacco laden breath, put his arm around me to console me I cringed. I no longer took it.

Death was unknown to me except what I saw in the movies or on TV; I certainly had never seen a dead body. Come to think of it, I never held a baby before either; that happened a few years later when my brother's wife had a son. Two givens in a human life span, birth and death, I never saw until my teens.

My grandmother, Dorothy, was my first death to deal with in my lifetime and I didn't know how to do it. Crouching next to the coffin with my cousin, I bravely touched her cold body. I often giggle when I am overcome with emotion. Sometimes I cry. For some reason, then, I giggled.

At first glance, she looked the same, my grandmother, save for the horizontal posture and closed eyes. She looked just like she did in her chair, surrounded by her ceramic figurines of boxer dogs, drinking scotch and water. When I touched her, she felt cold to the touch. Squirm. The cold, hygienic response to death struck me cold. Dread. Exhale. Dead. Even though the humidity outside created a warm and wet day, the feeling inside the funeral home was cold, inside me, cold, inside my grandmother, cold. Numb.

The memorial, the viewing, set up in a coffin-like-tightly-sealed (don't let the death leak out of here) room in the funeral home, invited time and space for more than a mere glance. She was made up all pretty like. She looked almost peaceful. The ersatz tranquility also stood out as a wee bit odd. Awkward gaping silence enshrouded the room. Walls thick with noise-cancelling, grief-absorbing qualities magically amped up my squirming, dreadful exhales for the dead. I sensed something in the room, a strange new calm. Her soul wasn't there, but admittedly, in my experience her soul wasn't really there, even when she was alive.

I was hungry to know her. What was her last exhale like? I loved her annual Christmas ornament gifts complete with my name and year written on the bottom, in her handwriting. Treasures. What was her most brave moment in her life? Her fierce love raised six incredible children. What made her giggle? Perhaps her husband fell in love with her smile.

I felt I didn't really know this person, my grandmother, without whom, I wouldn't be here.

I wanted to cry, but I laughed. Highly sensitive to the energies around me, the unspoken stories, the unlived lives, the forgotten dreams, I felt the intense confusion of grief. Laughing; that was my discharge. I don't remember any crying at the memorial. I remember the drinking afterward, of course. Family members drinking was customary, beer for the boys, scotch for the men, everything for the women. This was the only thing that was usual about this unusual day; the drinking.

The humidity outdoors turned to downpour. The energetic and electric release of the clouds with lightning and thunder gave my body permission to release.

I cried, in the car, in the backseat, alone, on the way home.

She died on a Sunday in May, Mother's Day, of cirrhosis. She was 72, mom was 48, I was 15. The multi-generational trauma of alcohol abuse carried forth. And so it is.

Years later, my mother shared with me her memories of her mother. The arguments, the drinking, the abusive acts. The image of my grandmother's face imprinted in a loaf of bread at the dinner table. The shouting. Ouch. My heart breaks as I type this. Years after her death, early in my sobriety, I tried to talk to my brothers about it, the chaos, but the denial was so thick, there was no room for truth or emotional processing. There was no room for the both, and. They were wonderful grandparents, and they suffered and their suffering caused pain. It was both, and, in my heart.

During the death process of my grandmother, I bore witness to *doing* as a response to any whiff of *being* that was out of the normal range required for functioning. For example, keep busy when you touch the suffering of life. I know it was hard for my mom. I've tasted her tears. But still, she kept busy. She moved mountains. My mom, the survivor, knew how to get shit done. Deal with it.

Do what needs to be done. Handle the funeral arrangements. Deal with the paperwork. Keep yourself busy and basically get over it.

My body heard the subtle messaging, *"constrict and pinch off emotions."* The weather, the stormy weather outside, gave me permission to release, inside. The environment reflects my mind. God doing for me what I could not do for myself. The storm released the pent up, built up condensation of the day's events.

The dominant culture I grew up in didn't deal with death regularly. We were protected from it. The dog didn't die, "he was taken to the country to live with open space." Did my grandmother go to live in the country, in wide open space? Oh God, I hoped so. She loved horses, or was it her mother who loved horses. May they both ride bareback and free, wild and wandering. May our ancestors experience release. May the ceramic figurines we cherish come to life, flesh and blood of warmth and love, pulsating with joy and the freedom to frolic, even in their death.

I blur past and present tense throughout this book. Apologies. Try as I might to fix it, it happens. Perhaps it is reflective of my imperfections. This is true, I'm far from perfect. I also know that my brain doesn't know the difference between the past and the present. Hence my imperative that we take ownership of our stories, question the validity of memory to build solid walls of woe, and write a new ending, because everything is malleable.

The first few chapters of despair segue into greater

compassion for myself. At the age of 24, I hit my bottom with Bacardi rum once again. It was a snowy night in Colorado and I was drunk, so drunk I passed out. In the morning, as I came to, I discovered I had thrown up on myself. Fortunately, I had passed out in an upright seated posture, on the tickle-me-Elmo red couch from the Salvation Army Thrift Store. I recall coming to. That's what you call waking up from being passed out or blacked out. Slowly, in suspended animation, and wickedly sharp pain, I cautiously crawled over the black and white tile of my apartment, braced myself near the porcelain God I had supplicated for a decade, and washed the dried remnants of visceral lining down the drain. I experienced a wave of gratitude in between the waves of nausea. Thank God, I escaped the Janis Joplin legacy, the deadly aspiration of choking on my own puke.

I prayed to God. "Please, not again."

This is the part of my story where I transitioned to back to grace. The death of my grandmother foreshadowed the death of a part of me. The death of my dignity first, then the death of the driver of my drinking. The driver was my inner critic, my self-aggressive tormentor. Finally, after countless attempts of trying to quit drinking alcohol on my own, I surrendered to win. Something clicked inside. Release. I turned my will and my life over to the care of a power greater than myself.

As I type this, questioning, how can I possibly publish my memoir? *It's too hard.* I once again surrender to win. I turn my will and my life over to the care of God as I understand God. This act of surrender is not a one-time-only event. It is a daily decision to release control, trust HP (Higher Power, sometimes I lovingly refer to as, "Honey Pie"), build a spiritual life, and surrender into success.

My life pivoted toward grace on November 27, 1994. And I haven't had an alcoholic drink since. Thanks to the "we" and the help of HP.

Today, I stay sober for my Grandmother, Dorothy, the

aforementioned cold corpse. May her spirit rekindle with the Source and support me during times of pain. She is part of my retinue. She is one of my angels. Part of my posse. I know this to be true. As much as I can find truth in the mystery of life, anything that has to do with love, grace, and tenderness, I let it in now.

I'm not afraid of death. I tell my boys regularly, if I don't see you again, remember that I have had a good life. We laugh and sure, it's a bit creepy, but I want to talk about death, and more importantly, I want to express my gratitude as much as possible. I have more blessings in my life than I can say grace over, and for this I am grateful. Or is it because I am grateful that I have more blessings in my life. Chicken or egg. It matters not. The point, I have a good life, indeed.

I've seen birth. I've seen death. I felt myself reborn multiple times.

Courageously, my husband and I discussed a different possibility for his father's death. He desires a natural death, complete with 72-hour home viewing. Vigil. Ritual. More involvement and hands on. More humane. Realistic. An opportunity for our sons to know death as a part of life. Natural burial. No embalming. Dry ice. Time. Space. Time and space for grace to enter our hearts and minds to work in a way that is indeed miraculous. The story is never really over, is it?

Being Mortal & Transitioning Gracefully

I want to die gracefully. Moving and transitioning with grace and ease is also how I wish to live my day to day life. How we transition reflects how we live. How we do one thing is how we do everything. My desire for greater connection with loved ones inspired me to allow space for grace.

In the past, transitions challenged my sense of calm and ease. From day one, I felt the pinch of forceps on my temples, hurrying me to a place I wasn't ready to be. (I'm talking about the birth process.) Therefore, I'd historically run a few minutes late. I'd rush past my beloveds, spill my coffee, and wonder which clock to believe. This frenetic energy didn't get me where I wanted to go. I always want to go to grace. Surrender. Release. Peaceful ease and loving calm abiding. You may hear me say, it didn't get me where I wanted to go, rather frequently. I case you wondered, that is where I long to be: calm abiding, as a tender, powerful, generous woman.

Developing an observing quality of mind, I saw myself racing around and my connections with others suffered. This woke me up. I began to slow down, say good-bye with a soft gaze, offer hugs, and guess what, grace and ease entered my heart... and I ended up being on time more of the time.

I highly recommend the book *Being Mortal* by Atul Gawande, which encourages us to find a new conversation around medicine and what matters most at the end. He describes the experiences of several of his patients' deaths and the deterioration of his own father. He explores new ways of working with others to empower them to contemplate their own death and the considerations of family before they find themselves in the "throes of crisis and fear." He highlights what I find myself infinitely curious about, which is, what is the story we tell ourselves about our lives?

This story I tell myself is that my Soul is my personal embodiment of Spirit, an incarnation of the Divine Spark of Universal Creation, of the Great Spirit that connects us all.

Where I'm from the only time I heard "soul" was in reference to a perfect mate I should obtain or in reference to something in me that needed saving. Neither of these things appealed to me. I didn't know about my soul, Spirit, or God consciousness. It wasn't taught. It wasn't discussed. In the absence of discussion, I lacked clarity around what it was exactly or even vaguely. What I heard was God had power, Jesus was the savior, Mary, was the virgin Mother, and something about the Holy Spirit that intrigued me. I felt it when I was outside, something special and unnamable.

As I'm sitting here I'm experiencing experiencing greater clarity of mind and a joyful soul, comfort in my skin and "vocational arousal," as Barbara Marx Hubbard, social pioneer, would call it. My soul has passion, purpose and manifests as a source of presence and power of light in my interactions with others. As Barbara says, "heal the earth, free the people, explore the universe."

A growing willingness to discuss the terms of the unseen powers at work wells up in me, crowding out the cringe-worthy condemnations of archaic beliefs. Committed to evolving, I recognize that shame, blame, and criticism no longer serve as working strategies in my life. Negativity simply doesn't get me where I want to go. The good little girl still wants to do the right thing, and presently the right thing to do is healing the dissociation from Spirit. Spirit is the connective tissue to Source. Source sources me.

Where I'd like us to be is tapping into the diversity of our individual zones of genius as well as the powers at hand to be source for a transformed world. I trust that diversity thrives with common purpose. We cannot all be the same, that is not true belonging. Yet we can scratch the surface of egoic judgment and find common ground.

My genius is for communication. I ask questions, and listen deeply. I listen for what is said and what is not said. I listen to the listening. I invite willingness and curiosity to guide me as I release the tenacious grip of judgment.

A sampling of questions I might mull over in a day: How do we get to clarity? Is an alcohol-free lifestyle an essential aspect of clarity? Does sugar cloud my mind? How essential is it for an extraordinary life? I leave space for different answers, and I rest in my truth: an alcohol-free lifestyle is an essential aspect of clarity in my life.

Yet in true acknowledgement, this genius of communication is not mine alone, it is a product of the sum of my experiences, my interactions, my ancestors, and of every person who has ever been kind to me and loved me. The essence of poets, professional athletes, musicians, artists, authors, rebels, laborers, ascetics, intermingle with my cells. My breath exchanges with many a thought leader and social pioneer. These energetic exchanges matter in terms of the essence of who I am today. And today, I feel more fully and truly myself. I have come home to myself. I no longer need to look out to others to find me, and I cannot evolve alone. It is both of these realities.

I love you. I need you. Uttering these simple phrases has altered my life immensely. The opportunity to bear witness to the amazing unfolding of my beloved husband, in his mysterious and steadfast state, gladdens my heart. Our relationship is both solid and evolving: a trusting monogamous relationship and a constantly evolving love affair with greater conscious connection.

What matters most is to trust in the agreements I make with myself. Something as simple as what time I say I'm going to sleep. Believe me, it matters. You see, if I don't trust myself, how can I trust you?

One thing I can do to get us there is strengthen my soul in sweet surrender, softening the edges of my presence while cultivating a culture of appreciation. In doing so, I can take the lid of the cap of my career, my vocation, my calling. We can blow the lid off mediocrity. Anything is possible. Endeavor to be a powerful point of presence and light and take a stand for aloha in every interaction. Then watch reality shift.

There is no tower of power lording over us unless we let it. We need boundaries, with ourselves, with others, with what is acceptable, and with what brings us up or down. Now, more than ever, we are needed. You matter. Now we get to show up to our lives with the proper mindset so that we can join genius, connect our thoughts and find power in partnership. Together, we can.

One thing I appreciate is the guidance of our *kūpuna*, our elders, toward clarity. Whether we see the world the way they do or not, they can certainly open our eyes to the secrets they hold. Forgiveness, evolutionary love, chronic curiosity, open-mindedness, open-heartedness, creative communities, daily movement, and deep appreciation of the natural world. I spend a lot of time with elders. I want to absorb their wisdom by osmosis. Whether it is my dear seventy-two-year-old friend whom I exchange messages with daily or my in-laws who smile and love us daily at the dinner table, I have daily interactions with elders. Weekly, I visited the wise and creative women of the Sellwood quilting group when I lived in Portland. I loved the water exercise class in Port Townsend, populated with retired seniors, where I went while pregnant. Now, I cherish the *kūpuna* paddling club I join several times a week. Elders show up to life in a way that is worthy of admiration and attention.

My life is infinitely richer because of these relationships. You see, how we treat each other is how we deserve to be treated; it's the golden rule. I long for enjoyment, passion, and purpose. They offer, I receive, then, I offer and others receive. We feed each other. In hell you can have long chopsticks and starve yourself. Or you can feed each other and experience bliss. I choose the latter.

The fifth distinction of an extraordinary life is clarity. What is one this you can do, Dear Reader, to clear your mind? I invite you to dive deep within to answer this question, so that you can cultivate core compassion. If you come up clueless at first attempt, go find an elder to spend time with in earnest.

Unburden my Heart, Clear my Mind

big trees towering
fresh beauty flowering
Vancouver, glorious.
the humming of commuters
entering the tunnel after a long-awaited pause,
a birth canal to a new self.
unburden my heart,
embark on the next adventure,
clear my mind,
interact with all that is around me,
prepare to discover myself anew.

Self, now whole,
reuniting forgotten parts
reclaiming lost parts
recovering denied parts
remembering hidden parts,
welcome home.
willing to strengthen
willing to soften
willing to see purity in all things
willing to move, sweat, write, pray,
daily
my senses alert
the tv across 13th street
beckoning
no need to focus there.
the chirp of the crosswalk
urging, saying, *GO NOW*
gently, in another language.

the coffee in the corner shop
rousing
the poetic thoughts
since, evaporated
trust the process of condensation and precipitation
the cycle of water – the cycle of creation – steady
constant
reliable
trustworthy

soft
positive
active
clear
energy

always available
infinitely accessible
readily ready
open my heart-mind to it now,
long time manifest.

this calm abiding
a result of inviting space for grace
to unburden my heart, clear my mind,
and work in a way
that is indeed,
miraculous.

no longer
an afterthought
to myself
claiming it all
relaxing now
having fun

hanging out
aiming high, diving deep
transforming the world,
starting with Self,
cheering, always cheering, for love.

~Amy Elizabeth Gordon, British Columbia, 2012

Chapter Six: Openness

openness-ordinary definition:
acceptance of or receptiveness to change or new ideas

openness-extraordinary definition:
acceptance of the present state of things and a tremendous desire to upgrade the quality of one's spiritual life

If you improve talking without judgement so that you can connect, you actually help satisfy the deepest yearning of the human heart.
~Harville Hendrix

A Natural State, Being at Ease

As I'm sitting here, the full moon beckons me, the cats cry in a cat fight outside the window, my hormonal flashes of prickly heat rouse me. Combine all of that with a book birthing process and I'm awake, not fully alert, but upright nonetheless.

The dark time of night breeds quiet and an invitation to restore. Life is settled. The proverbial snow globe sits in stillness on the shelf. The hand of my conscious mind no longer shakes the contents. When this natural stillness is perturbed, the fear committee rouses, its presence weighs heavy, as a stone.

Where I'm from, phone calls punctuate the hours. During my adolescence, day and night, the phone ringing breaks the moment and grabs attention. The middle of the night phone calls not only break the moment, they send out an alarm to my nervous system. No *good news* phone calls come in the middle of the night.

A vivid memory, as if it is present time, rouses.

Up late at a friend's party, I'm barely asleep when the phone rings, setting off the internal alarm. While I answer, I peek at the clock, 2:11 a.m. glows red in the corner of the room. An official sounding man says, "three minutes."

Then I hear my brother on the line, asking for mom.

Another drunk driving arrest in the family. Four brothers, four DUIs and counting. I can't recall if each one got one or one got more than one. I just know it was not an unfamiliar call. I wake my mom. I quickly pass the phone from my hand to my mom's but the burden of the news doesn't leave me; a sense of heaviness remains.

My heart feels burdened; heavy, like a stone.

In their heaviness, stones stay put unless an external force moves them; stones have a natural and definite steadfast sense of *leave me alone*. Fear gets wedged in my body like a stone; stubborn, stuck and seemingly solid. Leave me alone.

Where I'd like to be is in a natural state of being at ease, grounded, but not heavy.

When I experience fear, it contracts me from a natural state of being at ease to a tight place of pinch.

As a child, I didn't know how to move the fear, to shake the pinch. Fear piled up and connected to all the other fears, some inherited; alcoholism included. The stones gathering, forming a mountain of malaise. A foundation of discontentment formed the basis of my life. Living in the dominant culture I grew up in this discontentment strangled the growth of grace and gratitude, and fertilized consumerism and contempt.

Today, unlike my childhood, I choose not to have a bedside phone that can ring in the middle of the night, instead, I unplug. Yet even without the phone disruptions, self-generated negativity thunders loudest in the wee hours and this rainstorm waters the fallow fields of fear.

The experience of fear in my body is a tightening, a constriction, a pinch.

Doubt then invades my internal landscape as an invasive vine, crawling and tightening around the lung trees, constricting my safely nestled heart a little too tightly, quickening my breath, and disrupting my rest and digest slumber.

What matters most at these times is release. Release is a calming, soothing, settling, *ahhh*. I enter this portal of release when I focus on opening my heart, put my hand on my heart, and meditate on what I am grateful for, sometimes starting with the letter "A" and getting all the way to "Z." The itty-bitty-shitty committee quietens down and sleeps through the 2am to 4am rallying cry.

One thing I can do is to think about the creatures and features of the natural world.

I feel loved, safe, grateful, and happiest when I am outside; this is the saving grace I learned as a child. From this place of resourcefulness, of being resourced, I remember that my job is

Daily Tender to my soul. When I care for me, I care for you, and vice versa. My senses absorb all the natural beauty possible.

Appreciating stones, I feel solid.

Marveling at tree roots, I feel grounded.

Skipping down the beach, I feel free.

Indoors, my senses quickly cramp and I become irritable. I'm on hyper-alert. I notice when someone has been home; a pair of glasses moved, a dirty glass of milk forgotten, my favorite cookies eaten. Minor irritants eating away at the foundation of peace, the warm wash of existential anxiety feels cloying, so I clean to titrate it. The warm sudsy water wiping away the residue of neglect, temporarily. I get cabin-fevered; no amount of cleaning is enough.

A state of loneliness creeps into my heart, quietly, when I don't get outside.

One thing I appreciate is when I recall that life begins when I leave the house.

Then, just as a breath of fresh air works wonders for my psyche, I open the door, step outside and life begins anew again. Beyond the bars of my mental imprisonment of fears and anxieties, I am free to explore the natural state of great beauty around me. It penetrates me.

Skin and sun mingling.

Warmth within.

Illumination of possibilities.

Return to ease.

The sweetness of communing with the water element enlivens me. I frolic on the beach, the act of jumping foamy waves curling to the shore fills me with delight. This is the place, this shoreline, where, consciousness, symbolized by the land, and unconsciousness, the sea, mingle.

It is one of my favorite places on the planet.

Sensing the energies of the world around me, I live close to the bone, the deep marrow of being. These wake-up calls to natural great beauty save me from myself and recharge my energetic battery.

Reconnecting with bodies of water cleanses my soul.

Paddling on the rivers, the lessons of going with the flow and contemplating the journey come easier here. I also notice the muck and the mire that gets caught in the eddies. I love to philosophize with the question, which way is the future? Upriver, the rapids coming toward me, if I'm standing in the river. Or downriver, that flowing away from me, if I release and let go.

Swimming in the lakes, the eyes of the world, allows my perspective to shift as the lens widens. I grew up with lakes. When I study my genealogy, lakes figure prominently is where I'm from. I notice the ripples from each thought perturbing the surface of the lake. I notice the glassy reflections, the changing colors as sunrise shifts to noonday segues into dusk and dark.

Me, a psychic sponge of sorts, readily saturated with grace and beauty or conversely, with fear and doubt, I must be willing and able to squeeze out the toxins which flood the space between my thoughts. If I don't release the pinch, fear and doubt fester into a soup of shame, and that shame clogs my nervous system to the point of overwhelm.

Everything changes. As a teenager, I used to wear all black. Now I adore wearing all white. I even tolerate grey, in my wardrobe, in my hair, in my chain of thought. To me, this represents non-duality and non-attachment. I feel a sense of liberation. Adopting a fresh perspective free from polarities allows me a better chance of hanging out in the sweet spot of life.

Today, the rage I may experience from time to time is not so intense. The disagreements are not so disagreeable. The dread is not so dreadful. I know how to move the fear. I release the pinch. I unplug from dominant culture. My vagus nerve responds to singing and chanting. I tune into a different channel in my consciousness, I release the static of fear, and

I allow the higher vibration to keep the loft under my wings. Sometimes I soar, sometimes I glide, and for brief moments it feels like I am headed fast for the ground, plummeting. I breathe, deeply, and trust that this moment, too, shall pass. And it does.

Everything swirling and changing around me, the one thing throughout my life that is constant is the sunrise. It rises, every single day of my life. Not once in a while or when it was summer, but every day. The sun comes up behind the shadow of Maunakea or in the valley of mountains, depending on the time of year.

Wherever I am, it rises. The sun continues to rise, no matter what. It is not up to me whether this happens or not, which is a huge relief. I can rely on it. Sunrise is trustworthy and I surrender to this. It is a power greater than myself.

I woke early today, earlier than usual, 4am Instead of wrestling with my worries, some of which include: did I get enough sleep? How will I pay the bills? Is my mother okay? Will my son be alcoholic? Why do politics and environmental degradation polarize us? I go out on the lanai and look up at the sky. I join the stars and my spirit guides for prayer and meditation during this exquisite time.

Stars pierce the darkness, some swimming in a milky way, the big dipper in the east pouring purple cosmic chi over us. For a moment, I put my mental energies to a different task, learning to tell time based on the seasons and the constellations. Nature is a salve for my soul, I feel its restorative power immediately. The ambrosial hours of pre-dawn magnify this affect. Nature is the home of Grace.

I'm living a continual leap of faith and I jumped so high, it really is just one long free fall.

I have moments of feeling grounded, but perhaps I am temporarily resting on a cloud. The weather shifts, the clouds dissipate, for there really is no such thing as solid ground. The sun kisses my skin and reminds me of the Source of energy beyond the confines of my skin. Pulling me this way and that, the winds of this passing moment remind me of impermanence.

My life begins when I leave my house and allow my senses to play.

I ask myself, what is the most glorious thing I see in this moment, now? The new shoots on the fern? The wild turkey with feathers in full display, strutting through the yard? The lei of clouds ringing Maunakea?

I will remain active in the pursuit of my purpose, fueled by beauty and power of Nature around me, to heal the planet one relationship at a time. I am humbled to know there are some relationships I cannot heal, even within my own home, my own family. I didn't cause it, I can't cure it, I can't control it. Now one brother is sober, one is probably drunk; he has quietly disappeared. I send them all love.

The one relationship I can and do heal is the relationship with myself, dismounting the mountain of malaise.

From there, all things are possible.

I send love to all my brothers. I appreciate their fierce love and the biological bonding we share. When they remember my birthday, acknowledge my big heart, and accept me for who I am, my spirit soars. When I focus on our differences, notice the lack of connection, or remember the drunken times we shared together, or when I still see drunkenness, I feel the pinch. I can choose to release the pinch and return to the common denominator of love. I pause and reflect, holding my brothers in my heart with reverence and respect.

We all love sunrise.

We all love our mother.

We all want peace and happiness.

And we didn't all vote for the same president.

If I can't find common ground in my own family, how dare I give lip service to world peace. Regime change begins at home.

Tonight, I will put my head to my pillow in gratitude, remembering that this being here is enough. Forgiveness is better than sleeping aids.

I am in a natural state of calm abiding when I can unlock the pinch. Letting go of fear, doubt, and shame are essential to living in a place of relaxed pulsation, breathing with the wind, giving my exhale to the trees, receiving nourishment from the 'aina, the land, and surrendering to the flow of *wai*, the water. *Pu'u wai*, the hill of water, my heart center, hums in the heartbeat of space.

I am restored as the dark night breeds quiet. Tomorrow, I will rise again, like the sunrise, and do what must be done.

The Alluring Fix

As I'm sitting here, I find the allure of the fix is ubiquitous in American culture, it is everywhere. The allure of the fix is that pervasive desire for something different. The desire for something different deviates us from accepting our direct experiences. If times are good, we want them great. If times are bad, we want escape.

Where I'm from, alcohol and drugs provided the means of avoiding the direct experience, but these are no longer options for me. Spending decades of my recovery from alcoholism learning how to directly face life, continues to be a work in progress. Progress, not perfection. Learning how to simply just be, hasn't come easy.

Where I'd like to be is recognizing that my being here is enough. Maybe there's nothing to fix. Maybe I can dare to no longer see myself as broken. This is a game changer, a world view changer, and a veritable breath of fresh air. Distancing myself from ease, this is how Tommy Rosen, founder of Recovery 2.0, a generous resource blending yogic lifestyle and recovery, views addiction; with recovery being moving toward ease.

One thing I can do is notice my self-talk. I notice the phrase that gets the most air time in my head is, "if only." For example, "if only my sons remembered to do their chores, I wouldn't have to clean up after them. If only my husband created more discipline in his schedule, I wouldn't have to nag. If only I got more sleep, I wouldn't feel so tired. If only I adopted a vegan diet, I wouldn't have digestive problems." I notice the "if only" is coupled with the follow-up, "I wouldn't". It is an escape hatch. It removes personal responsibility from me in that moment. This trap of "if only" leads to the illusive future tense, "then I wouldn't have to postpone my happiness, kindness, and serenity."

What matters most is noticing the deeper desire for ease. We, collectively, crave a better life. We conclude on some level that if only the world were X, then we could feel Y. Logic and simple equations of X=Y are tempting considerations. They fuel the allure of fix; thin=happy; rich=content; diamond=worthy; pill=happiness.

One thing I appreciate is noticing that as I integrate my shadow self and dive deep into my unconscious mind, I seem to have more choice in my life how to decorate my inner world. I can then ask, with curiosity, what irksome thoughts comprise the furniture of my life?

The mainstream culture offers me a hectic pace with a self-driven motor that is not adapted for perpetual motion. Work. Laundry. Volunteer. You need help. I want to help. Yet sometimes, as I'm driving the ambulance to help others, I end up neglecting my needs, burn out, and run over innocent bystanders in the process. Ouch.

My first two decades of life in Florida laid the foundation for chronic busyness, a classic symptom of dominant culture. This spilled into my life in Colorado where I was literally and figuratively trying to climb every mountain. My first 14er, a mountain over 14, 000 feet high, was Long's Peak. The young sober woman I huffed and puffed all the way up with pulled out a cell phone to call her parents. I was aghast. It was sacrosanct. That was the mid-90s; cell phones were fairly new on the scene. I would be shocked now to find a moment in nature where someone doesn't have a phone to attempt to capture the beauty of the moment. Guilty as charged.

Things began to slow down a bit in the third decade of my life. Moving further northwest, the Pacific Northwest changed me on a cellular level. Expansive beauty liberated me and frontier energy soothed my soul. My nervous system unwound from a tight, hot, speedy frenzy to a greater sense of more frequent calm. Moving to Oregon, I drove the speed limit for the first time in my life. The big trees exuded a steady presence that beckoned me to slow day, to exchange breath with them. The bustle and hustle released over time. My time on the Olympic Peninsula, the first place I lived with very few, if any, billboards, stoplights or 24-hour joints, still offered me the Western epidemic of chronic busyness. It is not the fault of the highway. It is the chronic emptiness we run away from and it manifests as chronic disgruntlement.

When my present moment is laced with fears of the future or yearnings for a different past, I instinctually crave a fix, a change, a solution. When I stand with one foot in yesterday and one in tomorrow, I piss all over today. This posture doesn't ultimately get me where I want to go. Manufacturing my own suffering through trying to climb every proverbial mountain, trying to keep up with the illusive hustle, was exhausting.

Most of the time this suffering, this enduring, takes the form of dissatisfaction in relationships. And most of the time this relationship is with myself. Cultivate a relationship with myself, is possibly the greatest investment of my life. It implicitly enhances the quality of my other relationships. For a clear example, when I get a massage, it helps my husband, you bet!

My graduate degree training at Naropa, an independent school centered on Buddhist studies in Boulder, Colorado, was an unforgettable experience. Several great instructors and "world wisdom holders" opened my mind to new perspectives. Two lectures in particular relate to this topic of the allure of the fix.

Judith Zimmer Brown taught me that my mind is like a bowling alley. The ball releases, the thoughts meander. Without skillful means of mindfulness and awareness, the ball succumbs to the gutters: the gutter of hope on one side and the gutter of fear on the other.

What if I abandoned the notions of hope and fear and recognized the traps they are? What if I trained my mind to the present moment, ultimately gaining a shot at a strike—making the mark of feeling okay, right here, right now? This, Dear Reader, is key for extraordinary living.

When I see clearly the illusive nature of hope and fear, I recognize that hope and fear let us off the hook. They whisper sweet nothings…Hope says, "Someday things will be better, then and only then will you be okay." Fear says, "Someday you will lose something you cherish or you will never get what you want." Both shadowy voices imply, "What's the point in doing anything right NOW?" You'll be saved at some point in the future, or conversely, you're already doomed.

On the other hand, I find hope and fear in the present tense voice to be invaluable guides. Hope cheering me on through a 5k fun run: "You'll get through this," "keep on keeping on." Fear guiding me out of danger when a car swerves around a blind corner, "watch out" and "caution."

Unfortunately, sometimes these voices have moved beyond their present moment wisdom and tangle my nervous system in knots. I have to remind myself, "oh, I tripped over a rock" when my physiological reaction might be "ahhhh, I am falling over a cliff." Actually, I have a wide field around me. I am safe. Very rarely am I on the cliff, and if I am, I need my body to respond in a big way.

Another wonder lecture, at Naropa, shared by Rabbi Shalom-Shakter in which he explored our early desires for sweet nurturance, healed my addiction to ice cream. He tells the story of the innocent baby. The baby cries for help. Baby may be hungry, tired, cold, lonely and is offered milk. Sweet, creamy milk. No wonder I turn to the fridge when I am emotionally upset. Ben and Jerry's offers oxytocin rewards for my efforts. Cheese sure does please my mind. With awareness, I have greater choice to see if this behavior will get me where I want to go.

Twenty years ago, I was addicted to ice cream. It took me out of whatever malaise I experienced and brought a sugar rush and ersatz sense of okay-ness. Temporarily. Short-term benefits, but long-term consequences. My stomach ached. I bloated and gained weight. Looking to substances to do for me what alcohol did, for alcohol converts to a simple sugar, also. Getting chip-faced quit working, just like getting shit-faced quit working.

The quest for something outside of us to feel better makes a lot of sense because sometimes it works.

The chocolate ice cream cone tastes good and sends a neuro-chemical of pleasure. But if I can stop and pay attention to the way my teeth feel during the indulgence I notice they ache. My belly cramps. Afterward, my energy peaks, then plummets. If I notice this with curiosity, lovingkindness, and acceptance of myself, perhaps I make the decision to indulge a little after a healthy meal. Or perhaps I abstain altogether and enjoy the sweetness of life around me. This is a stark contrast to getting chip-faced in years past, when I ate an entire pint of ice cream.

The most radical thing is to stay put when I want to escape. It is to hug my beloved when I want to freeze. It is to open myself up when I want to shut down. In Dialectical Behavioral Therapy, we call it taking the Opposite Action. Our lives, these experimental orbits around the sun, can be full of fun, contentment, and thriving. Once we get past the mental mode of surviving (which is what I helped therapy clients with for decades), the molecules of the mind float a little more freely, a little more cleanly, and a little more serenely. This is how I help coaching clients move from surviving to thriving.

A large portion of my work with clients involves inviting them to inhabit the present moment. While working as a Licensed Mental Health Therapist, trained in Contemplative Psychotherapy, a blend of Eastern and Western Psychology, I heard many, many clients wrestling with their own inability to be ok in the present moment.

Rarely did I meet a client who was happy about taking psychotropic medications. Oftentimes, clients were not what we called, "med compliant," meaning they didn't take their prescribed meds.

One client, wanted off the meds. She hated taking them. I asked her, "What is the story you tell yourself as you put that Prozac in your mouth?" I explain that if she is riddled with self-aggression, mad at herself for having to take the pills, no pill in the world is going to help, in my non-medical provider opinion. At the time, I worked as a psychotherapist, and we did not prescribe meds, it was beyond our area of expertise. Those are psychiatrists or MDs who work in that realm. I merely helped people get familiar with their stories, the film that runs in their minds. If, however, she tells herself, "This is powerful medicine that is helping me through a dark time," well, that's another story entirely.

Another example:

A male client in his fifties, let's call him David, enters my office with a list of complaints, namely lacking energy, motivation, and hope.

"The anti-depressants aren't working," he reports straight away.

He goes on to report that his other meds are quite doing the trick, either. From high cholesterol to erectile dysfunction, he seems to have systemic inflammation in his body which is impairing his functioning. He states that the performance drugs are robbing his soul. He requests another med evaluation. I can't help him with that directly, it is beyond my area of professional expertise. I make a referral to a provider who can address all of us systems, from an integrated health perspective.

Being the silence breaker that I am, I point out that one of the most dangerous elements of dominant culture is the Standard American Diet. It is SAD. The cumulative effects of chronic stress and poor diet are essentially killing us (and the planet).

"I can't afford to buy quality food," he reports.

"Well, let's have a look at your cigarette, beer, coffee, and marijuana consumption, shall we?"

He laughs. We are building therapeutic rapport which is just as important as any treatment plan.

Then he tells me he works the night shift. Another symptom of our culture, the always on/always open for business framework which puts many into the impaired sleep category with their night shift schedules. I recently heard this type of work described as "carcinogenic."

In the past I worked night shift. Drinking at the 24-hour bar during my "lunch break" at midnight. Then I worked a day shift at another gig, starting at 8am after getting off at 3am. I hardly slept. This coupled with trying to pay rent and finding myself lost in the hustle of underearning and over-delivering; life in my early 20s was definitely unsustainable.

David and I explored the basic issues of survival that create daily stressors. Stable housing, harmony in the household, adequate physical health; these are the basics. He mentioned a recent job opportunity working day shift and spending more time with his kids. Then he said, "Well, I want therapy, too, not just meds, I have no one to talk to since my wife died." This opened up the opportunity for him to get more resourced, as I referred him to grief support group in addition to more therapy.

He had grief to metabolize. We, collectively, have grief to metabolize. Whether it is the loss of certain functions of our body, our landscape, or our family, we must acknowledge the heart ache and feel to heal.

Mental health, as provided in dominant culture has become a domain of pathologizing and prescribing, in my opinion, reflective of a broken system. Health care is predominantly symptom management. Thankfully, alternatives are growing in the collective awareness.

The saving grace of therapy is the heartfelt communication and healthy attachment it ideally provides. But it is a band-aid covering the gaping wound of family systems disintegration and social supports evaporation. It is reflective of a deeper problem. And many people serving as health care providers struggle with the notion of health in their own lives. Whew, it's messy.

Can I possibly do for David what Effexor, Prozac, Wellbutrin, Lipitor, and Viagra have not successfully done? He says he can't afford the time to come in regularly, to exercise, or to pay for organic whole foods. He is resistant to looking at other resources. Resistance is killing us, collectively. Period.

The treatment plan requires his input and energetic exchange. I can't fix his grief, his health, his broken spirit. Only he can, with willingness. He told me he doesn't have the motivation to do the inner work, talk a walk each day, and learn to deal with his emotions.

Clients often wait to feel better before acting in ways that can help. I point out that the goal is not to feel *better*, but to *feel* better. I encourage the client to act as if he had the motivation. To move from contemplating a better life to acting as if he had a better life. He must act his way into a new way of thinking, he cannot easily think his way into a new way of acting. The focus, initially, is on the relationship he has with himself. This is essential. There is no pill for every ill, though our drug store aisles tell us otherwise.

The complete holistic approach to mental well-being is not found solely in a pill. It consists of deep breathing, pure air, pure water, healthy food, exercise, sleep, training the mind, finding purpose, being a powerful presence of light, and cultivating a spiritual life. The benefits include a sense of worthiness and belonging, a connection with an inner guidance that grooms a grateful heart. The undercover agents of anti-sleep: guilt and shame, finally learn to quiet down and settle. A trust in oneself, pure, honest communication, and a life worth living are nutrition for the soul.

Things that help me deal with any lingering addictions to the dominant culture and the illusive idea of the alluring fix:

- Breathing deeply.
- Adopting and maintaining a strict media diet.
- Standing up straight.
- Waking up early; pre-dawn. Enjoying these "ambrosial hours."
- Stretching the spine. The hunched over posture mimics depressed posture. We're in this posture quite a bit when we are on our devices. Think: tech-neck.
- Hitting the RESET button at any time vs. waiting for the next day, the next Monday, the next month, of the next new year.
- Staying hydrated; water is vital for proper functioning on so many levels. Visiting the hydration station and remembering how much of our bodies are made of water.
- Marrying nature and movement. Motion is lotion and a walk in the woods does wonders.
- Writing. Long-hand or typing.
- Painting.
- Creating. Maybe even making a mess!
- Laughing, belly to belly, with someone, every night at bedtime.
- Relinquishing the notion of the "perfect" time.
- Engaging in the rose, thorn, rosebud ritual with loved ones nightly (what is beautiful, what hurts, what is anticipated).
- Communicating with transparency with others (honestly sharing my feelings and my thoughts, not what I think they want me to feel and think).

- Refraining from mind-altering substances. Integrity and authenticity grow each day of my life with continued and contented sobriety.

Mental health is a continuum we traverse daily. Some days I feel saner than others. Some days I feel more neurotic than others. Pockets of dispirited gloom float like scum on my reservoir of brilliant sanity. I habituate my brain into familiar grooves and gutters by cultivating thoughts and feelings that form my reality.

My training in Buddhist psychology and continued interest in neuroscience help me to move away from the need for a fix, to befriend the present moment. To open my heart and to shift away from the negativity bias allows me to pay attention to the beauty around me.

The sixth distinction of an extraordinary life is openness. The real danger is not in opening one's heart, but in keeping it closed in the prison of hurt. Allow the realm of resiliency to be the launching pad for the realm of compassion to soar. Dear Reader, I invite you to open your heart to feel the heartbeat of the divine.

A Blessing of the Heart Beat

Steady in sound
flexible in pace
tireless in presence
heart beats on and on
lub dub, lub dub.

New blood flows
headache goes away
laughter massages my heart
memory energizes life
lub dub, lub dub.

Healing oxygen enters each cell
lung tree expands and contracts
embodied presence calms
the lullaby of life
lub dub, lub dub.

~Amy Elizabeth Gordon, Waimea, 2017

Chapter Seven: Reactivation

reactivation-ordinary definition:
restore (something) to a state of activity; bring back into action

reactivation-extraordinary definition:
to receive charge and give charge to in an energetic exchange of excellence

Love is the extremely difficult realization
that something other than oneself is real.
Love...is the discovery of reality.
~Iris Murdoch

The Flounder and the Crab

It was a normal day. We donned our snorkels, masks and sun shirts to better observe the other worldly realm below. Marc, my husband, wanted to walk along the shore to the rocky coastline and then enter the water, to "allow for more immediate access" to tropical fish viewing. I wanted to dive right in and swim out to the point.

This is a familiar experience for us; a core scene in the film of our intertwined lives; my pressing immediacy, his more deliberate pace. I constrict with rigid demands. He expands with his own peace of mind. Oftentimes I run the soundtrack, *Marc hurry up* and I imagine he simultaneously runs *Amy, slow down, calm down, easy now.*

I fell in love with his calm nature and endless patience. On this day, I find myself wanting to vaporize him because of it. I typically want things done yesterday. He typically considers tomorrow soon enough. He perhaps fell in love with my energizing and activating presence. Presently, he shuts down, seething.

This is common in relationships. We fall in love with qualities we have denied in ourselves. As our awareness grows, we can move more quickly and painlessly out of our reactivity. In the past, we could stay stuck in this core scene, our bodies flooded with stress hormones, caught in lock down mode, enduring the silent treatment, waiting for time to show us some better thoughts.

"There's nothing there," he gestures to the brilliant turquoise clear water. "Let's walk down the beach before we get in." He continues along toward the southern edge of lava, toward the home of coral and abundant marine life.

"No, there is, and I want to swim," I argue. My body veers toward the ocean, my intuition knowing there is something there to see. My body knows what it knows and sometimes it is hard to translate this knowing to others.

Sometimes I convince myself that it would be "easier" to be uber-independent and make my own decisions and not have to communicate so much. Then, in the next breath, I realize how lonely that would feel. It wouldn't truly get me where I want to go; healthy relations with others, in harmony with the natural great beauty surrounding me.

Somehow beauty is enhanced when communally appreciated.

Somehow silence is more striking when shared with someone else.

Somehow being alone is restorative, whereas too much leads to loneliness, which I find utterly depleting of my life force. After-all, we are social creatures.

We get in after a few steps, a compromise of sorts.

Swimming our way to the coral, we see the exquisitely beautiful terrain below, the acres of oceanic pasture that changes with the tidal current and solar rays. Both empty and spacious, and yet full of life. We marvel at it all, flying above the depths, yet below the surface, the penetrating rays of sunshine connecting us in the in-between world of sea and sky.

Suddenly, I feel a tug on my flipper and I don't flip out on this unexpected contact. Unexpected events tend to freak me out but something about the embryonic, amniotic embrace of the ocean calms my nerves.

"Puffer fish right below us," Marc urges me down.

I look and see a crab. I don't say anything.

"No, it's a crab," he sputters after taking the snorkel out of his mouth.

We swim a bit farther.

A delightful sight of another crab comes into view. The ridges of the mini sand dunes parallel the shoreline and this crab cruises along, in her lane, sideways, crab-walking, pausing every few seconds. The sand behind her shimmers and shakes and a flounder fish form comes into focus, behind the crab, pausing when the crab pauses. Is this a snapshot of predatory behavior on the food chain or a snapshot of two unusual companions?

We float peacefully, magically and serenely suspended above the scene below, flounder following the crab, breathing fresh air effortlessly through a tube and enjoying the moment immensely. The sun warms my shoulders through my sun shirt. I hear the ambient sounds of fish eating tiny bites of coral. I thank the parrot fish for eating the coral, pooping it out, and making sand for the beach. Amazing to bear witness to the wonders of life.

Snorkeling is one of those other-worldly experiences. Not fully submerged below but not fully floating above, merging a bit of both worlds. This is how I see myself in our relationship. Not floundering on the bottom nor missing out on the magical worlds below by staying aloof. Rather, I simply take in the glory unfolding around me, relax with my breathing, and adjust my vision when necessary — I often need to get the water out of my mask or shift my perspective. In relationship, I often need to recall that we are not me, that my husband is an island of sovereignty to himself.

Snorkeling was new for me, I had never snorkeled before meeting Marc. Perhaps that is why this is another good metaphor for our relationship. In the past, in relationships, I had floundered and attempted to rise above, but with him I'm more fully present to him and to the miracles of snorkeling. Once, while snorkeling, I saw his grandmother's 94-year-old wrinkles undulate in majestic softness underwater. We heard the clicks of communication, and we saw the sinewy sleekness of dolphin play. Surrounding us, encouraging us to keep our nervous system relaxed, to remember to play and commune, commune and play, and always sleep with half our brain working!

As a young girl, I caught my first glimpse of the glorious underwater world when I saw my first coffee table book. Photos from Jacques Cousteau's *The Ocean World* leapt of the page and I dove right in with my imagination fired.

Cousteau said, "The sea, once it casts its spell, holds one in its net of wonder forever."

Growing up in Florida, held in that net of wonder, I spent lots of time in the Atlantic, but not really aware of what was below (and around) me. In fact, I recall feeling quite fearful when I could see below the surface, like the time I saw a big terrifying whale painted on the bottom of a hotel pool in Delray Beach.

Later, in my adulthood, while canoeing in the Atlantic off the coast of Maine with a dear friend, I felt my skin crawl when I saw crabs, lobsters, and flounders below me. Before my late twenties, I wasn't willing or able to invite curiosity to guide me as I looked to see what was happening underneath. I let terror call the shots. I lived a surface life. Now, as a sober woman of integrity, I live an extraordinary life, willing to dive deep into the whole-hearted reality of my relationships and my experiences, and discover how my this can benefit others.

Utterly fascinated that there are creatures in the dark deep that we don't even know about yet, today I no longer fear this vast world. That ocean covers much of our planet and we know very little about it, much like relationships. They comprise our realities and yet there are certainly dead zones and overconsumption and pollution concerns, much like relationships. Discovering, detoxing, and downright protecting, these are actions I apply to my relationships with others and with the ocean.

"Water and air, the two essential fluids on which all life depends, have become global garbage cans," Cousteau said.

Passionate about cleaning up my side of things, literally and figuratively, I volunteer time and actively contribute to being part of the solution rather than perpetuating the problem.

Save the ocean. Save the world. One relationship at a time.

Back in the ocean, I watch a flounder and a crab dance

below me. Is the crab trying to eat the flounder? Is the flounder trying to eat the crab? Are they friends cruising the highways of underwater commuting, looking for home?

Cousteau's idea that "When one man, for whatever reason, has the opportunity to lead an extraordinary life, he has no right to keep it to himself," inspires me to share my life and my breath, through story and written word, and through a willingness to be a part of the solution. The solution of H_2O and NaCl and the solution of engagement. In essence, to engage is the solution, and this is easier for me after I have been in the salt water solution.

Feeling Marc's awe and appreciation through the molecules of water separating us, I felt myself soften into the gravity of gratitude. It could have been a puffer fish, it could have been an eel, anything below was worthy of our attention. The warmth coming from above was worthy of our appreciation. The reality was, at that moment, we were communing with the natural great beauty around us, and that fed our love.

"You are the flounder and I'm the crab, " Marc proposed, the tropical breeze billowed his pareo.

"No, you are the flounder and I am the crab," I retorted. I scolded him with my gaze; eyes burned with saltwater, disapproval of public nudity burned my judgmental mind, residue of the grip of dominant culture's roots in sexual puritanism.

"But I am a crab astrologically speaking," he replied. "And, don't worry, no one can see me but you," releasing his pareo, his lightweight wrap, as he relishes in this moment of maximum skin to tropical breeze contact.

He lacks the sexual guilt I knew so well.

"But I don't flounder," I protest, and dried off quickly so I could get dressed. Yet the sensual-freedom-loving light within me turned on. Secretly I wondered if this were a nudist beach if I could pull it off, literally, or if I would, *gasp*, flounder.

There is something utterly refreshing about observing,

not interfering; appreciating, not fixing. There is something to learn about this moment to take with me into my life and foster appreciation instead of my tendency toward pushing for interaction and rushing to fix other people. It is both, and. Both cultivating awareness and being compassionate. Remembering that sweet spot of real responsibility, I pay attention and I provide positive support.

I am so familiar with my world orbiting around the scarcity sense of "Need more, yesterday" or "Hurry, rush."

Marc, on the other hand, seems more comfortable in his own orbit of "Do less, tomorrow."

Right or wrong? No. Good or bad? No. Simply different. A breath of ease flows through me when I recognize Marc is his own person. In other words, we are not me. He is a sovereign island to himself, as am I. We can snorkel over to each other. We can build bridges of connection through our conversations and nonverbal communication. We can enjoy making our own decisions, remaining aware of how it may influence the space between us.

Chøgyam Trungpa Rinpoche, the founder of the Naropa Institute, the birthplace of our love, said, "Good and bad, happy and sad, all thoughts vanish into emptiness like the imprint of the bird in the sky."

To this mind-blowing mantra I might add, "Here and there, the flounder and the crab, all feelings settle like the flounder in the sand at bottom of the sea."

Choosing Aloha Every Time

The volcano is erupting as I write this. Lava lakes are forming and magma is surfacing after years underground. That which was unseen is becoming visible. The unconscious is becoming conscious. When this happens, transformation is born.

Many moons ago, the leader of the American culture, John F. Kennedy, declared that we would get to the moon, that we would do the impossible. The moon represents the unknown, it also represents the unconscious, the emotional realm of dreams and liminal reality. Many rallied together and supported the proposal, many naysayers questioned the purpose, saying, "Let us tend to life on earth, the poverty, the addiction, the war." Yet we had to aim high, to reach for the extraordinary to find the Sea of Tranquility. This moonshot was an invitation to an extraordinary life.

This moonshot, nearly fifty years ago, allowed the perfect alignment of the stars to create my natal chart. My parents celebrated in extraordinary fashion, with four children under ten running down the beach at New Smyrna, Betty and Dan saw the glow in the sky, as the waxing gibbous moon sat poised at the ultimate target. The thrill of collective accomplishment swirled in their veins and fueled their lust. Love rekindled, once again, another egg and sperm, merged, and I was conceived. And I was conceived.

Where I'm from, my grandmother, mom's mom, took care of me at nine months old while my mom kept vigil at two hospitals. Mom was at Florida North Hospital for her husband, my father, who had his first heart attack under the age of 40. Mom was at Orange Memorial, the other hospital, for her father, my grandfather, who had his first mental breakdown requiring institutionalizing, in 1970. My parents divorced several years later, my grandmother died from alcoholism, and my grandfather died from colon cancer. Where I'm from is a lot of heart, ranging from heart-ache and dis-ease, to a powerful quality of love that surpasses my conscious understanding. The story I tell myself is that my ancestors lived and loved so hugely, sometimes so much, it hurt.

As I'm sitting here, I'm experiencing terrific health of mind, body, and spirit. I feel my feelings, intensely, when they arise, and I ride the emotional wave to the shore. I feel it to heal it while at the same time, I lead a purpose driven life and don't let my feelings call the shots. I carefully train my mind to notice what stories I'm entertaining which may prolong the emotional intensity. Curious about epigenetics, the study of biological mechanisms that switch genes on and off, as well as the quality of lifestyle to determine aspects of health, I take good care of my body. My body is host to a microbiome I respect and feed and care for, lovingly.

Where I'd like to be is reactivating women and men toward health: to be utterly free of heart dis-ease and the accompanying mental anguish, to break the multi-generational transmission of heart-ache in all its iterations. This is my moonshot. I'd like women to name that heart disease is the number one killer, and tame that disease by owning their richness of emotional reality, but not letting it pummel them to harmful consequences. I'd like to be in a culture that recognizes the power of epigenetics to enhance our wellbeing. May we treat the whole being, holistically, not just put time and effort into managing symptoms with medications or surgeries. I'd like wholesome lifestyles, healthy life living, to be the norm. The trends of heart disease, diabetes and cancer, as well as the epidemic of sleeplessness and chronic busyness, all of these diminish as a deeper knowing about the power of healing grows.

What matters most is being here now and living in the *na'au*--the guts, the intuition, the internal guidance system. From this core place, I am able to choose aloha every time, no matter what, over *pilikia*, the drama and the trauma. Even with the lava flowing, destroying homes and creating new land, gratitude is a way of life here, and it is intimately connected with generosity. People genuinely care. They give because it feels good and goes far in terms of what must be done.

One thing I can do is stay active in mind, body and spirit. By reactivating my connection with spirit, with my higher power, I'm thriving in optimal health. For me, that power used to be a male God, lording authority over my serenity and judging my afterlife. No longer do I believe in the patriarchy. No longer am I willing to allow male authority figures to call the shots for my quality of life.

One thing I appreciate is a good cup of black coffee from Ka'u, here on the island. The anti-inflammatory aspects of coffee alert my brain and enhance my wellbeing. Sounds good, now. (Talk about reactivation.)

Half-mast

I often want to help, I long to be of service. Sometimes, ironically, the most radical act is to do nothing. To stay put, perhaps to pray. The flagpole is at half-mast today. Adopting a fairly strict media diet, I trust I will hear what I need to hear. I observe the clouds, the waters, the flagpoles at the post office. If it is at half-mast, I say a prayer, then I may inquire, what happened? I can choose aloha first, feed compassion to my heart, rather than whet my appetite for the insatiable lust for terror that is the steady diet of many. Perhaps you are familiar with it? You drive by an accident and you cannot help but to gawk. Say a prayer, first.

The flagpole is at half-mast today. It is a school shooting in Texas, with a Pakistani girl dead. I hear the Pakistani response, *we know terror, we don't know kids shooting kids.* What to do? My mind, quick to act (and also quick to overwhelm), wants to fix this most obvious problem. Yet gun control is treating the symptom. I want to know the underlying causes and conditions. Saying it is "dominant culture" is vague, blaming, and relatively unhelpful. So, I breathe. Contemplation, nature, creativity, movement, yes, remember these jewels in life, Amy. I volunteer at my kids' school to teach mindfulness. I get the kiddos outside as much as possible. We engage in brain gym exercises to build neural networks and activate compassion. I become part of the solution, and in doing so, this lightens the load on my heart.

Much of our heart dis-ease is because when we care so much, it can turn to despair and overwhelm. Overwhelm is not going to pave the way for peace or generate health. The children's librarian tells me school shootings and fantasy are the two most popular genre of new literature coming out. Wow. I then engage in writing prompts with my kids. I talk to their friends. I engage in life, rather than disengage and watch the news, despair and wish it were all different. Not being a native healing from years of colonization and disempowerment, I'm still sensitive to the ripple effect of wounds; and feel it is time to break the silence. If we don't, we are silently condoning the present reality is a passive acceptance of what is.

When America is positioned as the "greatest fighting force on the planet that can create peace," I cringe. Fighting for peace is where we got it all wrong, in my opinion. How do I perpetuate this on a personal level? This is proper use of my energy versus judging how the world should be. The world starts with me. Fighting with my beloved right before bed or the next day, disagreeing about whether to take a nap, this is a clear example of the termites that eat the foundation of our peace. Sounds simple and perhaps silly, yet over time, this is as corrosive as "fighting for peace."

We fight ourselves daily when we think we should get better sleep, then stay up late on our devices out of habit or perceived necessity. Oprah gave a graduation address so practical, I love it. "Go to bed. Make your bed. Get your phone away from the table."

Release to Reactivate

In the past, my mom frequently suffered from back spasms. Cognizant of this, I went ahead and scheduled two massages, one for each of us, as preventative medicine. She went into the appointment saying, "I just don't know how to relax." She left the appointment saying, "I've never felt so relaxed." Talk about transformation, this was it. I went into that massage knowing how healed my mom was and it allowed *me* to release on a deeper level.

I heard recently from a yoga teacher, "relaxation is letting go of what's no longer necessary." I used to hold on to things that weren't mine in the first place. The story I make up is that moms are worriers.

When I used to try to get myself to relax, I actually felt myself tighten up, perhaps because, in the past, I heard folks tell me, "Relax" and it pissed me off.

After the birth of my second baby, my pelvic floor needed some physical therapy as my pubic symphysis did not go back together properly. While on the table in the women's health office, I was strapped to a biofeedback machine. Electrodes were around my perineum (look it up) and showed my response to certain stimuli.

The physical therapist told me to relax. She showed me a bar graph indicating I was not relaxing. I didn't get it. She then switched the visual display to show a full circle when the muscles were not taut. "Relax" and a tight dot appeared. Constriction. Visual proof. Proof of how tight-assed and uptight I really was.

"Find your own way of settling down", she suggested.

The therapist knew me in this small town where we lived and that at that time that I was a Contemplative Psychotherapist who specialized in Buddhist Psychology.

"Tell yourself you're meditating." Tight dot.

"Imagine you are walking." Tight dot.

"What the hell is wrong with me?" I asked myself, silently.

I had strong knowledge, strong will, strong abilities, and yet I couldn't relax and the monitor proved it.

She suggested I find my own word for the felt sense I was aiming for. Moonshot.

"Release." That is what came to me.

"Release," I answered her, from a clear and resounding intuitive place.

And the dot became the glowing large red orb humming on the screen. It was the most beautiful image I had ever created in my life, up until then. I sighed a deep sigh of release. Relief. *Release.*

In hindsight, I looked more closely at why her suggestions of meditating and walking failed to relax me. I hadn't realized just how tightly I was wound.

The way that meditation involved an upright posture created more tension in my body. I often held tension in my pelvis while trying to do it right. I had learned the notion of "not too tight, not too loose," from my meditation instructors about how I held my mind, but I had not applied it to all the way down to my pelvis. And I hadn't really released my mind. The body speaks the mind. My controlling mind tightened my pelvis. Here it was, on display in the therapist's office.

Was this why I needed augmentation during childbirth?

Walking had always been a form of exercise and "relaxation," in other words, I felt better afterward. Yet when the therapist told me to imagine walking, I instinctively held in my gut and tucked my pelvis, in some attempt to make my belly flatter and my butt smaller, another introjected message from the dominant culture, *suck it up, tuck it in.*

I was literally seeing on the screen how uptight and tight-assed I've been. Yikes and wow. Daunting and liberating. It was *both, and,* for sure.

I ruminate on what is really mine to own. I contract in fear and expand in faith. I ask my soul friends to show me the way to calm abiding. I've been told that there are a lot of unemployed angels out there waiting for us to ask for their help. Please help.

We are in the midst of a revolution in consciousness. As a social pioneer, I am living with extended family and all the joys and challenges that go along with that, including accepting that I need others. Surrender to win. This is big. I used to feel weak if I was needy. Mom told me we were survivors. Do survivors ever express need? I say yes. Acknowledging this need has transformed my relationships.

We are wounded in relationship and it is in relationship that we heal. I supplicate the creative intelligence, *"Please show me the way to enjoy calm abiding."* And as I hug my beloveds, I pray silently, *"Please show me how to embrace who I truly am, not who I think you think I should be. Please embrace who you truly are, not who you think I think you should be."*

What if you truly cease fighting anyone or anything? I believe you are stronger as a result. What if you let go of the notion of us and them? I believe we are interconnected and we can weave the web of peaceful coexistence on a daily basis. If you want world peace, you get to start in your home. What if you allow yourself to be more fully resourced and resilient? I believe in the Creative Power of the Universe to restore us to beauty, grace, and acceptance. What if we embrace the embrace that is offered? From this place, we are reactivated toward optimal heart health. I believe in the incredible inherent wisdom of the body to heal.

The seventh distinction of an extraordinary life is reactivation. Wake up. Take ownership of your state of health. I invite you to reactivate your connection with spirit to take you to new levels of joy and usefulness.

Where I'm from hurt people hurt people. I didn't want to hurt anyone, so luckily, I had no choice but to heal the hurt. Divorce roared through the family; I concluded I'd never marry. I thought another degree behind my name would give me the sense of worthiness and belonging I craved, thereby antidoting the loneliness that dominant culture subliminally fed me. When I'm hurt and lonely, I'm more likely to buy what you're buying, it hopes of having the life that you're having. I release the pinch of dominant culture's message that something outside of myself will cure me.

As I'm sitting here I'm experiencing more blessings in my life than I can say grace over; including the fact that I'm married for 17 years, many of them happily. We have two amazing boys, one of whom just attended his first high school dance last night, nearly the same age I was when I first got drunk. When I have an attitude of gratitude, I can turn frustrations into appreciations, and this, dear reader, is master's level in relational health. Instead of fueling the fire of frustration for my past, I appreciate the gift of being a sober mom today.

What matters most is activating compassion through forgiveness. Forgiveness, as a mentor once taught me, is letting go of the notion of ever having a different past. It breeds acceptance. It is liberating. It is for-giving. Forgive everyone, everything, including yourself, is a spiritual truth I heard a 98-year-old woman share. I've never forgotten it. Forgiveness equals a long life? Maybe not a direct correlation, but it certainly precedes a contented life, with no stones of resentment clogging up the heart.

Where I'd like to be is promoting power and passion in partnership through coaching the women and men who want to love their love life, and nurture their children to wholehearted purpose, so that they can be a powerful presence in the world. *Power in partnership* is the future. *Power over* others is the past. The relational paradigm is vitally essential to heal our broken world. When I get over my drama, I have more energy to get on with healing the planet, one relationship at a time.

One thing I can do to get me there is to continue writing, speaking, and living the magic of conscious couplehood and recognizing the inherent power in partnership. The energetic exchange I enjoy with my beloved husband feeds me in ways I didn't know I needed to be fed. I let myself need him, and this, dear reader, took Herculean effort in the early stages of our relationship. When I have more compassion for self, it means more skillful means with others; this basic tenet stoked my contemplative psychology education at Naropa University, where I trained in Buddhist Psychology, received a Master's Degree, and met the man of my dreams.

One thing I appreciate is that God did for me what I couldn't do for myself. I didn't adopt a monastic life, though I was close when I took Buddhist refuge vows. I didn't let self-aggression tear me down, though my tolerance for myself was slim. And I didn't know the journey of the full life of family and marriage would be composed of dignity, respect, sexuality, honor, curiosity and mystery; most of the time glued together with a big old dollop of grace. You see, God has entered into my heart and works in a way that is indeed miraculous.

The miracle here being that I can let go of worrying about using the word, "God," for fear of misrepresentation, and embrace the pure intention and inherent challenge of trying to define or label that which remains forever a mystery to me. And so it is, "God." I don't mean to confuse you, Dear Reader. Yes, I'm a Buddhist who believes in God, practices yoga and studies Hawai'i lifeways. It's beyond the both, and, it is everything.

Chapter Eight: Energy

energy-ordinary definition:
the strength and vitality required for sustained physical or mental activity

energy-extraordinary definition:
the current of vital information exchange that regenerates landscapes

Universe
Put me in the places you want me to be
With the people you want me to be with
Doing the thing you want me to do
I am grateful for the joys and challenges
In my life
Namaste
~Tommy Rosen, Recovery 2.0 prayer

Yoga Makes Me Feel

Where I'm from, I'm a small being on a big planet, a speck on the beach. Humble, I'm a baby, sitting in the lap of a parent, on the shore, waves tickling my feet, I thought, *there are more pelicans than people.* Full of wonder and awe of the Grace surrounding me, not consciously aware of it, but completely bathed in it, I go to sleep. Vibrant, I recall waking up to the next moment with eager anticipation. Hunting Easter eggs at age three, I feel unburdened by the struggles and demands of life. I sensed the burdens in others, this weight that filled their hearts and filled the nooks and crannies of the spaces around me, still, I was free for a time. Up to age four, I felt free.

Alive, I'm five, running down the beach. Cartwheeling. Singing. Soul smiling. Running. Moving. Away. Grateful, I'm six, sharing a sunrise with my dad, then pancakes on the beach, melting Cadbury eggs; a birthday party with friends riding the waves of the Atlantic. At seven, I'm in touch with the vibrancy of my senses and comfortable in my own skin. Sensing vertigo from being in the surf all day, this is what I imagine a washing machine feels like. I close my eyes at night, inner ear still moving, settling, recalibrating. Underwater, I feel safe, cradled, soothed. At eight, I'm growing tolerant of pain, I feel the burn of the sun. Too much sun. I enjoy the challenge of peeling the biggest swath of skin off my brother's burnt back. At a young age, making lemonade out of lemons, I'm learning resiliency. Powerful, at nine, I'm still riding the waves of the Atlantic with my body, attuned to the Natural Great Beauty surrounding me. Up until double digits, age 10, I feel so full of Divine Spirit. Life got infinitely more complex after that.

As I'm sitting here, I'm experiencing immense appreciation for the practice of yoga to return me to my youthful soul and the positive qualities of childhood. Yoga makes me feel humble, wonderful, vibrant, free, alive, grateful, sexy, tolerant of pain, powerful, still, and full of Divine Spirit. It's indeed that amazing and all encompassing. Seriously, I longed to feel this calm and energized, simultaneously at ease and ready, for my entire life. For much of my childhood I did feel this way. The rest of my life has been a daily reprieve back, based on committed contemplative action.

Yoga makes me feel an epic sense of self-realization. Writing this helps me realize how much a gift yoga is, how much a gift childhood is, and how easy it is to be detoured toward addictive behaviors while riding the stormy waves of birth, old age, sickness and death. In other words, no wonder I binge drank alcohol and experimented with altered states through taking various drugs into my sacred temple. My brain was already hijacked by surging hormones and my forehead tattooed with invisible "neocortex development under construction" signs until at least age twenty-five.

My hormones raced out of control, my emotions carried me on tidal waves of despair and elation, and I lacked the sense of calm abiding needed to sustain me. In the past, while behaving addictively, I was trying to connect with all of these aforementioned luscious qualities of my youth. I was seeking Spirit in a bottle of spirits. I was smoking to get high, a high my body could create on its own without chemical substances. I felt it as a child and now, as an adult, I understand yoga is a technology to assist me in self-generating these positive states of mind, body, and Spirit.

One thing I appreciate is that yoga makes me feel energized. I get energy from my yoga practice. Creating energy and space in my body and mind brings prana in an inter-cellular space. With prana, breath, in every cell of my being, wellness ensues. Significant results in a daily practice of even 10-20 minutes helped reduced anxiety and depression and improved my overall mental-health. It is wildly magical how I can start my practice feeling sleepy and lethargic and finish my practice feeling horny and alive. Movement, breath, relaxation all help me with self-regulation, *stepping into command central of*

Moonshot

my nervous system, as I like to say. Particularly with Kundalini yoga, one of the many kinds of yoga I have practiced over the last thirty years, I feel an awakening happening. I subtly sense the energy moving up my spine.

In my early 20s, that rising of energy got hijacked by destructive behaviors. I got stuck. Now, while enjoying freedom from (most) addictive behaviors, I feel free.

When my husband does yoga with me, I feel ecstatic. My energy is flowing, his energy is flowing; I am more turned on when we get our energies flowing together in these serpentine and seductive ways.

Where I'd like to be is feeling connected and protected. Yoga makes me feel connected and protected. **One thing I can do is** start my day with yoga chants by tuning in to the universal chanting, one that is continually riding the waves of worldwide sound currents. I tap into a source of energy beyond my own construction. I chant yoga chants to tune my brain. I chant yoga chants to join the lineage of all teachers and masters before me. I chant yoga chants to ask for protection, for creativity juiciness, for peace and harmony, for strength, for all imaginable and unimaginable guidance. I chant to honor my ancestors.

What matters most is action. Yoga is meditation in action. Yoga is finding prayer in posture. Yoga is meeting myself daily on the mat, the herculean act of simply showing up makes me feel successful; accepting myself wherever I am, and loving myself unconditionally.

Yoga makes me feel strong, like really strong, not work-out-at-the-gym-kinda strong. My core is active, my breathing is enhanced, my limbs limber and lean. The *pranayam,* the breath work, is central to my on-going yoga practice, which I carry with me at any time of the day. Deep breaths cure me of deep-seated anxiety. **One thing I appreciate** is that by expanding my breathing basket, my ribs, and inviting the soft tissue of my heart to truly allow itself to be cradled in the loving limbs of the lung tree, I release worry and invite calm. I am stronger now, after thirty years of yoga practice. For this, I am truly grateful, *sat nam* —truth is my identity.

The eighth distinction of an extraordinary life is an energized life. Explore what gives you juice, what enables you to feel resourced to do this gig called life with grace and ease.

Beloved God

Free our minds so we may know our hearts
that we may flow and go with Thee in Thy will
in Thy creation as you have made us all.
That in this way we may serve and love
and live for each other
in Harmony and Peace
recognizing Thy flow within us and all around us.
Sat Nam

~Snatam Kaur, Kundalini Yoga Prayer

Invitations to Reclaim Wellness

In summary, what happened was I practiced yoga, I got sober, I studied Buddhist Psychology, I got married, I had kids, and I moved to paradise. These are all powerful landmarks in my life. I developed core compassion with clarity of mind, openness of heart, reactivation of spirit and energizing my life.

Your landmarks will look different. Yet the invitation is to find portals into your own well-being. For me, the portals of yoga, sobriety, meditation, fidelity, family, and hula are all powerful entry points. Find yours now. If you want help, reach out.

I want to offer an invitation to reclaim wellness. It is our birthright. Here I offer is another perspective on some of the challenges we as privileged adults may encounter in our day to day lives within the realm of wellness. Having a different framework can open us up to new possibilities of workability. My invitation is to explore a new vernacular of the continuum of mental health we traverse daily.

The Five Buddha Families and The Six Realms

The Buddha families, which my husband and I learned about while studying Contemplative Psychology at Naropa University, describe five environments of the human mind. Each family has a color associated with it, and a particular trait. This trait can manifest in the human mind somewhere on a spectrum; the sane or wise end of the spectrum and a more dysfunctional or neurotic end of the spectrum.

At *Maitri* (Sanskrit word meaning lovingkindness), a month-long retreat of meditation each year of our graduate program, we enjoyed (and at times, endured) communal living and daily meditation practices and periods of silence. We worked together in the kitchen, tended to our cabins, and familiarized ourselves with the inner-workings of our own mind. In the Maitri rooms, we would spend days in each Buddha family. Each room a specific color, as well as a specific posture, all meant to evoke a specific emotion. Here is a very brief overview and an invitation to dive deeper:

- *Ratna* is the family of rich earthly substance, a golden yellow hue, the trait of resources. It manifests as abundance in wisdom, scarcity in neurosis. The sane side of this energetic manifestation implies a deep gratitude and appreciation for all the rich worldly delights, a sense of groundedness, a sense of full circle completion.
- **Invitation**—The next time you sense lack in your life, turn around, 180 degrees, and invite a sense of abundance into your mind.
- *Padma* is the family of relationships, a bright red hue, the trait of connection. It manifests as healthy passionate intimacy in wisdom, codependence in neurosis. The sane side of this energetic manifestation implies genuine, authentic connection with Self, Other, and Spirit.
- **Invitation**—The next time you find loving someone else is hurting you, step back a few steps and invite a deep, soft gaze into the mirror of your Soul and then out the window to the vast open sky above. Trust the truth that comes when you are connected honestly with yourself and open like the sky.
- *Karma* is the family of energy, a vibrant green hue, the trait of productivity. It manifests as steady, consistent energy in wisdom, speediness and absent mindedness and carelessness in neurosis. The sane side of this energetic manifestation implies adequate resourcefulness to activate when needed and to rest when needed.

- **Invitation**—The next time you are spinning out of control, stop, drop and breathe. Do less to get more. Trust that filling your reservoirs is a vital step in wellbeing.
- *Vajra* is the family of intellect, a brilliant blue hue, the trait of deep knowing. It manifests as discriminating wisdom or painful criticism that cuts like a knife, unskillfully dissecting another person or even oneself with sharp feedback. The sane side of this energetic manifestation implies keen awareness of timing, tone and technique when sharing information with others.
- **Invitation**—The next time you are critical of self or other, pause and notice the pain underneath your commentary. Consider that criticism is the adult cry. Try a creative expression of the hurt in a way that connects you to yourself and/or others more lovingly.
- *Buddha* is the family of presence, a bright pervasive white, the trait of omniscience. It manifests either as all-encompassing wisdom or dull vapidity. The sane side of this energetic manifestation implies a deep unconditional peace and love that contains all beings.
- **Invitation**—The next time you are disconnected from the present moment, surrender to the ever-present presence of gravity, holding you here, now. Breathe.

Buddhist Psychology has six realms. I offer a brief overview offer here as a further invitation to look at your daily mental states and aim high for an extraordinary life.

- The Hungry Ghost Realm—Picture a pencil thin neck on a bloated belly, a gaping mouth trying to jam stuff in that will never, ever, satiate the belly. Addictions. Wanting more. Fear of losing what you have (boyfriend, grades, money) or not getting what you want (boyfriend, grades, money).

- **Invitation**—Turn your attention to where you have enough: start a list, start with the small things, enough toilet paper, enough gas to get to the store, enough breath to make it up the stairs, and build from there.
- Write for 20 minutes on this topic. I have enough...
- The God Realm—floating around high on life with no ground of reality under you. Living high on the hog and wanting to remain removed from the earthly base in which we live.
- **Invitation**—Turn your attention to your connection with the earth. Go to the beach and walk barefoot. Go to your garden and dig in the earth and get dirt under your nails. Jump to feel the soar and land to feel the ground supporting you.
- Write for 20 minutes on this topic. I feel grounded when...
- The Human Realm—Wrestling with your reality and wanting to be somewhere you are not, then desirous of where you are and not wanting it to end. Utter discontent. Pulling geographical cures in where you live and where you work. Always thinking the grass is greener somewhere else.
- **Invitation**—Name the fact that you are caught in the samsaric wheel of life. Samsara is the cycle of death and rebirth to which the life in the material world is bound. Chasing after desires and running from revulsion and hanging out in ignorance are the three poisons. Passion, aggression, ignorance. Three poisons. Notice the things in your life you want more of, want less of, and the things you

are ignorant of, including people. For twenty minutes, see what emerges, notice. Without labeling anything good or bad, right or wrong, just noticing. This I'm drawn toward, this I'm drawn away from, this I could care less about. The point is to increase awareness.

- Write for 20 minutes on this topic. I cling to...I push from...I ignore...
- The Jealous Gods Realm—Wanting what someone else has and despising that person for having it. Based on scarcity, based on Hungry Ghost.
- **Invitation**—Experience equanimity, spontaneous joy for someone else's good fortune. Write a letter or text or email to express appreciation for this matter. Celebrate everyone's wins.
- Write for 20 minutes on this topic. I celebrate...
- The Animal Realm—Nose to the grindstone, doing what is next, not aware of surroundings, only wanting reward of in and out. Food in/ shit out. Pleasure on either end. Sex, in and out. Instinctual drives a primary motivation.
- **Invitation**—Free yourself from the grind by going out tonight and looking up. You may see stars, moon, clouds, lights, rainbows. Notice what happens when you shift your gaze. When you return to your work, set a timer to do a dance/ stretch break every 20 minutes. Bust free from mediocrity, blow the roof off the ordinary.
- Write for 20 minutes on this topic. When I look out the window, I see...
- The Hell Realm—icy hot, or fiery cold. The extremes of discomfort and suffering. The illusion that it will never end, that no one knows what you are experiencing. Feeling trapped by

circumstances beyond your control. Terminally unique and utterly alone.

- **Invitation**—Generate internal warmth and stimulate all 76,000 nerve endings in your body. Dry skin brushing up towards your heart first. Self-massage with sesame oil for real treat to self-soothe. Take a cold shower every morning for three weeks (unless you are on your menstrual cycle).
- Write for 20 minutes on this topic. I generate warmth by...

Exercises—4X4X4X4

Breathwork is a surefire way to bring integration in the moment. Sit quietly without distractions. That's polite way to say, put away your fucking devices for a spell. Turn off the screens around you. Inhale for a slow count of four. Pause at the peak of inhalation for a count of four. Exhale for a slow count of four. Pause at the bottom of the exhalation for four. Repeat for a total of four times. This breath is like a monster 4x4 truck crashing onto the scene of your mental movie. It grabs all the attention. It is commanding. It is powerful. Do not underestimate your ability to set yourself right in any moment. Your breath is always available to you. You don't need a script. You don't need money. You don't need anything, but your attention.

Writing Prompts

What message did you receive as a child? We name them to tame them.

- Consider the different neighborhoods of your mind—you could label them: core being, thinking, feeling, acting, and sensing.
- Think of five messages that sting. Negative messages of socialization. Notice when you recoil in reactivity.
- This is gold, very valuable information for your own transformation.
- Write them down.
- Now rewrite them. Give yourself positive messages that support you.

Next, look at the five people today to whom you have a reaction:

- Five positives, five negatives.
- Write down the qualities in that person you responded to.
- Possible positive reactions: beauty, fitness, generosity, wisdom, kindness.
- Possible negative reactions: loud, aggressive, bullying, brazen, controlling.
- Now pause for a moment.
- Consider that these traits are somewhere in you, too.
- Lost, disowned, and denied, perhaps, but in you, somewhere.
- The invitation is to integrate them now. If you spot it, you've got it.

A bridge of connection between the realm of compassion and the realm of service, is tuning in to my heart's desire. This is a fantastic writing prompt that a dear friend offered me and now I pass it along to you, along with a sampling of my desires.

My Heart's Desire …

My heart's desire is to live surrounded by beauty, peace and love. Today I have this.

My heart's desire is to feel the support of my family but not be dependent on them for my uprightness (or blame them for my uptightness). I need the help to raise my boys. I need family to hold, to comfort, to bond, to show how to live with each other.

My heart's desire is to return to gratitude, again and again. This is my religion, just like Oprah. An attitude of gratitude is the taproot of my life, and it miraculously goes with me regardless of where I am.

My heart's desire is to have a money tree, with roots sturdy and strong, based in the foundation of good values and collective wellbeing. The fruits of our labor are vast.

My heart's desire is to love up my family without getting stuck in the quagmire of their stuff. I feel deeply what is going on with other people. I notice the subtle innuendos as if they were billboards. I sense their energetic current running through me. I want to unplug without utterly disconnecting or flatlining.

My heart's desire is to allow the sweet bird song to gently bring me back to the present moment.

My heart's desire is to heal the relationship with myself in the present moment.

My heart's desire is live without the horror and unremitting need for redemption. They're the daily dismaying dalliances, the perennial angst that lies just under the surface and whispers to me in the morning, "how are you feeling now?"

My heart's desire is to allow the neurochemical cascade of my morning smile to imbue my being with an unflappable alrightness.

My heart's desire is to befriend the notion that "the obstacle is the way." If this is true my obstacle is myself. I get in the way of myself all the time. My husband said to me last week, "you make things so complicated." And so it is. I make things complicated. Whenever my self-aggression comes up, I'm going to say what Vonnegut says whenever somebody dies, "and so it is;" it's part of me dying: My self-aggression dying.

My heart's desire is to recall the decades of healing I've done. I've done work with shaman; Soul retrieval work, to gain back the little pieces of me that went with every guy that came inside of me. It dripped out, oozing. It being my self-esteem, my self-respect; dripping down my leg, the release of someone else precipitating the clenching down within me. The clench. A big part of my journey is to release this clench, release the pinch, release the grip. I hold myself so tightly. I analyze everything.

My heart's desire is to release the pinch.

My heart desire is to disrupt the parallel lines of the pleasure/pain pathway in my mind and enjoy sex more and more with each passing day. (And I do!)

My heart's desire is to remember every man and woman I made love with as giving me access to different aspects of myself. The artist, the pianist, the Swiss military, the African

American dancer, the Latino tennis instructor and actor, the green tea loving meditator, the singer, the stylist, the politician, the criminal.

My heart's desire is to return to calm and engage in fiery transformation, simultaneously, or at least in the same lifetime.

My heart's desire is to heal analysis paralysis.

My heart's desire is to fill the void within me with Spirit, not the spirits of Bacardi rum or the Jing of another person, but with the universal creative spark which unites all of us in a dazzling array of unique, yet patterned beauty. Murmuration at its finest.

My heart's desire is to cultivate the love that women are getting more empowered are waking up are finding their voice. I can say, "me too." Without the angst. Minus the shame, blame and criticism of another that is just that wounded part of me lashing out. Hurt people hurt people. It doesn't get me where I want to go.

My heart's desire is to be both being loving and forgiving. It's standing up for myself, speaking the truth, and not vilifying the other. Perhaps you vilify me for suggesting such a thing. And so it is.

My heart's desire is to allow (and possibly facilitate) the intentional dialogue so needed for healing and accepting power in partnership.

My heart's desire is to ask, "What would it be like if we (as wounded women) got curious, really curious what it is that these perpetrators need? Inquiry matters.

My heart's desire is to acknowledge that we all have unmet needs. What if I acknowledge they're all equally important?

My heart's desire is to seek the common denominator in those needs. Maybe this is groundbreaking, maybe crazy, but perpetuating the Us and Them mentality is the breeding ground for war, greed, scarcity, and suffering. Period. It doesn't work.

My heart's desire is to cease fighting anyone or anything, without being a doormat.

My heart's desire is to have someone hold my hand and kick me in the butt at the same time. By that I mean nurtured guidance.

My heart's desire is to know that when I am looking for God, I am already lost.

My heart's desire is to write a book with my husband, to teach with my husband, to do a lot with my husband.

My heart's desire is to say, "*Mahalo*," "thank you," many times a day, in every language imaginable.

My heart's desire is to embrace what comes.

My heart's desire is to not chase after anything.

My heart's desire is to let go of what goes.

My heart's desire is to enjoy the beauty of the hibiscus blooming in the middle of our garden that we have been chanting and blessing and tending to daily. It is a miracle that that little stump of a hibiscus produced such a beautiful blossom. We are growing good soil. We focus on the soil not a specific breed of person. This is non-attachment to the outcome. I'm talking about flowers and children, ideas and dreams. Cultivate good soil, daily, as a daily tender act of kindness.

My heart's desire is to pay attention to this new moon this night, this opportunity to see glorious stars and planets, possibilities and partnerships, and to release of worry and guilt.

My heart's desire is to feel the comfort of my own skin.

My heart's desire is to allow my willingness to show up in my life to tend to my side of the street and let other people find their own way. If they ask for help, if they want my services, if they want something of me I want them to ask. I read last night in Hawaiian book called *The Healers*, by Kimo Armitage, "any unwanted kindness is an unkindness." I think that's one of the reasons I get in a lot of trouble sometimes internally.

My heart's desire is to recognize the supports I have within my various communities.

My heart's desire is right livelihood; to earn good money, lead with generosity, and not overwork.

My heart's desire is to have my skin breathe, release, detox, and let go of the itch.

My heart's desire is to allow space for grace.

My heart's desire is to have information of how to best treat my right-wing (my shoulder girdle and arm) so I can integrate my masculine side. Strange I just said right wing I don't mean that in that Ultra conservative political sense. I mean it as the part of me the opposite of my left wing. Oh how funny this all sounds. I'm a human being I don't really have wings so maybe I need to let go of that analogy. But I do have a desire to store and to fly and feel the freedom within my own being.

My heart's desire is to have a wonderful lunch with my sponsor and her dear friend and celebrate recovery, celebrate life.

My heart's desire is to grow myself out of the way as a good enough mother and trust my boys know how to navigate their inner landscape (after attachment parenting).

My heart's desire is to drink good coffee, daily.

My heart's desire is to breathe fresh air.

My heart's desire is to enjoy foreign films.

My heart's desire is to ride bikes.

My heart's desire is to endorse the arts, I believe that art saves lives.

My heart's desire is to preserve Hawai'i lifeways.

My heart's desire is to fully comprehend aloha.

My heart's desire is to be embodied and loving and strong.

Part III: **What it's like now**

Realm of Service

service-ordinary definition:
the act of helping or doing work for someone

service-extraordinary definition:
the way of living that uplifts the world

Ask yourself, why am I here, now?

This is a new cosmology we create today. We are all family.

I'm only necessary because you are here.
~Kekuhi Keali'ikanaka'oleohailelani
Founder, Creator & Trainer of Hālau 'Ōhi'a

What it is like now is the life of aloha. I live with my husband, my boys, my in-laws, and my cats in a lovely island home in the tropical beauty in the middle of the Pacific Ocean; the most isolated place from other inhabited lands.

I throw myself into service because it is the quickest route out of egoic constriction and man-made misery. I create inner peace and harmonious relations to improve the health of the planet. As a dear friend said just yesterday, and I agree wholeheartedly, I'm committed to being beautifully self- abundant and outrageous, huge with the universe from a place of grounded abundance.

I can bring rain where we need rain, like on Kanaloa. I can bring creative destructive energies like the Pele. I can create and dwell in the calm of the storm and feel the ripple effects into the world.

And I've come to understand that how I do one thing is how I do everything. If I want a more beautiful world, why not start within and quit beating up on myself so fucking much? If I want world peace, why not love up my husband even though there are fleeting moments I want to vaporize him? If I wish to eliminate pollution, why not start with the internal environment and love up my in-laws and eliminate the toxic powerplants of dominant culture's story that spews plumes of derogatory pollution that hate is permitted and part of the mixture of these relations. I lovingly call, "bullshit."

I can choose aloha in each breath, to fill my heart with gladness, to fill my bowl of light. I can do this in order to enjoy life and, more importantly, to be of maximum service to God and my fellows.

Moving to Hawai'i afforded me a chance to slow down. In fact, each place I have moved affords me that to a greater degree. Perhaps this corresponds with getting older. Perhaps the environment reflects the mind.

I hold myself upright, not too tight, not too loose. I'm incredibly attached to my boys, but I don't helicopter or overbear. In certain pieces of my wardrobe, I have pockets of neuroses that hold a surprise $20 bill in them. I don't give up and I feel life fully in all of its immense intensity. I stay sober, no matter what. I trust all is well, no matter what.

What it's like now, is I live more in the space of "we" rather than "me."

Thanks to the encouragement of my editor, Sam, and all the others waiting for my Moonshot to crown, I ride the waves of anxiety with a wee bit more ease. Sounds oxymoronic, yes? My hard drive is full and my bank account is in the red, yet I'm not spiritually bankrupt. I'm rich beyond measure, just look at my smiling eyes. The anxiety of this book being wildly successful is present, as well as the concern it sits on the shelf of the thrift store collecting dust bunnies and gecko poop. If I may touch the life of at least one person in a positively transformative way to elevate human potential, I am happy. May it be so.

The life we have today is indeed extraordinary. It is one of recognizing our interconnection, being responsible for the way we show up in the world, sharing our lives generously with others, and cultivating conscious connections.

What it's like now is that the roof is burning off Notre Dame. May they reconstruct it after a fresh look at its contents, with fresh air blowing out the cobwebs. Blessings on the power of a new breath of meaning in the intrinsic beauty of all religions. Yes, all of them hold a core nugget worth restoring, regenerating, and reinvigorating.

We create amazing community and connection wherever we live, wherever we go. We love to host with meals, celebrations, tree plantings, beach clean-ups, and pulling over on the side of the road to pick up trash. We are committed to creating love, connection, and commitment in the world. It's service. Serving human relations to serve the greater good. We ignite generosity, compassion, and transformation for a united world.

Chapter Nine: Interdependence

interdependence-ordinary definition:
the dependence of two or more people on each other

interdependence-extraordinary definition:
the way of living that uplifts the world (yes, it's the same as service definition)

When you realize there is nothing lacking,
the whole world belongs to you.
~Lao Tzu

The greatest threat to our planet is the belief that someone else will save it.
~Robert Swan, English Explorer

I ola 'oe,
i ola mākou nei

My life is dependent on yours,
Your life is dependent on mine

Aloha to you, (from my *kumu*)
"*I ola 'oe, i ola mākou nei*" is a simple, yet profound thought that says, "I am interdependent on you, and you on interdependent on me." As island people, we know this to be true in the way we interact with each other, our families and our community. Sometimes we forget to include natural environment as a part of our community. Hawai'i lifeways, sometimes expressed as Hawaiian culture, teaches us that landscape, sky, and the ocean ARE our family—just like our "family" family! By learning a little more about the Hawai'i lifeways, language, ritual, music, hula, poetry, chant, wahi pana or pulsing places, the arts and many other aspects—we learn more about how to express aloha for the POTENTIAL of our island home...AND, for ourselves.

~Kekuhi Keali'ikanaka'oleohaililani, Founder & Trainer of Hālau 'Ōhi'a.

Aloha Defined

Aloha—love, affection, compassion, mercy, sympathy, pity, kindness, sentiment, grace, charity; greeting, salutation, regards; sweetheart, lover, loved one; beloved, loving, kind, compassionate, charitable, lovable; to love, be fond of; to show kindness, mercy, pity, charity, affection; to venerate; to remember with affection; to greet, hail. Greetings! Hello! Good-by! Farewell! Alas!

~Mary Kawena Pukui, Hawaiian Dictionary

The word *aloha* itself stands for principles and guiding forces. Spell it out; A–L–O–H–A; look at each letter.

Ahonui–Patience, expressed with perseverance (literally the great breath).
Lokahi–Unity, expressed harmoniously.
'Olu'olu–Agreeableness, expressed with pleasantness.
Ha'a ha'a–Humility, expressed with modesty.
Akahai–Gentle kindness, expressed with tenderness.

Hālau 'Ohi'a

Another possible definition of aloha is *alo-ha*. *Alo* is face and *hā* is breath. This is the beautiful practice of sharing breath with the Natural Great Beauty. I've shared aloha with our world. I've always communicated with the natural world. Moving here, and living the Island consciousness, I found an amazing community, called ***Hālau 'Ōhi'a***, where this is the norm.

Joining ***Hālau 'Ōhi'a***, a unique professional development opportunity, and engaging with our landscape through Hawai'i lifeways, positions me to learn more about communicating with the natural world. This is the group of folks I went with to the remote island that was a previous target for military bombing. My classmates are primarily employed with natural resource management. My particular spin on natural resource management has to do with managing ourselves, our breath, and our relationships. Together, we are foundational to the well-being of the landscape. Together, we learn skills we can apply to our professional and personal lives.

Hālau 'Ōhi'a, Hawai'i Stewardship Training, is a unique, personal and professional development program, developed and taught by Kekuhi Keali'ikanaka'oleohaililani, master *kumu*, teacher and trainer, for stewards of the Hawai'i landscape. *Hālau* translates to traditional school of learning. *Hālau* literally means "many breaths" and is often focused on the traditional art of hula. *'Ōhi'a*, literally "to gather," is the name of the most bio-culturally important native tree in Hawai'i.

Here, in *Hālau 'Ōhi'a*, we have the great good fortune of learning, as well as unlearning. Through remembering and recognizing that our function on this planet is foundational to the well-being of our landscapes, we focus on deepening our connections for the well-being of ourselves and *honua*, earth. When we see our trees as our ancestors we unlearn the notion of us/them and we tend to our relationships with respectful protection and care.

We focus on this communication and the reciprocity of our energetic exchanges with all aspects of life. In our formal training in *Hālau 'Ōhi'a*, we chant for permission to enter a space. We chant to encourage things to grow. We chant to welcome the sunrise. We pay attention to the energetic exchanges with all creatures, great and small, seen and unseen.

I've received permission to reprint some of our chants. Below is our chant when we are excited to see something grow. I'm excited to see your transform grow, and I'm encouraging it full out, utterly and completely, and so it is that I offer this.

Pule Ho'oulu

He mele ku'una Traditional text. Date Unknown.
Source: Unwritten Literature, N. Emerson, 1918
Published: Edith Kanaka'ole Foundation, 2005

E ulu ē
E ulu kini o ke akua
Ulu a'e 'o Kāne me Kanaloa
Ulu ka 'ōhi'a a lau ka wai
Ka 'ie'ie
Ulu a'e ke akua a noho i kona kahu
E ia ka wai lā
He wai ola
E ola ia'u i ke kumu
E ola i ke po'o, ke po'o pua'a
E ola i ka pae, ka paepae
E ola i nā haumana, nā haumana a pau
'Eli'eli kapu, 'eli'eli noa

One translation offered:

Increase our knowledge, multitude of gods
Inspire us, Kāne and Kanaloa
Grow and nourish us like the 'ōhi'a leaf and the 'ie'ie
Inspire the guardian to stay and persevere
Here is the water, the `ceremonial `awa, the water of life
Give life to the source
Give life to the leader
Give life to the hula assistant
Life to all the students
Profound the kapu, profound its lifting

I chant for those things I want to see grow and thrive. Finding a chant that connects me more fully to my life is a true gift. I chant *E Ulu E* as I water the garden. I plant special plant friends with names and symbols that mean something to me.

The plant, *Brunfelsia grandiflora*, has flowers that change color, symbolizing *yesterday, today, tomorrow*; in fact, that's its common name, yesterday, today, tomorrow. I gave this to my beloved husband, Marc, on our sweet sixteen wedding anniversary and it is that I water the love of our marriage when I water this plant.

I bought a plant called, Thevetia peruviana, "be still," at my younger son, Toby's, school plant sale. I painted a sign that says "be still" and it reminds me that I'm a human being not a human doing. I transplanted the plant to a bigger pot and it went on a growing spree. It is ready to expand even more. Presently, it is growing near a local plant called "*hau*" which is pronounced, "how." It is fun to communicate with the creatures and features of the landscape.

Profound wisdom exists in the question, "How?" and the reply, "Be still."

Tucking orchids in the armpits of trees and watching them bloom, I have fun in the garden. I plant *mamaki* and *kokola'au* to make plant medicine tea for us. We have *la'i* or ti leaves, which are good friends to have nearby, for all sorts of reasons. We love our *'ōhi'a* trees in the front yard; the bees also love them.

What I water grows, both in the garden and in the mind. The landscape in Hawai'i is resilient and everything loves to grow. Even when the house was tented for termites, the vegetation near the front door came back, strong and resilient.

I've heard often that what we need is right in front of us. I need strong and reliant influencers in my life. I need to answer "how?" with "be still." I need love. I need strong blood. Yesterday, today and tomorrow.

As I'm sitting here, I'm reminded that diversity thrives when there is common purpose. The common purpose of *Hālau ʻŌhiʻa* is preserving Hawaiʻi lifeways.

I was invited by a former client to join *Hālau ʻŌhiʻa*, a class led by a well-known *kumu* (teacher) in Hilo, Hawaiʻi. Curious about Hawaiian cultural protocol and how to be a part of the solution of preserving and protecting the wellness of the islands, I joined. I checked my ego at the door and I felt a deeper sense of belonging and purpose. **Where I'd like to be** is living and breathing the power of ritual to connect with life in powerful ways beyond measure.

Most other *haumana*, students, were somehow involved in natural resources and conservation organizations. **One thing I can do** is to continue learning the protocols and myths of all the cultures of this fascinating planet. There is so much commonality. The common denominator of mankind is Mother Earth.

Fear of not belonging once held me prisoner within myself, there is some residual fear, but I am grateful it now fits in a pocket and is not the big cage that constricted me and blocked my authentic presence.

What matters most is that I trusted myself to not abandon myself, and through the reality of interdependence, I trusted others to not abandon me either.

Where I'm from, the story I would have told myself was that I was an outsider and didn't belong because of the color of my skin, or the fact that I didn't fit as a conservation employee under the umbrella of an organization.

I took a stand for myself and focused on myself and in doing so, I stood for others and focused on the whole planet. As a relationship health coach, I got to walk my talk. I embraced courage. By this I mean I drove myself 1.5 hours to Hilo, and brought my pocket-sized fear, which seemed to grow larger on the commute. I would stop on Saddle Road and hike a beautiful spot, *puʻu huluʻhulu,* for a sunrise. Resourced. After buying a healthy lunch at the store, I would walk in, nervous as all get out, and join, even with loud chorus of "NO" ringing in my head.

This class was unlike any other class. As a Master's level student in the perpetual school of life, I have attended and taught a fair number of classes. The introduction and background of each student is typically a part of that process. Even with online classes nowadays, you type in who you are and where you are from at the beginning of class.

There was no role call in our first class of *Papa Hui* (the seedling of the *'ohia* tree). We sat on *lauhala* (woven plant) mats in an indoor/outdoor classroom at the University of Hilo. We laughed. We laughed a lot and this helped us remember what *kumu* was saying. I believe memories get lodged in the brain, the hippocampus, much more readily if they are bathed in an emotional bath at the time of learning.

Our kumu admitted that she was nervous. Her rock star persona that I had built up in my head after hearing who she was brought back to the earthly plane when she shared her humanness with us. We are interdependent.

To me, she is humbly fantastic. For this I am truly grateful, because my history of putting people on a pedestal of-better-than inevitably implies that I am less than and I don't like this self-talk anymore. I have changed the channel on it, though the static of it sometimes tries to overtake the other channels now. When I hear the static, I do what needs to be done to tune in what I would rather hear.

The message of wise counsel was clearly transmitted and received once again. Kumu Kekuhi was super skillful at engaging us, I sometimes couldn't believe how long we sat on the floor, enthralled in the teaching. Her exploration of the triple layer of meaning of myths and images was downright fascinating to me. The layers of meaning was how I have always viewed my life without actually naming it that, easily seeing the bigger meaning to things. Viewing *ka'ao*, myths, this way really resonated with me in a way that enhanced my sense of belonging in *Hālau 'Ōhi'a*.

The chants we learned and performed in each class had an immediate and transformative effect. They erased my fear- and ego-filled insecurities fed to me by the dominant culture of my upbringing. I was no longer an outsider, in class or in my mind. I was no longer anxious. I was connected, transported to the portal of existence that transcends time and space to a place within myself that is pure love and light.

We traveled together as a class for our *hua'ka'i*, field trip, around the island. I brought my *keiki*, children, with me. Everett and Toby learned chanting and proper protocol for entering the *hei'au*, sacred site. We all slept in common space on cots with thirty other people, ate what was offered, and what we offered. We did the hard work and they played just as hard.

It warmed my heart to see them engaged in this way of life. Easy-going, present, aware, helpful, joyful. My boys taught me so much, and continue to do so, and together we learn so much.

Kumu told us repeatedly, "I don't care if you were born here or not, or the color of your skin, if you are here now, that is what matters. Any time the static distorted my sense of belonging, she cleared it with this clear and kind message. On the first *hua'ka'i*, we formed work trains of people to carry out old cut ironwood trees for farm land restoration in Hāmākū'a.

This cooperation, *laulima*, is a traditional way of efficiently getting things done, the need to move things over a distance happens through many hands.

The rocks handed from one person to the next, as well as the logs that need to be moved.

Na lima e malamalama hana, many hands make light work.

This effective practice impressed me and brought up my insecurities. The strong local guy across from me on the train of hands dropped the log before I could securely hold it. Over and over again, he dropped the log I was supposed to gather from him. My paranoid mind kicked in and felt mistreated because of the lightness of my skin, my *malahini*, newcomer, status. Feeling a wave of negative emotions welling up in my heart, I took positive action by moving closer to him so he would be less likely to drop it. He still dropped it.

Learning to cut people slack and quit being offended has been vital to my wellbeing. I spoke with this person, the log-dropper, now a friend, some years later, and learned that my fearful and paranoid thinking creates lies, untruths, and suffering. He meant no harm to me.

In Hawai'i, there is a beautiful relationship healing practice called *ho'oponopono*. Ho'oponopono means to correct. *Pono* means excellence, wellbeing, true condition or nature. I started this practice with myself.

To return to this sense of well-being is the spirit behind this traditional practice. These are the essential ingredients needed in resolving conflict through repair:

- I'm sorry.
- Please forgive me.
- Thank you.
- I love you.

The next day another *kanaka*, local guy, was passing around dried ahi snacks to others. He did not pass to me or my boys. I am a sensitive person and all this may be my wild imagination, but I told myself that he was ignoring us. I saw it happen for several rounds of sharing. The assertive girl in me spoke up and asked for snack for my boys. He shared with them.

When I have faith in the goodness of others, life feels less shaky and uncertain.

As I look at my certificate from two years ago for Proof of Professional Development Training, *Palapala 'Anu'u*. It states in part–

> …It is with the greatest joy, aloha, and gratitude that I, Kekuhikuhipu'uoneonaali'ioKohala Kanae Kanahele Keali'ikanakaoleolilikalaniohaililani, thank YOU, your supervisors & your family for supporting you in Hālau 'Ōhi'a, Papa Hua; and formally invite you to continue Hālau 'Ōhi'a at the next level of engagement in Papa A'a.
> 'Ie Holo Ē!

And so we have continued for many years, my husband and Toby still actively participate while I write my book and serve others in relationship health. From my kumu, Kekuhi, "While Liz (her name of endearment) has had to turn her focus to her profession and her particular contribution to the community, we miss her authenticity and presence in Hālau 'Ōhi'a."

In *Hālau 'Ōhi'a*, we explore the journey of *Pele* and *Hi'iaka*, a fantastic myth of relatable proportions. We dive deep into the chants of upheaval, *huli'hia*, and the chants of restoration, *kulia*, and we recognize the destructive quality of creation. We look at *ka po*, the darkness, in a way that stirs the imagination away from the dominant culture's graphic displays of darkness, into the deep creative soup of massive chaos and infinite possibilities. Pushing it underground doesn't honor its significance in daily life.

Dominant culture suppresses darkness, the reality of death, the reality of loss and aging, the reality that we need support transitioning in various life stages, therefore it shows up as a corroding moral fabric with sexual abuse allegations, lies, and disruption in social supports that many of us recognize feed the downriver cleanup of our society.

Underground, the dark matter, the wonderfully creative energies of life, pushed and pushed further down, at least in the dominant culture that I grew up in, the soup with which I've been simmered, it pushed the Shadow deeper into the dark. It is the creative place often destructive before birthing something new. This is where we are, this is where we're emerging from, this is where we must wake up.

Alternatively, we acknowledge death, honor again, employ rites of passage, and stitch together the fat quarters of life with infused meaning, purpose and the common denominator of deep loving connection. In essence, we recognize the darkness in the light. We identify the shadows as a part of life, without trying to push them down in a suppressing fashion, nor ramp them up, trying to live in the outrage of a shadowy identity.

My kumu introduced me to a language and structure to explore the lens of perspective I have seen the world much of my life. There is the personal image of the story, the regional image and the global image...the micro, macro and meta levels of life experiences. Kumu said, I can teach what my understanding is of all this, thus far.

Please be advised, Dear Reader, that I am sharing my interpretation of my life and my vision for the planet and relational health. I am by no means an expert of indigeneous culture, island consciousness or Hawai'i lifeways. I realize I know only a little, and that is what I share and humbly offer you here.

Hawai'i Lifeways
Ki'i Ākea

I say all of this on a very global level, there's so much darkness, I don't even need to name it. In the past we have said about rules and proscriptions around sex, religion, health, all void of ritual chanting-dancing-connection with the elements. This is dark stuff, but see the Alchemy of how to use it for good because creation lies within the darkness. Let's look now at our *na'au,* (pronounced na-ow), which is a marvelous word meaning guts, mind, heart, the seat of feelings and intuition. Let's explore how to be *pono,* righteous and disciplined, consider our *manao,* our thoughts, and learn to continually choose *aloha,* love, grace, compassion over *pilikia,* drama and trauma.

Ki'i Honua

I say all this from a very local level which is close around me. This includes my two growing boys tiptoeing into adolescence, my own hormonal shifts carrying me towards menopause, my in-laws and the late-life challenges of memory loss, physical limitations, relationship fulfillment and/or lack thereof. This includes my husband in his heart-wrenching work up close and personal into people's lives coupled with his 10 + hour commute per week. He wants to bake bread, to make love, to walk the beach, to bask in the glory of his family's presence. So he does this on weekends, squeezed in, while the dominant culture tells him he must work more, to earn more, to secure health insurance and paid time off, to do the grind.

Our island is creating land, destroying homes, enduring hurricanes. Our nation, or shall I say the mainland America, is dealing with ineptitude of far-reaching proportions. As a recovering American, I write this out of love. My resentment toward my homeland is a weight in my heart. I must drop the stones from my heart, and take appropriate action, whether it is preserving the lifeways of Hawai'i or working the election; I do both.

Ki'i 'Iaka

I say all of this on a very personal level as the upheaval throughout the past four-plus decades of my life had lots of darkness; the dark night of the soul, the nervous breakdown, the rapes, the binge drinking, the trauma and abuse. I was a little girl convinced she was going to hell, when actually I was already in it.

Living in Hawai'i, I'm learning a foreign language. Even though I live in the United States still, and we share the same postage stamps, the same currency, and drive on the same side of the road, I still feel I'm in a different culture altogether.

Hawai'i Lifeways: reactivation

Pele, the fire goddess, has moments of rage and destruction and tenderness and compassion. Pele's fierce tenderness is described as "a spasm of tenderness that smiles like an oasis in her life, in Nathaniel B. Emerson's translation of Pele and Hi'iaka: A Myth from Hawai'i.

Just as Pele does, it is important to acknowledge the people and places that brought us to where we are today. I say Aloha to the places I lived even though they didn't serve my function.

Aloha Florida, mahalo to the rivers, lakes, aquifers, springs, ocean, and alligators.

Aloha Colorado, mahalo to the flatirons, rock climbing, river rafting, and aspen.

Aloha Oregon, mahalo to the evergreens, trillium, chard, and ferny friends.

Aloha Washington, mahalo to the salmon, cedars, eagles, and trumpeter swans.

Like Pele's journey to find home, I traveled. Like her sister, Hi'iakaikepoliopele, I served and I battled the demons that didn't serve my function anymore. Whether it was the places I lived, the men I loved, the alcohol and drugs that obscured my mind and fed the wrong kind of spirits, the striving to better myself, yea that, too, I even had to let go of that.

I get distracted with subconscious teasers and testers along the journey, for sure. They are the eddies that I swim around in for a while before I get back in the flow of life. Crushes or resentments tangle my heart in knots, slow my digestion, and basically back up my system.

Sometimes I flop up on a bank of the river and engage in rigid and controlling behavior, and when I see that doesn't get me where I want to go, then I slide back in the river of life, and I go with the flow. Sometimes I flop up on the other bank on the other side of the river and wreak havoc all around me in a chaotic swirl of energy, then finally spin back in, and let the water carry me.

I dive down deep within, to expand the reservoirs of my soul, the carrying capacity for more spirit that can always be expanded. I see my soul as my personal manifestation of the great spirit that connects us all.

Things need to evolve. Indigenous wisdom often stands in tradition, of what the ancestors have done. As a socially evolving human, I appreciate the respect for tradition and the willingness to bring the present moment, with all of her joys and challenges, to the efforts. At the same time, what we've been doing also gets to evolve.

There is a consciousness movement in the world, we can see the events as fertilizer to grow what we want to grow. There is a point, a condition, at which there is a revolution. The Earth is suffering. The *huli heia*, the upheaval, is happening, and certain chapters are pau, done. Destruction and creation are messy processes.

How do we make sense of the information? Kumu asks, "Look at your creative Self, your pregnant Self, what are you birthing?" We contemplate the *Uli*, part of the cosmos that we cannot see. It is that state of pregnancy, whether we are a man or a woman.

"Cannot have a life of constant *huli hia*," chaos, Kekuhi assured us. The land needs time to regenerate. I chime in that we as humans need that time, too. We need fallow time. Just as we need the land to have fallow time.

Kumu says, "Just do what your Spirit needs to do, take care of it at different levels." She discusses the different levels we must tend. *Ki'i iaka*, the personal level, our personal shrine. *Ki'i honua*, the communal or regional level, our communal shrine. *Ki'i ikea*, the global level, our worldly shrine.

Moonshot

When we own the reality that EVERYTHING is my universe, we cultivate things carefully, mindfully, skillfully. Is the current function worth recreating, restoring, rededicating?

Sometimes transformation means leave it alone. This has been a vital step in the unlearning process for me. Non-action can indeed be a skillful intervention. How profound!

Ask yourself, "What is the function?" The process, the way we go about things, restoring the function, is more important than the thing we are restoring. Learning the chants of *Pele* and her sister, *Hi'iaka*, is an integral part of our learning process and I can apply it to my life now. The portal opens, I step in, I recognize the resources are all around me. The 40,000 deities in mythology means 80,000 eyes willing to watch and offer presence and deep guidance when I ask. I must ask. Pray. Visualize the return of health, order, an end to the chaos. What will it look like, sound like, feel like? To begin life, the end of life, and the rebirth of life; the cycle of life continues. We are grateful for this journey.

Kumu asks us the questions, she doesn't necessarily answer the questions. She is a "puller-outer." She reminds us that many practices and cultural objects came from across the water, yet we consider them indigenous. Are we indigenous to ourselves? That is my curiosity. *Heiau*, sacred site, practice comes from across the water. *Kalo*, taro, is vital to the island diet, and we needed to bring from across the Pacific Ocean.

Where we live is the most remote place on the planet in terms of geographical distance from other living people. If those of us who transplanted here can be a part of the solution vs. part of the problem, if we can claim our genealogy and weave that web of all of our ancestors, we basically connect the dots to be here now. Wherever you are is the center of the universe. Claim that. Respect that. Know that deep in your bones. I not telling you to move to Hawai'i Island or some other remote place to find your place on the planet. I suggest developing a sense of place WHEREEVER you are NOW.

We did this before we moved here. In the Pacific Northwest with working the land, digging my hands in, picking at dirt under my nails for days, communing with the elements, the plant friends and creatures, seen and unseen, belonging happened. I joined the community of the Earth Institute to do a curriculum called Sense of Place to feed my head what my fingernails were already wise to. I socialized with farmers, with creatives, with like-minded folk.

Our children went to a Waldorf school on a biodynamic farm. They didn't have computers, or plastic toys or mandatory testing. They had daily walks in the "Ferny Woods," which in the Pacific Northwest meant oftentimes in the rain. Rainboots and wool undergarments were our big purchases every year. The rest of the clothes showed up on our doorstop from friends and neighbors or we hosted a clothing exchange and shopped at thrift stores. We shared our resources. We made big meals and took some to neighbors on Mondays and they came and brought their bounty on Tuesdays and Wednesdays. Thursdays we fended for ourselves. Fridays we hosted big potlucks.

Cultivation is the energetic exchange of *kanaka*, people, with the elements, the feelings, the stories we tell ourselves. The old stories of us vs. them don't work anymore. The story of how to come together for a common ground, honoring diversity as an essential feature of thriving environments? This matters most. "No need hold head," kumu told me after I, once again, anguished at trying to figure something out or got caught up in worry that I did not know all the *ahupua'a*, land divisions, of our *moku*, region.

Diversity thrives in common purpose, let us look underneath for the commonality. We must relate through the color of our blood. We are all warm-blooded. We all have red blood. We have different skin colors, hair, clothing, preferences. We are all one. With the earth. We must rally together to care for the earth.

Where I'm from, there was never enough time to simply

be. There was the rush and the hustle. The hurry up to wait. It came from within me. When I succumb to the chronic busyness of dominant culture, as Brené Brown says, exhaustion is a status symbol, I am not really present to my life. I'm always late, always rushing, always planning the next great event.

As I'm sitting here I'm experiencing tremendous gratitude for my life and a profound relationship with enough. Unfamiliar to me as an addict, this is a relationship, the relationship with enough, which I've cultivated in my journey of recovery. When I feel contentment, I'm more awake, aware, and alive. When I feel content, I relinquish the need for hope and fear in my life's narrative. Hope is "if only" and fear is "what if"—neither of which gets me where I want to go, to the sweet surrender of the present moment, the soft spot of the eternal now.

Where I'd like to be is enjoying the patient pleasure of pause punctuating my daily vibe. I want less hustle, less bustle. I want to tolerate the wait without filling it with email checking and texting (and now, social media). The liminal space, the space between events, between thoughts, between information coming in, is a vital step in life, in order to assimilate what we're experiencing. Momentary moments of fallow time help immensely. My business coach, Shanda Sumpter, takes a week off each month for integration or flex time.

One thing I can do to help get me there is leave the phone in the back of the car. Then the temptation to check emails and texts while waiting for kiddos at school or soccer pick-ups evaporates. Then I'm certain not to be on a device while driving. It's better for me, and safer for everyone. You see, I must protect and preserve my attention, the world is becoming inattentively blind, meaning we don't see what is right in front of us, and it is fucking scary.

What matters most is being present where ever I am and enjoy the company I keep with myself. "Your legacy is who you are behind closed doors, not who you are on screen" (social media), this is a quote from my coach, Shanda. Basically, do my insides match my outsides? Yes. From this place, I can enjoy the company of others and be of maximum service to the situation. Admittedly, the competitive girl in me wants to win. I need to be present to accomplish this. *Must be present to win,* I think of this often. I adore being alone, it is loneliness that I detest. Being in public with everyone on their devices is lonely, scary, and ugly, in my humble opinion.

One thing I appreciate is that we're living the dream of intentional living and conscious connection and taking the steps to move us forward and trusting the world will hold us. I meditated in natural great beauty today with the sound of fresh water trickling under me. Two towering 'Ōhi'a trees stood guard, listening to the wind tell the stories of yesterday while the rocks stayed still to tell the stories of tomorrow. Here, in the *na'au*, the emotional center/the guts, is where I experience the eternal moment. Now. I stand here, now. Because when I stand with one foot in yesterday and one foot in tomorrow, I piss all over today.

The ninth distinction of an extraordinary life is interdependence. This key feature of my life both creates a sense of warmth and security, as well as holding others and providing safety. I am in the web and I am the spider weaving the web. Where do you enjoy a sense of deep connection with the world around you? The invitation is to surrender into the security of the web of interbeing and to stay on your toes to provide the structure for others. This is the heart of calm abiding, active pulsation, and relaxed joyfulness. Think of it as effortless existence with all the demands of conscious presence woven into your state of being.

Chapter Ten: **Responsibility**

responsibility-ordinary definition:
the state or fact having a duty to deal with something or having control over someone

responsibility-extraordinary definition:
the state of owning your world and how you show up in it; response-ability

The single most important predictor
of how you will behave as a parent
is how you were parented as a child.
~Harville Hendrix/Helen LaKelly Hunt

Eye of the Storm

This is where the magic happens for me. In the eye of the storm I find the calm. It seems so fearful to go into the unknown, the dark and stormy environs, and still I heed the advice, "walk through the fear." Then magic happens. I meander through the mental chatter of memories and meanness. I roar through the raging red effort of struggle into a clear sky blue of effortless existence. I dive under the mighty waves of emotional tsunamis and still surface for air. I cannot tip-toe around fear. Tip-toeing around people, places, and things doesn't get me where I want to go. I must go into the eye of the storm. Considering myself a fairly courageous and adventuresome person, it's funny to notice that I still get cold feet before doing something new. Momentarily I may want to back out of the plan. Instead, I notice the noticing and do something new regardless. I act my way into a new way of thinking.

I stay committed to living an extraordinary life.

I feel it to heal it.

I feel the fear and act in faith, anyways, knowing that the universe is conspiring tirelessly in my favor.

Yes, tirelessly in my favor, how is that for a mindset shift towards extraordinary? Quite simply, it's extraordinary.

Here I write about both my husband's family as well as my biological family.

Living with extended family was a huge experience of going into the eye of the storm.

"You're living with your in-laws, are you serious, why would you do that?"

Sentiments similar to this sounded so familiar to me. In the past, I heard it all the time. It is almost as if we are culturally trained to dislike in-laws. This is another pinch of dominant culture I am releasing. In fact, my beloved mother-in-law is the one I credit with that phrase, "release the pinch." She wisely holds the space for me to release, to trust, and to feel her support. She is a wellspring of kindness and generosity. We would not live here without her kindness and generosity. I'm a better person having gotten over myself and my perceived needs for space and my needs for things a certain way, whether it is dinner menu, or the décor. We give and take, beautifully.

My willingness to surrender to win, to speak from an open-heart of compassion and commitment to be of service makes all this possible for me to show up fully, as I am. I know she is downstairs cheering me on my next Masterclass called, "Your Relationships, Reimagined," or writing my books. I also know she has ideas that she holds in a respectful way. In other words, she does not try to parent our boys, and yet she is a support to them in being their best selves. She is skillful in this regard and for that I'm truly grateful. I've heard stories of in-law relationships that are not that way and she and I made an agreement early-on to do this differently. To embrace the distinctions of interdependence and responsibility with day to day actions.

My friend Jenn once said, "Yay, Amy, you're a Renaissance woman, please write about what you are embarking on, we want to learn from you."

This, Dear Reader, is the voice I tune into when the doubt doubles up and bubbles up inside me. I listen to a more encouraging and supportive voice of "You got this, Do this, Amy."

Living with my in-laws is good for the planet. We travel less to see each other at holidays because we are already together. We have found a shared vision, A Star of Gladness if you will, which serves as our North Star, our compass for our lives together.

We all care for the planet and enjoy time in nature together. We have generosity in our genes and we want to serve in powerfully positive ways. One way we did this recently was to join forces to help our local canoe club transition away from single use plastic water bottles and plastic forks at our events. My father-in-law is getting the stainless water filters, my mother-in-law is getting the silverware from local thrift stores. I am stepping more fully into leadership as a compassionate woman willing to take charge and ask for help and move away from the disposable mindset of our culture.

In our family living situation, we share resources, joys, challenges, and energies. It is crazy-making at times, but truly I find the calm in the eye of the storm. Nancy Levin says that "We create chaos when we don't tell the truth." I think this quote sums up why my household feels chaotic to me at times. When there is truth, there is calm. The simple termites that erode the foundation of trust are worth getting rid of; this is pest extermination that I support.

At mealtimes, one ritual of connection is when we engage in the practice of "www", what went well. For us each to learn from each other is priceless. With my father-in-law I practice the act of leaning in, setting boundaries, showing up, and backing off. We need not react so intensely to someone's reactivity. It is like being mad at being mad. The double-layered negative emotion is too tough to chew and impossible to digest. I like my emotions in bite-sized chunks.

When I pace myself, I am less likely to let someone else's energies run through my circuit. This is definitely progress, not perfection. My sensitivity is a gift and a curse. Some would say, "Why don't you live alone so you can recharge your batteries?" Living alone would not get me where I want to go. I turn toward the storm, face it and find calm and joy in the center.

Traveling to the Mainland to enjoy a family reunion with my mother was another recent example of going into the eye of the storm. I thought I needed my own space. In fact, I thought I needed the 4,684 miles of space. In other words, I originally replied that we "couldn't go" to the reunion.

My mother said, "you will come."

Of course, we went.

I asked for our own private cabin for our family of four. This did not occur. Instead, we stayed in a home of 13 bedrooms with twice as many people as there were bedrooms. Talk about going into the eye of the storm. I could picture the storm before I even got to the reunion. The dark clouds of drinking (not everyone in my family is sober) and the lightning bolts of tension. These memories of previous family get-togethers fueled my sleeplessness prior to our departure. Then I started losing sleep about losing sleep. Talk about a double layer of negative emotion!

My practice is to bring myself to this moment, forgive and forget the past, and invite my genuine self to suit up and show up to be a point of presence and light. Allowing myself to simply be automatically generates grace to allow others to simply be. My state of being has become a contract with myself. I am a tender, powerful, generous woman. I live and breathe my contract. And life becomes extraordinary.

Leaving the island for the first time since we moved here, feeling a wee bit nervous, I said goodbye to the cloud people and look forward to seeing how their migration across the ocean changes them. The same sun and the moon and the stars go with us, though they may appear different. Nature keeps me grounded, no matter where I am. For this I am grateful.

In preparation for our travels, in my imagination, I'm back in the Pacific Northwest. Greeting the variegated thrush, vireo, raven and bald eagle in my mind's eye. Appreciating the efforts of the trees, the red cedar, Douglas fir and big-leafed maple, this deep breath I take here now is in part due to them, the lungs of the planet. I anticipate the familiar summer serenade to friendship and camping at Dosewallips Elkhorn campground. The glacier blue snow melt shows the passage of time as the river roars past and commands deep respect lest we get swept away by the powerful deep beauty and gray force of nature. The moss. The fern. The soft earth that receives my soul's sole tenderly and bounces back to rise for the next step and the next.

I take my island consciousness with me, wherever I go. I am an island, I enjoy sovereignty, and I build the bridges of connection to others through communication and care. I never leave the island of myself for long. My breath tethers me back. Again, and again.

On the plane from one place to the next, I move, fidget, and adjust. I'm simply recalibrating to the gyroscope of serenity within while traveling 500 miles per hour, ending up in a different time zone, hoping to keep circulation circulating and gaining gainful rest.

Travel is a big deal that doesn't get recognized as such. Since the iron bird took to the skies, we privileged humans take it for granted that we get to go wherever we want to go. I *pule*, I pray, not because I am afraid, but to give thanks, to ask for protection and to send good vibes to all the travelers with me who may be suffering, whether it is fear of flying or baby's ears plugging, I send love and light.

I dwell on the great good fortune of beauty within and all around. I will seek and find it on the plane, in the six airports we visit. I want to rent a big car, I want to release the carbon footprint guilt of flying so I return to gratitude for small notions of comfort.

Is it possible to have comfort and consciousness? That is a path I am seeking in life. Guilt is a scratchy surface and ignorance is a dark pit. Enlightened self-interest for the benefit of others… let's head that direction, shall we Dear Reader?

When we get off the plane, I tune into my surroundings. My first mountains ever in my life were in North Carolina, in Cashiers, back when I was nine years old, and I wonder if we will get there. I'd like to, but I'm not attached to the outcome. This lack of attachment to my wish list is an indicator we are in for a mighty fine time.

Here is a great example of what an amazing time I had at this family reunion. One pink-hued sunrise morning on the balcony overlooking the gentle rolling hills of the Appalachians, my brother put down his iPad, joined me, and practiced yoga for the first time in his life. At dinner he thanked me in front of everyone for my leadership in "lining up his chakras." He told me he felt nicer to his wife that day and it just might spill over into tomorrow. I pictured him finding a Carolina waterfall that cascaded peace down his spine, as he smiled inwardly, and enjoyed the moment immensely with his beloved.

Part of my pre-flight jiggers stemmed from fear of our differences, who drinks, who doesn't, who voted for Trump, who didn't, who is still going to church, who isn't. Differences polarize and breed anxiety. This us and them mentality creates good moment and bad moments and a hell of a lot of breath holding moments in between. I want to breathe deeply in each moment, regardless of who I am with or what topic is up for discussion. Afterall, who in their right mind actually enjoys walking on eggshells?

In my family, we all love nature. Both my family of origin and my in-laws. I return to this as common ground of acceptance for all of us. I set my sights high on the *Hōkūle'a*, the star of gladness, that brings me back to aloha. This star of gladness brings celestial navigators back home to Hawai'i. My blessing is that we all return to Gladness, that we gladden our heart with what matters most.

It was as if our diversity, our different political and religious views, met respect in the common ground of sunrise. This is a theme in my life. Let sunrise teach me how to be. Bold, unstoppable, consistent, soft and transformative all at the same time. The soft hues of pink and purple haze melted the sharp points of discord between us.

These can be so sharp as to sever the ties in many families. My guardian angels had different ideas. Yoga. That transformative experience with my look-how-different-we-are brother was in and of itself a transformative experience. Later that night, he was intoxicated and threw logs on the fire all night during a raging rainstorm, but you know what? I did a positive reframe on that, too. *He was willing to keep the flames of love going despite all obstacles. And he was safe and not driving on the roads.* It didn't matter to me in that moment that he was drinking, and this, Dear Reader, is a new chapter in the story I tell myself.

Another brother operates in a different orbit than I do, though we are in the same solar system of recovery from alcoholism. At the family reunion, we showed up in a spin free zone, no news on and no discussion of politics. A truce of neutrality left an unusual silence in the space between us. It was both pleasant to not be verbally disagreeing about the state of the world, and at the same time, it was disappointing to not fully connect.

In my endeavors to be a gentle presence on this planet, I get to show up differently around my family today, and therefore I'm actively re-writing the ending. I'd rather be sober than right. I'd rather be happy than right. I'd rather have harmony than discord. All of this in effort to experience the peace that passes all understanding.

Today, I am willing and able to reclaim the lost parts of me. The parts that skinheads took when I was raped. The parts that strangers took when I was robbed. The parts that teachers took when I was told I didn't know the correct interpretation of a poem or piece of art.

My come from is riddled with racial violence, drugs, alcohol, and an adolescent mind hijacked by hormones mixed with an overwhelming desire to help and love and serve and not enough proper channels for it to flow out of me. I blocked it. I gave it away. I drank it away. I raged it away. I knotted myself up into tightly-wound perturbations.

I reclaim wellness through a long and worthwhile healing journey. I go into the eye of the storm. I got sober. I stay sober. I got sane. I stay sane. I got real. I stay real. And now I speak out for compassion and stand up for transformation.

It is music to my eyes when I read a party invite from someone that spells out, "Your presence is enough." No presents needed. I don't have to buy my way into a friendship.

I don't have to register for the perfect gift. I don't have to have another thing to do in order to accept this thing to do. I can simply show up.

This is how I live my life now. I simply show up and trust that my presence is enough. It works in my home. It works at my family reunion. Being a point of presence and light is powerful and transformative. It is enough. My state of being is enough.

The Softening

A golden nugget of my meditation practice is the notion, "not too tight, not too loose." This relates not only to how I hold myself in the meditation posture, but also how I hold my perspective, my beliefs, my view on how life should be. This gentle reminder is incredibly helpful when I am taking myself too seriously; rather common, or slacking off entirely, rather uncommon. It helps me to stay alert and upright without becoming rigid, inflexible and overly constricted. It feels good in my body when I remember to hold myself "not too tight, not too loose."

When I am in conscious contact with my higher power, thereby activating the softening, I can indeed:

- enjoy the alignment of a tender heart with an attuned mind
- cut myself some slack and ease up on others
- set goals and aspirations without letting the striving create strife

This place of not too tight, not too loose is comfortable and invites calm abiding and relaxed pulsation of my energy. Too tight and I am constricted, pent up, uptight and tight-assed. Too loose and I am uninspired, unmotivated, and bordering on despair, hopelessness and the all too contagious, *why bother?*

How do I feel this calm abiding? My fists soften. My gaze and eyes soften. My hips soften. My work flows. My energy feels alive and sustainable, well-fed and rested, yet active and alert. I like having space, particularly space within my own skin. I need rhythm, scheduling and routine, at the same time I love pushing through with the eternal whisperings of doing what comes naturally, wondering how reliably that will get me where I want to go?

The answer comes if I can be in the present moment, if I can turn down the volume on my inner dialogue, lessen the chaotic static of wondering what home life is like when I am working and vice versa, wondering what work life is like when I am emerged in home life. The pull to be two places at once or wearing two hats at once is a single cause of great stress.

How do you feel in your body temple, now? My yoga instructor asks each of us to use this as an immediate present moment check-in.

I am calm. I am peaceful. I am safe. Here. Now.

My gaze matters. Your gaze matters. I do believe we communicate way beyond words. I speak powerfully, you know a lot about how I am feeling, even when I am not moving my lips. This social instrument signifies contempt if I am rolling my eyes, a message of disgust that you are somehow less than human. I am working on not rolling my eyes so much, as a practice of acting my way into a new way of thinking. Because this facial response can feel automatic, I practice smiling throughout the day. Smiles soften my gaze. Interruptive smiles change my neurochemistry and my mood.

My eyes communicate vast amounts of information about my internal weather patterns. My handwriting communicates whether I am tired or engaged, angry or content. Oftentimes if I am outside, I am content. That's a good idea for my next handwriting analysis; journal while outside. My breathing communicates if I am calm or hyper, grateful or annoyed. The heavy sighs are exclamation points to punctuate this state of being.

If I continue to practice the character traits of heavy sigh, cold hard stare, eye-rolling or scribbling chronic disgruntlement into my journal, I am essentially hardwiring this trait, this tendency to feel overwhelmed, into a state of being that is hard, calloused, inflexible and bitter. This is not at all my goal in life.

My goal is to cultivate an authentic caring and gentle presence on this planet who is simultaneously active, engaged, dynamic, flexible, bold, and strong. I long to dwell in alignment with a strong spine, tender heart, and connection with the Divine.

I hurt other people even when I don't intend to. I can fire up someone's amygdala. The nervous system hijacked by fear requires me to tend and befriend. From the time of perceived energy, when I hurt someone's feelings, to making the repair, is a crucial window of opportunity to strengthen the relationship. The longer I wait, the more time that passes, the more harm sets into grooves of erosion in the space between. We can learn to regulate each other's nervous system.

Today, in an up close, knees touching, eye to eye intentional dialogue (see Appendix VI for a wealth of information on the intentional dialogue) with my husband, I engaged the system of repair and watering the space between so the fiery topic of money didn't set fire to our well-being. When my threat system is activated, especially when driving, it can feel deadly. Eye to eye contact brings in resonance, entrainment, attunement. It is essential for healthy relations. If I can look you in the eye and feel the softening, all things are possible. If I can take the higher road and say, "I am sorry. Please forgive me. Thank you. I love you," not only to others, but also to myself, I have a goldmine of resources that will feed me forever. I enjoy the relief of the disentanglement. A mentor told me "sorry" is not an eraser. Do you get it?

What would it be like if it were that simple?

What if I could wear life like a loose garment?

Resilience of Kaho'olawe

As I'm sitting here, I'm loving my feet for where they have brought me in life, for carrying me safely into the world.

Where I'm from is a pattern of choosing isolation vs. engagement and limiting what I feel responsible for. Sometimes I would hibernate in my home, especially when I didn't want to engage with the world, with life. And pretty darn soon I started feeling what I refer to as, "cabin fever" and I needed to leave the house. It was a pull to greater service calling me forth.

In this day and age of internet, I don't feel cabin fever as much. I can hunker down and settle in with work, entertainment, learning, yoga and meditation, all without leaving my bedroom. It is amazing and terrifying all at once. Then the story I tell myself is that "this is enough, this is as good as it gets." It's all an illusion.

There is more to life. I face this distraction recognize I don't want a virtual life.

Where I'd like to be is in the realm of service in this extraordinary reality of life. I want to sweat. I want to get dirty. And I have an insatiable appetite to commune with the Natural Great Beauty surrounding us. I can't get my Nature fix while in my bedroom, though I do have an excellent view of Maunakea during the day and the Southern Cross constellation at dawn.

What matters most is that I'm grateful, for all of it.

One thing I can do is be 100% responsible for life, 100% of the time. By keeping this commitment to myself, I don't waver, I don't get exhausted or overwhelmed. I stay in a place of trust and focus. As I am more and more resourced in my life, I have more and more to give.

Filling my reservoirs before I launched into a summer of travel, I grounded at home, tidying, packing, planning, and praying. In the past, I got fairly anxious when I travelled. And I had not been doing much of it over the last couple of years. It was time.

Soon I was unplugged, with no phone, no internet, no Netflix originals.

Going to an uninhabited island stretched me beyond my comfort zone. This is where transformation takes place, so I'm very familiar with it. I took really good care of the soles of my feet and the soul of my being. Going to an ancient place, the eighth major island of this archipelago, transformed me. This place that has served many purposes, including a bombing range for the U.S. military, bore the scars of devastation and the power of healing and resilience.

Planning for Kaho'olawe, also known as Kanaloa, we received special training. and a special invitation. This invitation is essential to going.

My dreamscape opened up into wide vistas and I saw myself stretching into the elemental world at an even deeper level.

My kumu invited my husband to come, as an opening came up. He happened to be at the safety training and he could not resist this incredible opportunity. Many people who live here have not yet received this invitation, this incredible opportunity to go to this island.

Wear protective footgear, this was the main take home message from the safety training we attended recently for the June full moon trip to Kaho'olawe. At least that is what I paid attention to. Sure, there are unexploded ordinance to watch out for, UXOs, but the take care of your feet message really landed with me. There was a particular emphasis on how much we need our feet to guide us, carry us, and lead us. There was no dock to land the boat and no doc to tend to wounds. My feet, my soles of my feet have done an amazing job, so has my soul. My focus was on my soles and my soul: protect and care for daily, be mindful of movements and give gratitude always.

Let me back up a bit. **Where I'm from**, I have felt compelled to make this world a better place my entire life. I have volunteered in beach clean-ups, tree plantings, trail maintenance, and political protests to preserve our planet. This is why this chapter on responsibility is the longest of the entire memoir.

My soul's exposure to and interaction with the raw, primal, spiritual energy of the most sacred of all of the Hawai'i Islands, *Kaho'olawe*, is something I treasure as sacred. Sacred like the *wiliwili* tree on the island that survived the storms and the bombs. Presently, there are so many storms swirling about in the world, relationally, environmentally, socially, I find comfort in the restoration of this island. The uninhabited island of Kaho'olawe: she is the place of hope in my mind. I feel blessed to go there. To do my part to repair the wrongs of humans. To give and receive the spiritual *mana*, power, of Kanaloa. She represents conflict between peace/war, life/death, cultural perpetuation/forced assimilation. She calls on all of us to reflect in natural great beauty.

Where I'd like to be is the calm in the eye of the storm. This is how I wish to approach my mission in life, to heal the planet, by healing relationships.

I did that on this journey. We, our group of 30 or so adults and children, engaged in proper protocol for this experience on Kaho'olawe. Chanting during the transitions, we chant to ask permission to enter this sacred space as well as to leave this sacred space. We readied ourselves completely.

Ravaged by years of U.S. military bombing and "training for peace through destructive means," this island is evidence of government taking over and destroying, temporarily, the natural great beauty of our earth. Peace through destructive means makes no sense to me.

I want world peace. It seems, the mark of progress is not an external indication that world looks like I would like it look, with respectable leaders and genuine aloha circumnavigating the globe in all directions, rather, it boils down to my relationship with myself. I have grown my patience and expanded my reservoir of calm. All in the midst of the storms of life.

Is it futile to believe that if we all did this inner work we wouldn't have such a devastating storm of moral bankruptcy on our hands? I think not. It is the work that must be done.

We all want protection and safety. My intention is that it be based on love and caring and mutual respect for the inherent worth and dignity of all human beings. I don't want war, fighting, missiles. I don't want to feed the insatiable hunger of the hungry ghost. Imagine a beast with a pencil-thin neck and bloated belly that never gets enough of whatever it thinks it is lacking, this is the hungry ghost. Therefore, because it thinks it is lacking, its hunger is never-ending. That hunger is rooted in fear.

One thing I can do is to replace the fear with faith. This breaks the cycle of the habitual hydraulics of our paranoid mind. May it be so. I can ask myself, how can I be a point of power and light, be a part of the solution, restoration of the mind and the landscape vs. be a part of the problem, the paranoia of the human mind?

The ritual of our conservation work during *huaka'i*, journey, to Kaho'olawe began with individual preparation of mind, body, and spirit prior to our travel. For me, I got extra sleep. I paid attention to my dreams. I took extra good care of my feet, trimming the nails straight across to avoid ingrown infections, walking more gingerly on the earth to avoid stubbed toes, massaging my feet nightly to thank them for all the miles we had walked in our lifetime and the many more to come.

We flew to Maui and had the day to explore before we met our group and slept on the beach. When we landed in Kahalui Airport on Maui I was curious about going to the top of *Haleakalā*.

House of the Sun. *Haleakalā*. The place atop Maui that you now need reservations to go see sunrise. It seemed a fine way to capture the best of our 12 hours in Maui. We found our way to Down to Earth health food store and consumed a healthy assortment of food. We decided not to drive up and instead followed suggestion of a friend to hit a secret beach. The smell, strong. The wind, strong. The beauty, strong. A great way to land, getting Down to Earth and feet in the sand.

After a coffee and fruit refill in Pa'ia, we ventured on to Haiku. We meandered our way up the mountain to find ourselves at the Haleakalā Waldorf School. Our friend teaches there and happily gave us a tour. It was magical. Hot and beautiful terraced terrain. We drove further up the mountain to her home and the weather changed. The cloud people surrounded us. We visited her animals and home and walked the trails up Haleakalā. We saw Oprah's property and sent her big love aloha. My sons were thrilled to be that close. The house of the sun was surrounded by clouds, then it cleared. I felt grateful for the walk, the stretch, and then the clearing of the vista toward Kaho'olawe.

That's where we are going, I thought. I spoke of it cautiously. I have wanted to go on this *huaka'i* since Kumu Kekuhi first mentioned the possibility. I really knew nothing about it until moving to Hawai'i two years ago. I knew it is uninhabited. I knew it was a bombing target for the U.S. military.

Resentful about our military for decades, I longed to heal this. Every time I think of military I think of war. I think of puffing ourselves up to hide our vulnerability. What if we whispered, "I need you to help me." What if we were strong enough to ask for help? What if we, as humanity, adopted the fifth article of NATO, the principle of collective defence, which says, concern for one country is concern for all.

This is starkly different from put America first.

Prior to our travels, I gazed upon the Hawaiian Koa wood carved bookends that are on my desk. My grandfather picked them up while he was here in the Pacific region during his career in the military. I never met him on this earthly plane. He died of heart complications before I was born. Yes, another in the legacy of heart disease in my family. My father held such adoration for him and respect for the military, even though his father was not home during his youth due to his military career and the military did not accept my father due to physical limitations. My father referred to his dad as the great man of this century. I ponder what makes men great.

I reflect on the need for forgiveness and the resilience of life. I release the burden of white man's guilt. In my dreamscape, I met my grandfather and remembered he was a Naval Commander for the Pacific Fleet. I welcomed the releasing of guilt and shame.

One thing I appreciate is that I simply do what I can. And this is what I did.

We chanted for permission to access this sacred and scarred land. We engaged in ritualistic cleansing, *kapu kai*, to release the stuck hurriedness, *pilikia*, and built up grime we collect in our mundane activities to prepare us for the work of being fully present. We let go of the mundane chit chat, the ordinary distractions that fill our minds and days. We invited silence to be the fertilizer for the *kapu*, sacred. We unplugged from media and devices, we tuned into *Kanaka*, person, Vision, and we sank more fully into the moment. We drank *olena*, turmeric, water to hydrate. We hiked at pre-dawn, a gentle invitation to kilo, to pay greater attention to the clouds, the wind, the quality of this moment, now. We chanted for sunrise, *E ala ē*, we marked the high noon connection with high ritual, a portal opened that fed immense energy to our open beings, and the *au'au* ritual of cleansing in the *kai*, ocean, marked the days' end.

With each *huaka'i*, I let go of the need for "alone time" and recognize, in advance, that part of the *huaka'i* process is traveling as 35 individuals, a 70-foot unit, without getting enmeshed in other people's *pilikia*. It truly is a remarkable thing, when we bring our best selves forward, body, mind and spirit, and when we recognize our inter-connectedness with each other, we maintain healthy boundaries and attuned hearts. In other words, we *care* for each other, but we don't try to *take care* of each other. We all *malama the keiki,* take care of the children. We all carry each other's *ukana,* luggage, on the landing at the island and the departure with the *okala,* rubbish.

We tuned into *Kanaka* Vision and we saw the cloud people march across the landscape and bring the rains back to Kanaloa. We chanted the *moʻokūʻauhau* of *Hokuleʻa.* We sat in the navigator's chair and recognized the need to look up, not just out. The trash we saw in bays, resultant of the currents bringing the detritus of humanity to our shores, was intense, especially since this island is uninhabited; there is no escape from the fingerprint of humanity. I let this serve as a call to action. There is no "away" that we can throw things. Looking up, out, in and around, the shift in perspective continues in our re-entry with the rest of our lives.

A huge part of being *hanaiʻd,* adopted, by place is the spirit of forgiveness of self and other. A grandfather, a Naval commander in the Pacific Fleet, resides in my ancestry. The knowing and remembering came in a dream. How do we clean up the wreckage of our past? We cultivate awareness of what is, we accept this moment is exactly as it is, and we clean it up, restore, and cultivate wellness with mana enhancing engagement with the landscape. Let us bring the subconscious to the conscious, let us discuss the significance of discovering coral up on the *heiau,* sacred spot, the *Kanaloa* and the *Kane* integrating. Kanaloa is a major god of the ocean, Kane is a major god of the land. Kanaloa also represents the subconscious, Kane represents the conscious mind. I personally think this is why so many humans love the beach, the shoreline of the integration of both important qualities of mind.

"No need hold head." She taught me this. My fears of going to a previous military site were small enough to fit in my pocket and I trusting my vulnerable nature to be tough enough to handle the various challenges presented.

We made it. We, my two sons and my husband, have joined a new *ʻohana,* PKO, Protect Kahoʻolawe ʻOhana. This is the non-profit organization that supports infrastructure and schedules for those parties invited to come to this sacred land. The support staff, the *kua*, literally meaning spine, delighted and uplifted us immensely, and we, in turn, reciprocated this energetic exchange.

We had another orientation meeting and then secured our bags with 3 ml contractor bags and duct tape, as they would be floating in the *kai*, sea, to get to shore. Throwing a pad on the beach in Maui and attempting to sleep under a full moon, with a belly full of nerves and a mind full of excitement, I was grateful to get a few winks here and there. The cool offshore breeze urged me to open my sleeping bag. The jack hammer tearing up one of Maui's busy streets at a "quiet" time was a surreal backdrop to the experience. The boys passed out. My headlamp cast a glow on a squashed centipede. My default fear response did not kick into high gear. I simply noticed, a centipede. Stepped on centipede. A small voice inside wanted to question if someone put it near my pad to harm me. The ever-vigilant negativity bias of my brain looking for traction. I choose to tune to a different channel.

Forgive my repetitiveness of this topic, I have to learn faith and unlearn fear over and over again as the Daily Tender of my life.

The beauty of gratitude. I have the great good fortune of waking up before the *pu*, conch shell, blow to put in my contacts, use the *lu*, toilet, tidy up my camp. All before the boys woke up. Being on Sacred Land is an invitation to the senses. Turning down the volume on my fearful egoic mind, tuning into my *na'au*, the currents, the guts, intuition.

We were on the boat, Synammon III, which meant we waited while boats ferried people and *ukana*, baggage, back and forth. We explored the Kihei boat harbor. We fueled up with fruit and water, water, water. Dangers of dehydration addressed repeatedly.

Kapu kai. Set up camp. Eat breaky. Rest. Adore, admire, appreciate. Sunrise.

Justified labor. History. Deep *manao*, sharing of thoughts. Well restoration, aloe removal, 4 scorpions spotted. Coffee. Rest. *Pilli hale. Au au.* Chanting. *'Awa.* Food. Beach restoration and the discovery of plastic was the most evident damage to this island.

Here we tuned into a different channel, *Kanaka* Vision. Bringing ourselves back to the present moment. Again, and again. It was like a Buddhist retreat but "for real kine." It was like a yoga retreat but "for real kine." It was like an ecological restoration retreat but "for real kine." We were invited to the present moment, to be fully embodied, to *malama* the *aina*, without it feeling like a mental focus, body focus, earth focus narrowing our energy.

I have been involved in various types of retreats for over two decades of my life. I love the structure and the intentionality. This *huaka'i* was by far the best one yet. I didn't bring my ego and her fear baggage with me. When she showed up to question my belonging, my worth, my being, I simply whispered to her and reminded her to drop the baggage and do the work, the justified labor of restoration. Do not step on unexploded ordinance and stay within the established boundaries. This challenge to not wander off kept me focused on the honor and privilege of being on this *piko*, belly button, of the archipelago.

My habit is to pick up trash when I see it on trails or roadsides or beaches. When we were on these trails, we were instructed not to. "If you didn't drop it, don't pick it up." This idea is revolutionary. Literally and figuratively, my entire life I've been trying to clean up other people's trash and it's not always my job. That said, we did a huge, communal beach clean-up which we readily participated in. The bigger vision is significant, in that I can use my energy to clean up my side of the street and help others not litter in the first place. This is what I call upriver cleanup. It's a paradigm shift from needing programs and services to deal with the symptoms vs. shift the energies in the first place, to address the underlying causes and conditions.

Kaho'olawe is not a wasteland, though many who fly over may look down and think so. This is a unique place where 240 different winds converge, and where the currents exist to guide one more speedily in the direction one wishes to go. Here heaven meets earth and the sun comes out of the top of the *hale*, house, certain times of the year.

She is an island waiting and responsive to every effort to bring this land back. This is how I see my own journey of personal transformation and human potential. This is how I see other humans. Let us celebrate our trauma in order to give fertilizer to our rebirth. This is revolutionary. This is necessary.

If sovereignty is sought by some locals, I sometimes wonder why am I included in these important rituals? I include this here because it is something you may wonder, I used to question this, but no more.

There are two types of business in life, my business and none of my business. "Just do you," is what we heard over and over throughout our time together. I hear it in all corners of my life which now infiltrate my mind. Take the leadership of my own life. Serve others from that place of leadership. *Ola!* And bring it back to gratitude every single time.

Chanting

I sometimes pray internally, tuning into the self-talk of supplication. Other times, I pray out loud, in various languages. One form of prayer is chanting. Chanting does something to my brain. I tap into both hemispheres and enjoy an oasis of ease in my soul which calms the chaos of a controlling mind. Especially if I am chanting in a different language. I let go and I let it rip. I feel my *na'au*, my inner guidance, ignite its dominion once again. My judgmental mind silences and observes the unfolding of universal energies communing.

This reminds me of how I had to get quiet when I entered the church and watch the old white men in robes do all the significant stuff. I didn't matter, yet I did because I was the audience. I tell myself my judgmental mind doesn't matter but it does. My judgmental mind is the audience in the play of life. It heckles and shouts to try to disrupt the flow of what is going on on-stage but it cannot stop the continual unfolding of intermingling energies when I am chanting.

In other words, it doesn't heckle.

My Kundalini yoga teachers tell me the sound current of all the ages is a continuous stream of energy. When I chant I am joining forces with this vital energy. I need to join forces with bigger energy than myself, otherwise my judgmental mind calls the shots and next thing you know I feel alone, isolated, fearful and uncertain what to do.

I can simply ask my guides, in the form of a chant, for help. It is almost like a prayer loaded with energetic life force. In yoga, we chant, mostly in another language, Gurmukhi, to ask protection while traveling, to seek healing and to give thanks. It's all about receiving the love and light of those who shed light on the darkness.

One of my favorite ways to recalibrate to the present moment is a six-minute chant with Snatam Kaur, Ek Ong Kaur, that not only activates my vagus nerve (central for a calm state) but also invites deep inhales and long and slow exhales. The benefits of chanting are many. When we pop in the CD in the soccer van, within moments the entire family can be attuned, it is marvelous. Sometime it provokes groans from the backseat as it starts, but not too often. We, as a family, have come to recognize what a powerful restart button a bit of time chanting can be.

In the Hawai'i lifeways I am learning chanting, it is *da same kine ting*. Chanting opens the portal to something else. Hula opens the portal to something else. Ritual opens the portal to something else. That something else is the connection to spirits, connection to landscape, connection to aloha that my magnifying egoic mind can convince me is all a bit woo-woo. It's not. It's real.

The rain didn't come because some Hawaiian lady did a chant. The cloud people sensed the energy of us all, heard our voices, felt our *na'au*, paid us a visit. When I was on top of Mo'u nui, on Kaho'olawee, I had the great good fortune to chant the transition from Kekuhi chanting to the other folks chanting, all sharing the journey of *Hōkūle'a,*.

My line was *Huli iho nei ka wa'a a Kanaloanuiakea. Holo.*

Bringing my full self to pay attention to when it was time for me to begin was essential. Kekuhi can change her chant as she is moved in the moment. I got to listen and comprehend, to the best of my ability. *Hōkūle'a*, literally translated as clear or happy star, was the Polynesian Voyaging Society canoe that sailed a worldwide voyage of weaving a lei of aloha around the planet, navigating only with the ancestral skills of celestial navigation. Her voyage culminated in the *mo'okū'auhau* that my classmates chanted. Hearing different voices, and sensing different energies, super-charged energetic exchange ensued.

The energy that coursed through my body as our *kihea*'s billowed in the wind and the cloud friends marched over to us was unlike anything I had actively participated in before. It was high ritual on sacred ground at a memorable moment in the time space continuum. Beyond honored to participate, I had an inward climb to get there, as well as the physical hike to the summit.

Leading up to this was hard. I volunteered to do the chant in *olelo Hawai'i*, the Hawaiian language, not my native tongue. (See Appendix III for more on the language.) Kekuhi, our *kumu*, teacher, did not assign it to us, rather if we felt moved to participate, we could. She asked if the boys were going to do it with me. I asked them. Everett, my oldest, and Marc, my husband, said yes. Toby, no. We practiced. Marc is even less familiar with the language than we are. Part of my character defect is that I can, at times, be impatient and perfectionistic. It got a bit messy during our rehearsal. I offended my husband by saying, "this isn't going to work" in a particular controlling tone that did not get me where I wanted to go. I heard other people practicing and realized most were chanting by themselves. Some families shared lines, each going separate. We were wedded to the idea of unison, if possible.

How to chant is different depending on the *oli* or *mele*, chant or song. I was trying to sing and scrambling the words with other chants I kind of know. I would stop if someone messed up, including myself. At first, I froze when Kekuhi did her chant and said *"atua"* instead of *"akua"* which is what was written on my cheat sheet. The more ancient form of the language uses the letter *t* where now it is often the letter *k*. I missed the beat where I was supposed to chant. She said, "Come on guys" and I still froze. The little girl had done something wrong, I had messed up and I found myself in hell, the cold and pitiful state of analysis paralysis. She said if there is ever a gap of 3 one-thousandths I am probably *pau*, done.

I didn't know how to chant in unison with my husband and eldest son. Angry, I wanted to go it alone, which is often my egoic response to hurt feelings. I didn't rush to apologize. I didn't want to practice again and again. I stayed at the camp with the other folks and drank *awa*, kava drink (used to reduce anxiety and promote mental calmness, as well as ritualistically). As a recovering alcoholic I was aware what I was doing and reassured myself it was not alcohol and I wasn't planning to get inebriated. I did what I do with my anxieties in my recovery, instead of blotting them out with a substance, I talked about them.

A bit of background is that I hardly knew my classmates at that time. In other words, I didn't have a confidant or best buddy there. We blessed in that we don't have cliques or that kind of vibe that supports or promotes drama.

I opened up by saying, "I don't know how to chant with others. I really messed up." One fellow said, "no need for self-judgment." "Let it go." Then someone suggested I start the chant with the first word and the others can join in. This was a terrific idea. Take charge. Be a leader. Trust yourself. Just do me but invite others in. I loved the feedback. I dropped it, this issue that was somehow no longer an issue. My heart felt lighter. I didn't have to blame or shame my beloveds. I didn't have to beat myself up. I could initiate and then feel the support swell up around me.

It worked. The fiery tingling up-swelling wonderment I felt afterward was incredible. I was in the portal. I was connected with the *akua*, gods, and the elemental energies of life. Kekuhi says chanting is a magical communication device and the fire in the belly was good. I was not the director, I was not the audience, I was a willing participant. I was not in control, yet my presence mattered. For this I am truly grateful.

Chanting has enriched my life beyond measure and strengthened my soul to be a worthy and warm vessel for the Great Spirit to land. We chant to seek permission to enter a space, a forest, the ocean, a party. I ask for my best self to come forward and see what I can learn from this experience, this energetic exchange, and to see what I can offer. This is an important piece to the conservation work we do here on the island.

What follows are some ideas inspired by Hālau ʻŌhiʻa's article "Sustainability Science? A Portal into the Science of Aloha," a collaborative writing process blending ideas and experiences of over thirty people interested in "sacred ecology and biocultural conservation" here in Hawaiʻi: There is indeed a "collective resurgence of sacred commitment to the places and processes we steward through remembering" our relationship with the landscapes as if the landscapes are our ancestors, because they are.

Whether you are from a particular landscape or not, if you live and breathe, and sleep, and eat, and eliminate in that place, you are connected. The land feeds you like a family member would and you take care of the land like you would a family member. This is revolutionary thinking for most Americans who see land as something to own, to build upon, to "cultivate" in a way that suits individual styles and preferences. I see this way of thinking as disrespectful and flawed.

Where I'm from I have always entered the portal of Spirit most readily when I am outdoors. The sunlight permeates my cells. The wind caresses my skin. The stars inspire great ideas. The trees give and take in mutual equanimity. The mountains represent a steadfastness and solidity that illuminates safety. The rivers teach flow, and letting go of past and future concerns and invite the now to be as beautiful and impermanent and amazing as it truly is. I could go on and on about the sacredness of the natural world. Perhaps you could, too.

As I'm sitting here, I'm experiencing a dissolving of who I've been and a surrendering into the success of who I am now.

Tired of trying to be a good girl.

Tired of my original-sinner-egoic mind telling me I am a bad girl.

Tired of the dominant culture telling me we are all fucked, but go shopping, buy this anti-aging cream, drink some wine, pop this pill and watch this blockbuster assault your nervous system just to pass the time. The dominant culture messaging gets louder, scarier and more graphic every year. We, collectively, have numbed to the madness. And we need to wake up. Now.

There is a conscious shift happening, I live it, I feel it. I am, as Barbara Marx Hubbard calls it and is herself, a social pioneer.

Where I'd like to be is a leader in the cultural revolution. I live with less stuff. We have one TV in the house and didn't have that the first decade of our son's life. We have no devices at the dinner table. We eat home cooked food more nights of the week than not, with three generations at the table. We live together. We share our resources and skills and talents. We share our joys and challenges with each other. We clean our own house and grow some of our own food. We absolutely adore car-free days. We write poetry together as a family.

One thing I can do is talk about real life stuff at the dinner table, yes regular meals together make a difference. We discuss a family member's declining memory, the news and our reaction to Anthony Bourdain's suicide, how to soften the competitive bent that hijacks our minds from winner/loser into win-win-win, and how to promote compassion in every interaction. We talk about hugging and what it means in the dominant culture to ask permission and have a come from of consent and respect.

We delight in the awards and recognition that comes with responsibility and proper use of the will, but we don't attach our own worth or our son's worth to them. For example, our sons both earned scholarships to attend private school. Everett's scholarship is called, *po'o kela*, which translates as reaching high with the head. He also received the compassion award, various academic and athletic honors, and headmaster's list. I questioned how many awards his school doles out, ruminating on the praise and blame trap that our educational system sometimes exacerbates. Are we awarding them for being decent children, which is now somehow beyond the norm.

Release, Amy, release. The school's mission statement is based on the principles of excellence, integrity, and compassion, and these are indeed worthy of recognition. My system flooded with positivity when he went on stage, taking a stand for compassion. Yes! My younger son won the scholarship, *ulu pono*, growing righteousness, an exceptional award of great significance and financial assistance. Yes! Letting go of my judgment of over-awarding children, appreciating ritual and intentions in the academic setting, and returning to a grateful heart once again, yes.

What matters most is to be of maximum service and infuse life with compassion, and gratitude.

These all sound small -- hardly a hero's journey. But let me tell you what. It is the little things that matter. **One thing I appreciate** is that they add up. The termites that erode the foundation of a life worth living are eliminated, one breath, one positive interaction, one smile, at a time. Daily tenderizing of the heart can save the world. Fertilizing the space between grows good soil. From this place, all things are possible.

Where I'm from we threw McDonald's wrappers out the Buick station wagon window while careening down Interstate I-4. Five kids in the car made an unwanted mess and therefore, firmly ingrained with the idea that we need to throw trash "away," we threw it out the window.

As I'm sitting here I'm experiencing a greater understanding of reduce, reuse, recycle in the dominant culture, but it seems too little awareness and a whole lot of denial. Many of us want to save the planet and we don't want to go crazy in the process. We do our best with the information we have. It's when we have new information to counter old behaviors that we started to feel a bit scrambled, caught between the walls of guilt and apathy.

Where I'd like us to be is experiencing greater coherence between these two desires. We wholeheartedly care about the planet, ourselves, and we are motivated to do something about it. One small act of compassion toward self sends seismic ripples of wholesomeness to the planet. She hears us, feels us and knows.

What matters most is evolving as a conscious consumer on this planet, while enjoying pleasure and abundant joyfulness. It's possible to be and do both, and. This is a new understanding which I'm wholeheartedly embracing. In the past, I struggled with right livelihood and seeing money as a powerful tool. It is, and the philanthropic benefactor within me is ready to feast and to feed others. I'm taking a stand as source for a transformed world, and from this heart-centric place, I invite wealth into my life. Poor people can't help poor people, I've heard. Trust, serve, receive, as I release the pinch of greed and the squeeze of scarcity.

One thing I can do to get us there to save the planet is to eliminate single use plastics in my life. Using them again, bringing my own container, even if it's not convenient, and buying less prepared food and drink. Plastic in the ocean, on the beach, in the landfill; it's not going anywhere. Knowing there is no "away" to throw my trash, realizing there is no "away" to throw my relationships, I can eliminate single use relationships in my life, also.

One thing I appreciate is the devoted commitment so many of my friends have toward saving habitat for Pacific Northwest Salmon, habitat for *Palila* bird on the slopes of Maunakea, the ancient fishponds of Kiholo, the *Kauri* trees of Aotearoa. These efforts make a difference. Sharing appreciations, energy, and efforts makes a difference. Your appreciative relationships with the land and mountains, the sea and the stars, matter. We can help by clearing up the space between; by noticing the quality of our conscious partnerships with Self, Other, and Spirit; our Surrounding are our family. Let us treat each other and the landscapes with this consideration. This is what needs our attention first and foremost. Stop polluting our inner waterways, the atmosphere around us and cultivate good soil for transformation to flourish.

The tenth distinction of an extraordinary life is responsibility. Here the invitation is to focus (pun intended) on just one thing, your gaze. Soften your gaze and notice how you feel. Soften your gaze and notice how others respond to you. You are powerful. Cultivate a soft gaze and watch loving thoughts flow and generate a magnetic resonance of reciprocity. In other words, you become a magnet for loving kindness, when that is within you and reflected in your gaze. It really is an inside job, that's not just spiritual jargon. It's an inside job with external benefits.

Chapter Eleven:
Generosity

generous-ordinary definition:
the quality of being kind and generous

generous-extraordinary definition:
the quality of being kind and generous despite feeling otherwise

One does not become enlightened by imagining figures of light, but by making the darkness conscious. The latter procedure, however, is disagreeable and therefore not popular.
~C.G. Jung, Swiss psychoanalyst

Smitten By Kitten (or how surrender breeds serenity)

Whispering in each boy's ear at night while sleeping, "may you grow stronger every day and stronger in every way;" is a ritual I have done for thirteen plus years. Now I find myself whispering this same sweet sentiment into kittens' ears. Kittens that are a new addition to our family. Kittens that require bottle feeding and monitoring. They need an adult to make decisions for them, like the wet warm cotton ball on pee and poop private parts to stimulate reflexes.

May you grow stronger every day and stronger in every way.

Just over a week ago, I heard a coqui tree frog in the woods next to our house. I would go outside after hearing it for a few seconds and it would cease, immediately. This was curious because, to date, our home on the island, did not harbor coqui. This invasive species with no natural predator and the accompanying high-decibel nighttime noise was not here before.

I was compelled, as many residents here are compelled, to stop this creature from establishing a population of other coqui. This is akin to negative thoughts popping up in the neighborhood of my mind. I love quiet nights; I don't want coqui in my backyard. I love the native serenity of my mind in its pure state, not invasive negative annoyances of worry and outrage, perfection and doubt.

In order to flush out the coqui, and in effort to preserve nighttime serenity (and sanity), I got to work on the debris piled by our neighbor's fence under the trees. I asked for help. My teenager came to help, barefoot and ungloved. I pulled up big branches and handed them to him. Even without shoes on, he wanted to go down deeper into the debris and pull it out. I was hesitant and I wanted to control him and say, "put your shoes on," and then something whispered in my ear, "he is getting stronger every day and stronger in every way, let him decide."

I let him.

Now to fully set the stage, I should tell you that I really wanted to be miffed that the debris was piled up on the edge of our yard. Was it our neighbor who put it there? Was it my husband who put it there? I felt the warm wash of outrage prodding me. Instead of raging, however, I simply took a deep breath after a powerful exhale and observed my thoughts. It was a crystal clear example of meditation in action.

For that split second, I didn't react with a nasty tone of voice. It felt so freeing to not get personally offended by something that someone does or does not do. Part of me really wanted to blame someone for this mess. But, more importantly, a bigger part of me didn't want to cast blame. *Alhamdu-lillah,* an Arabic phrase meaning thanks be to God- to show gratefulness of a situation. I long to know this phrase in each world wisdom tradition. If I had a bucket list, this accomplishment would appear there.

It was profound, yet simple. I simply did what was in front of me to do. Pulled out a branch, broke it into smaller pieces, placed it in the yard waste can. Immersing myself in my surroundings, I whispered to the elusive coqui, *please find a new home, not here.*

My mother-in-law wondered who I was talking to. I talk to nature a lot; practically all day long and sometimes audibly. Something darted across my field of vision. I reassured myself it was not a rat, ruled out that it was not a mongoose, and decided, it was, indeed, a feral cat.

Still working, feeling strong, my older son continued helping me. He noticed. "Gosh, Mom, that's a big load."

"Thanks," I replied. In hindsight, I realized that it wasn't a compliment, rather a "watch out for your back," guiding comment.

I find it interesting to observe that the stronger in physical body I get, the softer in my demeanor I get. The softer I get with my gaze, my tone of voice, my reactivity, the stronger in spirit

I get. Vulnerability, a place of soft and supple willingness, is a sign of strength. Releasing the grip of how things should be and embracing things as they are I considered letting go of the coqui eradication project. I laughed when I recognized that having more than one coqui would be preferable, almost symphony like, rather than the lone instrument of the high frequency anomaly.

I was taking another load of yard debris to the truck when I saw a look on my son's face I had never seen before. I heard a murmuring that I had never heard before. Once my brain figured out that he wasn't hurt, I concluded he was elated. Another negative thought—silenced.

The strange sound coming from him exuded pure excitement, no words, just a cooing, wooing sound. Finally, he uttered something coherent. "They are so cute," he cried.

He found kittens. Under the truck-load of debris we had pulled out together. A nest. A den. Kittens. The cat I had witnessed dart away was the mama cat. We had unearthed a natural birth place.

More striking to me was just how this little bundle of cuteness ignited the dry kindling that had been growing in my boy, ready to ignite in a heartbeat; for he had wanted something to nurture for so very long. Our trips to PetSmart ended up empty-handed. Here was a furry animal to cuddle, times two. One black. One tiger-striped. He told his nine-year-old brother and within moments they were both smitten by kitten.

My mama instinct told me to leave them be. I stopped pulling out the debris around them. They were tucked away, safe in the cave of branches; granted they had more exposure than previously. We had unearthed them. We had disrupted the natural process, I worried. I trusted that mama, that feral cat, to do the work that needed to be done to raise these kittens. We need to leave them be.

While I was hauling the debris, my husband apparently was giving our sons a different message. He told them to go ahead and pick up the kittens. Of course, they wanted to pick them up and the next thing I knew they were in the house, drawing the *ooooohs* and *aaaaahs* of other family members. The kittens cannot walk, their eyes are barely open, they are vulnerable and needy.

I was concerned. We were essentially cultivating housecats out of feral beings, was this our *kuleana*, our responsibility? I have a client who engages in feral cat sterilization practices to help assuage this very real problem of too many wild cats here in the islands. There are no natural predators for the cats. *What is the right thing to do?* Quickly falling into analysis paralysis, I felt immobilized, drowning in the intentions of doing the right thing.

This is a core scene in my life. I am flowing along the river of life and I get caught on an errant branch reaching out from the banks. The branch of DO THE RIGHT THING ensnares me repeatedly. The eddy I swirl around in gets mucky and yucky very quickly. When I am stuck, I really am not where I want to be, I've learned this over time.

One way to get back in the flow of life is to surrender to what is, to unhook from the analysis that there is only ONE RIGHT THING. The way this shows up in interpersonal relations is to ask myself, *how important is it, anyway?* To choose my battles carefully. I want to be right, damnit, often. I want to be happy, however, more often. I have discovered the most powerful phrase in keeping harmony in the household, *"you might be right."*

My husband thinks we should adopt them. *You might be right.* My sister-in-law is calling the drug store to see if they carry little bottles in order to bottle feed them. *You might be right.* My father-in-law is calling the vet to inquire about kitten formula, and when we should bring them in to be checked. *You might be right.* My boys are in love. *Yes.*

Then I noticed these little bundles that each fit in the palm of my hand remind me of the kittens my father and brothers brought to me when I was four, a black kitten I named him Pitch and a tabby I named Tiger. This touched an even softer spot within me; a sweet memory. Love, nurturance, cuddling soft, tenderness. Having kittens tenderizes my heart. I, too, was smitten by kitten.

A week prior to their arrival, at our Sunday family meeting, the vibe couldn't have been farther from this current vibe of unconditional tenderness. Tense and painful interactions landed heavy like a load of debris harboring coqui, as we discussed the difficulties of living together multi-generationally, and troubles with communication.

This Sunday, the vibe was one of rallying together, albeit cautiously, to take care of these two helpless creatures who were now our *kuleana*, our responsibility.

The mama cat walked by our sliding door, mewing and searching for her babies. A cool trade wind blew through the yard, carrying her cries. I did my Buddhist meditation practice of *tong len*, sending and receiving. I breathed in her distress and sent out freedom and ease. I breathed in her concerns and sent out reassurance. I breathed, repeatedly, intentionally, to calm myself down and send good vibes to mama (me and the cat).

My beloved brought me a cup of coffee, bringing me out of my mental meanderings and back to the moment with a delicious aroma.

The kittens were already *hanai*'ed, adopted, by humans.

What could I do?

Embrace what comes. Let go of what goes. Don't chase after anything.

I would not have asked for it to be this way, with multiple feedings per day and pulls on our energy. Personally, I would have let the kittens nurse with the mama and work out potential adoption later, and after a family meeting to discuss it. Again, though I wanted to be miffed with what was right in front of me, I felt the angel of acceptance whispering in my ear, "let it be. Tend and befriend. Be gentle. This is a gift to the boys. They want to nurture. Let them nurture."

I held one pound of cute in each hand, the furry balls of kitten, for the first time. I found myself smitten by kitten, I softened to this situation, and I surrendered to win.

We eventually showed the mama cat the kittens through the door. She saw them, smelled them, and hopefully knew they were safe. Perhaps I'm anthropomorphizing. We eventually trapped her and had her fixed. She passed the health exam and was set free again. We eventually trapped the father and took him in. He didn't make it out again. We eventually saw another kitten with a weeping eye and diminished size, obviously living but not thriving. Everett wanted to adopt it, too. I had to set a limit. No more kittens.

We cannot save all beings. It is not our *kuleana*, our responsibility. That was hard to explain. Find that balance, that sweet spot in the middle, between altruistic kindness towards everything and altruistic kindness towards self and what is reasonable in our household. These are important life lessons.

I am reminded of the Cherokee fable of the two wolves inside each of us, one representing peaceful positivity, the other negative outrage. We observe these two creatures, living, growing, fighting, every day, in each of us. The observer asks, who will win? The moral of the story is that the one you feed wins, the one you pay attention to with soft and tender nurturance grows stronger every day and stronger in every way.

To personally abstain from wanting to feed the angry wolf of reactivity and blame was a relief. There are many times in my life when I have quickly fed the negativity that lives within me, the insatiable wolf of perfection and judgment, who is so righteously convinced she must win. I now release the grip of winner/loser. By feeding the other wolf, the more loving wolf, more nutritious quantities of food, strengthens it.

May you grow stronger and softer, more vulnerable and more powerful, every day, in every way.

As I'm sitting here, I realize that what Marc and I source in the space between us, is the playground for Everett and Toby to grow. Put broadly, the relationship of the parents is the playground of the child.

Where I'm from, I needed connection and I needed independence. Humans need to feel emotional attunement and be able to self-soothe and learn from mistakes. Little by little, tending to the small moments of life, I moved continuously in a direction of independence (not always healthy mind you), rooted in the belief that we are all connected all the time; interconnectedness has always resonated with me.

Where I'd like to be is knowing that we're doing a good job as parents if we enjoy healthy connection with our children and we grow ourselves out of the way; this fosters healthy independence for the child, which is essential for wellbeing; it is both, and.

One thing I can do is to release the grip of controlling. When I contract, I literally constrict my lifeforce. When I get more controlling, and I actually create push back from what I most want in that moment.

What matters most is setting boundaries as a parent who is willing to take charge. Then our children have the freedom to explore fully the life in front of them, knowing where the edges are.

One thing I appreciate is the ability to release the competitive edge of right/wrong and winning/losing. What if life really were a win/win game? Seeing in through that lens is a literal game changer.

Journey to Aotearoa

My family and I had the great good fortune of joining our classmates, in our collective intention of saving the planet, for an epic trip to Aotearoa earlier this year. I didn't know much about this exquisite landscape and incredible culture until a year ago. Aotearoa is the Maori name for the long white cloud; it's also known as New Zealand.

We collectively helped each other get there. We fund-raised $20k and shared mileage. We trust that as others helped pay it forward for us to go, we will do the same in the future.

To share with you my ignorance, I thought I might see kangaroos because I thought New Zealand was the lush shadow of Australia. Little did I know that it is its own country, a few hours by flight away. Learning about other countries and cultures was not part of my dominant cultural education. The indoctrination of America being the focal point of extreme power and importance clouded my knowing of other places beyond what I saw in National Geographic.

Crossing the International Dateline and the Equator in our journey to Aotearoa, my head discombobulated just thinking about it, we carried our excitement within us, though it spilled out from time to time. The dateline is arbitrarily drawn down the Pacific Ocean, with Pago Pago on one side and us on the other. We were chasing the sunset as our 2:40 pm departure from Honolulu made its way to Auckland.

Choosing to unplug for this entire ten-day journey, no phone, no computer, no tablet, meant no camera or work. I found it a liberating decision. As Anne Lamot says, and I paraphrase, when we need to reboot an electronic device, we unplug it, and it's the same with humans.

My habitual reach for a device took time to disappear during the journey. I questioned whether or not I knew how to properly be bored anymore. In the past, I would reach for a device to pass the time, to fill the time, to "make use" of the time. I don't allow the *puka*, the hole, to remain empty. I fill it with checking email or posts or taking photos. Deliberate unplugging from tech, habitual reaching during wait, the ghost limb sensation haunted me for the first few days. Eventually, I tapped a resource of patience I had forgotten deep inside myself. I allowed my curiosity of others and the world be real time, not headlines, snapchats, or snapshots.

In U.S. airports we were mostly in front of computer screens. In Auckland airport there was a mixture of screens and real person-to-person interactions. We are hardwired to connect, and it is dreadfully easy to do with devices in such a way we might miss the energetic exchange with the people around us.

In the *Marae*, the traditional meeting place of the Maori, is sacredness; no screens, no TV, no alcohol, no drugs. Just people serving and singing and honoring us, the extended family, the Polynesian ancestors, with open arms. The Marae has wooden beams that literally extend down, serving as arms to welcome. Sleeping under the spine and ribs of the building in the home of the ancestors, photos of the deceased on the walls. The carvings of the storied ones surrounding us in our sleep. Prior to the trip, it was daunting to imagine sleeping with 34 others in one room. Gratefully, it was a pleasant surprise to feel the warmth, the love, the acceptance. (And the earplugs helped with the snoring!)

The family we have created in Hālau 'Ōhi'a is a chosen family, *'ohana*. I have my recovery 'ohana, my paddling 'ohana, and my writer's support group 'ohana. My great good fortune is that I have real sense of connecting with family everywhere. On this journey, the different *Iwi*, the tribal organizations of the different Maori that we visited, enriched our lives immensely. Feeling connected heals the split of disconnectedness I grew up with on the mainland.

The ride into the first Marae was along a dirt road, to a pick-up truck that was waiting for us at the end. A big, toothless

Maori guy got out of the truck and I felt relieved to not have to get out to greet him straight away. Being shy and scared of bigger guys is hard-wired in me, and this too, requires healing. Would he accept me, a Caucasian woman, a relative, perhaps, of the colonists, the settlers that came to his land and caused major chaos? Checking my guilt at the door, the possibility that everything was okay surfaced like the beautiful moon behind the ginger-covered hills. The bird greeted us; this reminded me to be in the present moment, which is a great antidote to fearful egoic mind.

Choosing to live in this moment without fear, I did not need to puff myself or shrink back for any false sense of protection and be right sized. Healing the multi-generational transmission of greed, of hunt and take, or imbalance and disrespect. Instead of marrying myself to the inner narrative of all that happened with colonialism, I named it to tame it. After, I discussed it with others, cried about it, and left it to compost in the garden of unwanted emotional states. Instead of residing in fear and the funk of the past, I returned to the present moment. I offered kindness, willingness, honesty, help and jolly good discussion about all manner of things.

Mana Enhancing Agreements

Mana means spiritual power and presence, a dignified life force. Before going on this journey, I had not experienced the presence of a culture that lives and breathes with this truth of recognizing it in each other. I picked up on this Mana as I greeted, *Hongi*, Maori elders and children and women like me, raising a family, and longing for peace and happiness. I ate their delicious food. This solidified our bond on a deeper level.

Many people in the Waipou Iwi in Aotearoa are busy reclaiming land, conserving the forests, ambassadoring the giant Kauri trees, and raising families. They taught me about mana enhancing agreements. Basically, I understand this to mean, what can we engage in that is mutually beneficial? In other words, how do we bring out the best in each other? How do we benefit each other and truly understand what support looks like for all parties involved in an agreement? The acronym, MEA, Mana Enhancing Agreements, inspires us to bring our best self forth and once again dedicate to be a part of the solution rather than part of the problem.

Here's an example, while we were waiting for mealtime, one of my fellow learners, a native of Hawai'i, offered me an opportunity to practice an MEA (without naming it as such). He told me, "You know Liz, when you talk, I kinda cringe, like what is she doing talking? I realized that growing up I rarely talked and I had to know about what I was talking about, but you just go for it, even asking questions and stuff. I realized, after listening to you, that you are really tuned in to what is going on. I'm sorry I had that reaction to you, but I really appreciate what you had to say."

This shut me up, I could feel the familiar whip of self-flagellation readying itself to attack me. Yet, gracefully, gratefully, I didn't cave. I lacked the ability to pick up that whip and aim for him or me or anyone else. I had intuitively sensed his irritation with me earlier in our time of getting to know each other. I shut down the fear and showed up in loving presence instead. Rather than reacting defensively, I listened, I truly listened. *Mahalo.*

My understanding is that he was to be seen and not heard growing up. I had heard that from others growing up here. Conversely, my cultural upbringing in Western schooling and assertiveness in my family of all boys makes me different, not better or worse, than what he was used to on the island where he grew up. Together, we learn from each other, we shared breath, and a moment of diversity with a common purpose of love and service.

I gave him an appreciation. I reminded him of how he told me to not be self-critical of myself when I was learning a chant on Kanaloa. I was mad at my family who couldn't get the timing down right with me. He told me, "Don't beat up on yourself. You a leader. Just lead and they will follow, they will join in after you start." I share this example again because this is my brain getting rewired. Right there and then I was constructing new pathways with the help of the positive feedback of my environment. I didn't have to ride the story of guilt, instead I got rid of it.

Beating up on myself never got me where I wanted to go and I am less inclined to do it these days. I cried as I grappled with the multigenerational transmission of trauma and guilt I hauled around to every interaction I had with folks. I didn't know how to introduce myself as a person of European descent when the Polynesians were calling me ancestor. Way back, however, we are of the same blood. One blood. One ocean. One canoe. Painful as the growth is while emerging from a cocoon of self-loathing, I see how self-loathing and self-aggression is the root of my dis-ease. Saving the planet starts with myself, inhaling and exhaling in loving treatment to myself.

When we greeted the Maori, the formal ritual of greeting involved naming the mountain, the river and the *waka* or canoe that each Maori identified with. A connection. A sense of place. A sense of belonging. Not rooted in the ego of I, which breeds illness, but the collective consciousness of we, which fosters wellness.

We are rooted in the land. They are people of the land. They shared an insight with us, many of us who are conservation workers healing the land, "When the people are okay, the land will be okay."

We must unlearn the destructive habits to relearn how to truly care. Our unlearning begins when we release the strongly held inbuilt distrust of ourselves and each other. Taking full responsibility for the vision of life we want, we uplift ourselves and the world. Our commitment to the vision begins.

These sentiments speak volumes to me of the integrity

Moonshot

and grit of The Tūhoe people of Aotearoa. They struggle with the costs of colonization, with the depth of brokenness, with worry and despair. And still, meeting with them, seeing their land, literally standing on the edge of civilization, and sharing our breath, was one of the most uplifting experiences of my life.

Social media introduced me to an indigenous hero, Tame Iti. His passion for change, his creative spark, and his deep compassion transmitted across the internet as I watched a TED talk; *Mana, the power of knowing who you are* prior to our trip. Then I saw him on YouTube in his self-professed "butting heads" days, attempting to regain traditional lands from the Crown government of New Zealand. He was, in my mind, an iconic powerful figure who stood loud and proud for his life, his land, and his love.

The punk rocker in me (leftover from my teenage years) found him admirable. Little did I know that I would get to meet him, share breath, and gaze into his purple cataracted eyes at his art studio/gallery. In the past, Tame Iti was known as an activist, considered a trouble-maker by some, jailed, and freed. His people, the Tūhoe, have attained sovereignty from the Crown, and are now doing the vital work of restoring peace to the people and the land.

He shared, "I'm done butting heads, I've done it for 40 years, art heals me." He was the embodiment of a principle I had seen on bumper stickers. "Art saves lives."

Personally, I find art is an expression of our creative juices. It keeps our inner waters flowing. Fueling my creative fire keeps my soul happy and my spirit free.

When I first saw him, Tame Iti, in his high hat during our *powhitteri*, official greeting, I was in awe. I wondered how to get a chance to talk with him. It reminded me of seeing famous people and the fluttery vibrations detected throughout my body. But this rang deeper, with greater resonance than mere flutters. It shook me to my bones. The Tūhoe in me responded favorably. The meeting is not about the ego, the self, it is about the place. Introductions start with your mountain and the river. The felt sense of respect in every pore of my being, connected to the Tūhoe. We're interconnected. Though when you look at us, at first glance, it is too easy to simply see the differences.

I heard the presenters talk about colonization turning the Maori into something they are not. I'm going to be so bold as to say it does the same thing to descendants of the white colonists. I'm not what I imagine colonists to generally be: a person who believes my life to be more valuable and honorable than yours therefore I have the right to take from you without regard for your welfare. This is not me, and at the same precious moment, it is. We are all connected and what I reject in myself or in you lives in the shadows of me.

I heard from a Maori presenter whom I greatly respect, "Countries that ignore indigenous [people and plants] are going to fail." During discussions in Aotearoa, we explored ideas of culture. Culture civilizes people, makes people gentle. Culture fosters courage and confidence and kinship—we are connected forever. This interaction inspired many questions. What is the Tūhoe part in all of us? How does that unify us? What causes us to want to be kind and generous to each other and how does this save the planet?

We, collectively, are beset by loneliness and disconnection. The job of culture is to convince young people that nature is the most wonderful thing to hold on to. A new way of binding ideas in a written form; friendship agreements.

Friendship agreements last longer than contracts. We are the ones involved in the agreements, not a business, not a corporation, rather, a kinship organization. According to the Tūhoe—

"In the face of Western ideals of success, we search for our truth and restore our honor. Restore ourselves to who we should be. Colonization turned us into something other than ourselves. Addicted to the system. Beneficiaries and subjects to the Crown. Greatest enemy is ourselves. [we must] accept full responsibility for ourselves. The land is okay, the people are not. Common sense then comes common practice. You are the last born of the natures children. Every Day Brings Hope. With Unity there will be no darkness. We then argue that you do not need to own anything to be stewards of land. Therefore, deep in Nature lies our understanding of everything."

Whew. Pause. Read it all over again. Turning to Nature for understanding, this is the common denominator of all cultures. This is my hope for mankind. Finding universality, honoring our differences, and tending to our relations with love and respect.

Every Iwi thinks this: "This is the Center of the Universe. That's 'cause we look out, not in." I appreciate this perspective. Rather than egocentric, it is empowering.

"Some will die angry," For they do not agree with letting go of the resentments. Shift the focus toward healing these resentments, we go a long way toward healing the environment. After all, how can we have a healthy planet whilst polluting our cells, and ourselves?

This bears repeating: According to one person of the Tūhoe Nation, when the people work out their relationships, the land will be restored. On a very deep level I get this. As a relational health coach, my focus is on people, though I also care passionately about the land. This is what I propose; When we are okay, the land is okay. And so it is that we reach these considerations from our epic travel, which fortify previous leanings—

- Stop polluting the environment of your relational life.
- We can wait for the world to change (for the worse) or we can act (for the better).
- Start cultivating a more beautiful life.
- Choose to contribute to or take from the quality of any moment. Now.

The Living Building, on the Tūhoe Nation, a building that gives more than it takes, is indeed remarkable. As we walked through the space, past the gardens, water filtration and compostable toilets, we discovered much about the purpose, the vision behind it. The impetus, as I understand it, was to demonstrate what is possible. A decision of a community who was tired of looking backwards several generations and that had decided to look forward several generations. They knew they could not do anything about the past, they could only do something completely different about the future.

The meeting space dug into the earth, a space that honored the energy and the mana of the place, built with such care and consideration; I could taste the reverence and respect on my palate. The afternoon tea was delicious, so was the atmosphere created in this space.

The Living Building impressed upon me the importance of having a vision, a purpose for living. While many still live in poverty and struggle with addictions and unhealthy conditions, the question of the use of resources to build this feat of wonder surfaced. The building matched the beauty of this vision, like a flower composting itself, harnessing what it needs from the sun and giving back more than it takes. Impressive, to say the least.

Part of my unlearning has been to give up striving,

striving for more, for perfection, for winning. Instead, I have a relationship with enough, with good enough, with cooperation, and, ironically, all of this invites abundance. Abundance of spirit, of connection, of time, of health, and of willingness to keep on keeping on, saving the planet one relationship at a time. Letting go of the dominant grip of greed and speed, we slowed down and saw what was possible.

Still, I had moments of addictive tendencies resurfacing.

Turning to food is a milder form of self-medication than drinking alcohol, but self-medication nonetheless. I ate more pizza than I needed, not wanting to drink the fancy vodka that shimmered brightly like the lights on Lake Taupo, that night we had free in the middle of our trip to Aotearoa. As my beloved husband said to my seemingly pregnant looking pizza belly later that evening, "better bloated than loaded." Amen.

And with me, I demonstrate what is possible. I live as a sober woman of integrity, in a committed and happy marriage. I am well-rested, fit, awake, and fully alive. I work on my relationship vision, which grows to encompass family, both offspring and parents, landscapes and Hawai'i lifeways, vocations and creative pursuits. I want a lot from life, and I give a lot to it.

Yet, ironically, I no longer strive. Striving begets strife. I'm led by a divine calling, to be of maximum service to those around me, to lead a heart-centric life of aloha.

Tame Iti showed us around his art studio. Depictions of the artist Frida Kahlo peered at me as he told me he quit banging his head against the wall with his activism. How I interpreted that, was he quit fighting anyone or anything, and in the process, he quit hurting himself.

He sees clearly. He understands we are all the same.

He looked me in the eyes, thoughtfully. I commented on his purple eyes, he told me they were cataracts and he was due for surgery next month. And yet, his vision is clear. He knows what matters most. To tap the creative spirit within all of us to create a better world, to restore the land, to heal the minds. We tend to the relationship with Self and we have a powerful, positive impact on the planet. Bluntly, the world doesn't need us to be aggressive. It's counter-productive to making restoration work successful. Evolution involves emptying myself of myself to be of maximum service to others. It may sound paradoxical, but healthy, or enlightened self-interest paves the way for me to get over myself.

To unlearn the role of colonizer and the accompanying guilt, remorse, and shame I feel as a relative of one who colonized, I pray to release the negativity. To unlearn addiction and the subsequent numbing out, I pray to instead show up lovingly to the present moment. To remember where I'm from grounds me and empowers me to tend to the land and the space between wherever I am.

The importance of mana, knowing who we are and where we come from, is vital. When I told Tame Iti that I was a recovering alcoholic, he replied, yes, but where is your Tūhoe? In other words, I am remembering that I am more than a recovering alcoholic, a recovering colonist (via my ancestors), and a recovering American. More than, not less than.

My husband shared with me a book his mother had when he was a child. It described the geology of North America, the glaciers carving the plains, melting to grow the grass, feeding the buffalo who numbered in thousands. Heavy hooves massaged the earth and heavy piss aerated the earth and mounds of shit fertilized the earth to grow the richest soil on the mainland. The bountiful breadbasket now grows monoculture chemical laden crops to feed big animals to feed us.

Social evolution is needed for the internal thaw of frigidity and ignorance. Allow the deep penetration of big events to massage our psyche and let all the shit of our mistakes be the manure in the field of awakening. We must awaken, together. Diversity thrives in common purpose, we cannot survive on monoculture crops or monotheism or ethnic domination.

Let us write our story, our creation story. Let us imagine the Living Building like the Tūhoe Tribe in Aotearoa. Questioned why they would spend the resources to build such an elaborate building while simultaneously people lived in poverty and addiction, the elders cast a call to vision, to envision, to visualize the future. We look at the past to inform us, we look to the future to inspire us. May it be so.

Ideally, culture civilizes people, and that doesn't translate into making them something they are not. It gives structures and framework for living together peacefully. Sharing knowledge, sharing resources, sharing work, these are ideal in a culture. Inherent in this is a sense of worthiness and belonging. Culture makes people gentle. It fosters deep connections with courage, confidence and kinship.

This Power Has Touched the Great Ones on Earth

This Power has touched the Great Ones on Earth. This power is freely available to you, rendering you great. You are already on Earth. You are already One. Now is the time to be made ready to receive the touch of the Power.

This Power enables you to sustain connection with others and not lose connection with yourself. This Power enables you to know yourself and cultivate a garden of delight in the space between Self and Other. This Power enables clear, assertive communication to fill the space at times, while at other times, preserving the sacred element of silence. This Power enables active listening, with engagement, allowing a soft gaze and receptive, respectful body language inviting of deep respect.

This Power enables you to sustain energetic connection with what matters most— to see the potential in what you can do and do it without getting burnt out. This requires a simultaneous awareness of the internal as well as external landscapes. This Power guides the process of holding yourself to a high bar regarding standards of behavior and cut yourself some slack when you fall short; you will. Forgo moral weight-lifting which leaves you battered with guilt. Turn inward to your inner guidance system and surrender there.

This Power whispers, "I am me and you are you. We are not me, yet there is no we without me."

How to cultivate receptivity to this power, to strengthen your soul and invite Spirit home is simple. Become right sized, cognizant of your greatness and at home in your humility. It is both, and. Lord not over others, neither lean too heavily on or dominate. Awaken aloha. Invite it all, grace, humility, love, openness, honor, acceptance.

How to manifest it, the Power, in your life is straightforward and simple. Move. Sleep. Detox your mind regularly. Hydrate wildly. Hum with abandon. Love fiercely. Advocate for your partner's wellbeing.

What would it sound like if I told you that you can craft a magnificent life according to your own chosen standards? You might call that a moonshot, aiming high to a magnificence beyond your grasp. You might doubt me, judge me, vilify me, or want to vaporize me. You might wait until you have the motivation for such an endeavor. Well the time is now, Dear

Reader, now. Spirit is guiding me, my soul is safe at home, my own little neighborhood for Spirit to reside. Healing is indeed possible, no matter what. Spirit is resilient, when we tend to our soul.

Make a home for your soul. Emit respect. Act in love. Forgiveness is a push-up that makes you stronger. Practice plank pose (like holding the top of the push-up) and bask yourself in what you are thankful for. Thank plank for this moment, too. Adopt alternate nostril breathing (see the end of section one for instructions if you are unfamiliar with it). Do this simple breathing practice daily while you are waiting for the hot water to boil for your hot lemon water to start the day. When our toolkit is over-flowing with ideas to strengthen our soul, it is as if the ground is literally littered with them, and we see the opportunities everywhere. Rejoice and be glad to have these opportunities.

One way I open to this Power is simple: My body is a temple; I care deeply for its upkeep, daily. I am well rested. My spirit guides commune with my soul guards during my slumber. Occasionally the itty-bitty-shitty committee rouses me and interrupts their connection. Doing my level best to limit their meeting time, I focus back on gratitude instead of feeding the doubt and fear that want to rob me of my serenity.

Are you well rested? Does your IBS create IBS symptoms in your digestion? Is it easier and more socially acceptable to talk about how exhausted you are and connect to other people's pain points than it is to let yourself feel good and share the joy in that?

Well rested, indeed, I actually am getting good night's sleep much of the time. Healthy, strong, physically active doing enjoyable things, and within five pounds of my ideal weight, these result from being well rested. Healthy sex life with my husband and daily self-massage and yoga practice wake up my nervous system feed my sensuality a healthy appetite.

Power in Partnership

This Power has Touched the Great Ones on Earth. Power in Partnership. The strongest women I see today are those that accept they cannot do it all alone. I honor them. I have dear friends who fry themselves with over-doing, over-compensating, and quite frankly, martyrdom. Been there, done that.

Women are taking charge, with good men in association, and they are training the children. We are moving to a partnership society, not a matriarchy. Rianne Eisler, a powerful voice in this conversation, says this, as do many other great thought leaders of our time.

Someone recently asked me, if your soul were on stage, what would it be talking about? If my soul were on stage, it would share about the power in partnership, the importance of tending to our relationships, relationships matter most, we need each other to evolve into our best selves.

We create each other and the assembly instructions need a revision. Our personal OS (operating system) needs a reboot. Unplug to recharge. Tune inward in introspective awareness.

I'm going big, dreaming big, and living the life of healthy relationships with most people in my life. This strengthens my soul.

Recently I updated my virtual altar, my website, and I continue to actively participate in the internet, the nervous system of the planet. The workaholic in me no longer shouts, but rather whispers: "Come on honey, do more, you are due more in life but you must do more to get it..." whispering. When it does create static in my serenity, it's easier to turn down the knob on the volume of this now. Moments of peaceful remembering of the Sea of Tranquility; it's truly okay to be a human being and not base my self-worth on what I am doing (or what I am not doing...)

Images of past and present bring me to this place

immediately. A place of being at peace, being. Moss. Being. An elusive, yet perennial image of moss hanging above me. Dappled sunlight streaming through the clouds as the trees sway. My soul is sparkling and simmering in a soup of joy. This inner and outer landscape image grounds me in marvel and wonder.

Cherish your sense of wonder. Wonder is sustenance for the soul.

I have loving connection with my sons. We just enjoyed a lovely spring break of car-free time, hiking, beaching, and doing art and cooking together. I first wrote that a year a half ago. My son is on fall break now, and we are planning tickets to Bruno Mars! I am in the birthing process of writing and publishing this book. It feels as painful as the child-birthing process with my two boys, but way longer.

I have to ask for help, daily. It is actually one of my strengths. I asked my mother-in-law to make chili for dinner. She offered to cook two nights this week because she knows I'm keeping my book deadline. Asking for help is a strengthening prayer, asking for help from people, both seen and unseen. Recognizing that I cannot do this gig called life alone makes me stronger, not weaker. This is another way I release the pinch of dominant culture.

From the text, *Kanaka Hawai'i Cartography*, Renee Puanlani Louis, states, "The more you seek from the divine entity, the more the need to give up something of value, a sacrifice, a simply daily *pule*," prayer.

To receive the power, we have to ask. Ask for the power to be Known. To be Visible. To be a part of Life. To suit up and show up in a way that is indeed miraculous. I can. You can, too.

I pray to my ancestors to watch over me, gently guide me in the right direction, and enjoy life with me. They love the interactions, the act of staying connected; I hear them in birdsong, I feel them in clouds, I see them in the shimmer of moonlight on the water.

'Aumākua, guardian ancestral spirits, are widely recognized by families in Hawai'i. The honoring and devotion to relatives, dead or alive, is inspiring to me. Living here taps me into my roots more respectfully, more graciously, and more attentively. I no longer live in judgment of how I think my ancestors could have lived a better life. Been there, done that.

Now I see how I can keep their spirit alive and well, by feeding the dreamlife, feeding the energetic exchange, feeding the animals I think represent my beloveds. It is watering a garden that continues to feed my soul. Without the generosity of my parents, my in-laws, and my dear Aunt Judy, I would not have the great good fortune of calling Hawai'i home. Not only does the financial support make this possible, but the courage and commitment to living a life worth living is integral in the spirit of my ancestors. For that, I am doubly grateful.

I rise and shine each day, though the weight of my bones may feel awkward and strange. I stretch and smile and act as if this moment, too, matters.

You rise and shine each day, though the weight of your bones may feel awkward and strange. You stretch and smile and act as if this moment, too, matters.

Whenever the ever-present presence of gravity feels daunting, instead of pushing, I surrender. You surrender. The Great Ones know this truth. Be with what is. Rise and shine, no matter what. Invite space for grace to enter our hearts and minds and embrace what comes, let go of what goes, and don't chase after anything.

Hiking in moonlight with glistening patterns covering the terrain just outside *Halema'uma'u,* the crater of an active volcano, the spiders' webs' crisscross the path in front of me. I know I'm within six feet of this power at any time. I've heard we are always within six feet of a spider. In the past, this would have spooked me, my arachnophobia so paralyzing.

Today, I don't have that fear. I have transcended fear into appreciation. Spiders are amazing. A tarantula on the trail in

Sedona stopped me in my tracks. Absolute admiration instead of abhorrent aberration coursed through my veins.

The Natural Great Beauty around us touches the Great Ones on Earth by the reminder: we are them.

Pele, the goddess of fire on the Island of Hawai'i, flares up from time to time. She is still present on our island, an active flowing volcano, active, then quiet. Building consciousness cross-culturally, Pele builds earth; we are a growing island. Pele inspires beauty, generates awe, and demands respect. This Power has touched the Great Ones on Earth.

Sitting in Sedona, Arizona, at the ChocoTree Restaurant. The menu of this charming place espouses that "one person in unconditional love is more powerful than 300,000 people living in fear." I shiver, chicken skin, in the bone truth of this statement. My beloved shines his soft gaze on me as Snatam Kaur's melodic voice chants *On Namo* on the stereo system. I weep, with joy, in the light of the truth.

Where I'm from, I had a lot of time alone. In the woods, in the lake, at the beach. In general, it was a good thing. I carved spaciousness in my mind which I later craved.

As I'm sitting here, I know how much time alone can be restorative, rejuvenating, and downright refreshing. When I like the company with myself, it feels luxuriously simple to delight in the wonder of being, the wonder of being alive.

Too much time alone, well, that's a different story, that starts tipping into loneliness. There are those moments when loneliness creeps in, even in a roomful of people. The space between feels unsafe and uncomfortable. At those times, I ask myself, how connected am I to myself right now? Tune into myself to cultivate that self-compassion, from here, from this home within myself, I can be my own best friend to antidote loneliness.

Then I ask myself, how connected am I to my surroundings? Tune into the elements which surround me to antidote loneliness. Put down the smartphone. Leave the house to antidote isolation. Say hello to the birds and the trees. My grandmother-in-law, my Nonnie, always said, "you can never be lonely if you like birds."

Where I'd like to be is grounded in the gladness of being outdoors. This brings a wellspring of energy and aliveness that is better than any church service I ever went to.

One thing I can do to antidote loneliness is to turn outward, to pick up the 500- pound phone and call someone and ask them to get outside with me. In giving, we are receiving.

What matters most is to ask myself, upon awakening, what is the story I'm telling?

Smile upon awakening, before my feet hit the floor. This sets off a neurochemical cascade of good connections in my entire being. (Thank you, Thich Nhat Hahn for this pearl of wisdom.) No longer do I put the pillow over my head and wrestle with gravity, for I know I won't win, and more importantly, wrestling with the dawn doesn't get me where I want to go. Ask my husband, I'm better off during the day if I don't try to sleep in and succumb to bed. Rise, smile, and act as if I have the energy. What inspires me is that I love the opportunities to make a difference in the world on this morning. Transitioning into the day with grace and feeling the energy surface to do the important work that needs to be done, makes it very hard to not smile and not feel grace, ease, calm.

One thing I appreciate is this quality of being that I'm describing as relaxed joyfulness, calm abiding, energetic aliveness. When I quit taking responsibility for everything in life and just did me, I receive abundant energy to do what needs to be done with calm and ease and intense commitment, rigor, and excellence. Believe it or not, it is both, and.

Next, I make my bed. Seriously, this simple act is super potent. I begin anew, close the chapter of sleep, and transition to the day ahead. This simple activity has transformed the lives of many of my clients and friends. Clear out the space under your bed so your dreamscape is open, with no hiding spaces for the monsters.

Our *kuleana*, our responsibility, is to be true to ourselves, so that we can be true to others. When we inhabit our lives fully, enjoy our own embodied presence, then we can show up in conscious connection. From here, we can be amazing partners and feel higher love.

Here's something else I do, a simple act that benefits me and countless others; I drink water regularly and stay hydrated. Hydrating wildly, I keep my internal waterways flowing and clear.

I breathe deeply into my heart center. I fully exhale what is no longer needed in this moment. I willingly inhale the sweetness of this moment, right here, right now. Then, my friend, when I do these things, I'm stepping into Command Central of my nervous system.

As I promote the power of partnership in my life, I start with my relationship with myself. When this thrives, so does my marriage. Marriage matters, for the children are watching, and I want them, all children, to have the best possible world to grow up in.

We are social creatures. We need each other to fully self-actualize and live to our fullest potential. In Imago Therapy, a wonderful method of working with couples developed by Harville Hendrix and Helen LaKelly Hunt, we explore this key concept, "we are wounded in relationships and we heal in relationships." As a relational health coach and Certified Imago Relationship Therapist, I am passionate about tending to relationships, to "the space between."

In my own marriage, our romantic relationship cycled through lust, attraction and attachment, all the way into a satisfying long-term marriage. The romantic phase gave us the juice to experience the transformative power of love. For us it started hot, it burned wildly, and it still keeps us warm inside. Our marriage and our mutual commitment provide the most rewarding opportunity to grow and heal; to give and receive love. It is our responsibility to show up and do this.

We're really expecting a lot from our romantic partners. On one hand, we want stability in our partner. Reliability, predicable safety and security. On the other hand, we want a sense of fresh aliveness. Wild, erotic, new, mysterious wonder and amazement. In one person!

Esther Perel, an erotic desire expert, explores this conundrum in her groundbreaking work on couples and partnerships. She explores the crisis of desire by asking, "can we love what we already have?" Check out her book *Mating in Captivity* or her many TED Talks if you want more about this.

Many couples cycle through the romantic phase and wind up in the power struggle phase only to split up because the illusion of finding the perfect partner which fuels the search for someone better.

We live in a disposable society. This mindset is killing us and robbing us of an opportunity to shift the drift and activate renewable resources, in the realm of relationships as well as the material world.

Let's look at this more closely.

We know there is no away, we can't throw it away. All the past relationships in your life linger longer when we have attachment to them. We attach with positive memories or negative resentments. Let us regenerate that energy into our present relationships. I'm a huge fan of the notion, love the one you're with. And my hubbie is a lucky man because of it. I used to think I was weird because I didn't hold resentments to former lovers (or those who violated me) or even more weird because I didn't stay in touch with past lovers or hold fantasies of them in my psyche. I feel clear. I feel clean. I feel pure and whole.

(And you have heard where I've come from, at least a few highlights of my story, believe me, there's more. I am a sober woman of integrity and as my dear friend said to me this week,

"Amy, you are all heart." This is for you, Dad. All heart, no holding back, going for the moonshot of an extraordinary life.)

Let's get back to this idea of cultivating conscious connection. Couplehood mindset is what I call it. In the early stages of couplehood, we want perfection, we fall in love with the potential of someone (and ourselves). We tell ourselves we will be okay only if he changes.

In conscious partnership, instead of looking for the right partner, we become the right partner. Instead of placing conditions on ourselves and expectations on others, we allow the warm embrace of unconditional love to bring out the best in us. Over and over and over again.

Today, I am responsible for my own happiness. And yet I still manufacture my own misery whenever I want my husband to be different than he is. It typically happens when I want myself to be different than I am. It's a contagion. It fuels the power struggle. In early power struggle stages, I often blamed my husband. It wasn't until I was 100% responsible for my part of the dynamic that awareness grew and true love blossomed. Responsibility, *kuleana*, is essential in committed relationships.

Communication breeds safety for more vulnerable expression of desires, preferences and dislikes. Sex gets better when we express our needs, our desires, both in the bedroom and outside. More intimacy, *in-to-me-see*, more pleasure. When I give and receive in all aspects of our relationship, I am freer to give and receive while making love. It's so yummy. Make it safe, connect, and feel the joy.

The sex of long term committed relationship blows my mind. The juice from our mutual integrity and commitment fueled with the curiosity and mystery of the continual evolution of self and other is enticing. Big words, I know. Here's the funny thing, I don't lead with a sexual appetite, in fact, I tell myself I could easily go without, but I wonder how true this is.

As a teen and young adult, I was voracious. My sexual

appetite contributed to some unhealthy interactions in my life. In hindsight, I think I was desperately seeking AMY. I was hungry for my wholeness. Now that I have reclaimed it, I don't crave like I did. The unfolding opportunity for me is that pleasure is a birthright, and embodied pleasure is glorious, why I drop out of my head and into my heart, or my yoni. I have created two amazing human beings and the fertile real estate could be regentrified into oil paintings, writing, and other creative expressions, for sure. And, I am open to the reality that I want to advocate for my partner's needs. And when he's happy, I'm happy. And I think I want sex more than I recognize. I'm just such a heady gal, still.

Remember, conscious partnership is recognizing *we* are not *me*. Incompatibility is really good news. We are two distinct islands and we meet in the sea of consciousness. I'm a recovering alcoholic. My husband is not. I'm a controlling driven entrepreneur. My husband is supportive, steady-paced nurturer. We are different. Thank God. When I presence myself from an embodied presence, drop out of my thinking and into my sensing, I recognize differences with curiosity instead of struggle. The journey of the head dropping into the heart sometimes feels like a free fall, and you can learn to surrender to the grace of gravity, and trust you won't fall hard.

Incompatibility in marriage is a common complaint. The myth perpetuated around incompatibility is that with differences, there is the inability of harmonious coexistence, and this myth fuels the power struggle. Yet most relationships have some level of incompatibility. I know mine does, and still, we have harmonious coexistence much of the time. We do share basic values and sense of purpose in life, and how we express that for ourselves may look very different. I'm a sober woman of integrity. Marc is a casual drinker. I seek spiritual truths and converse about this topic regularly. Marc lives spiritual truths without much fanfare.

A basic tenet of truth in partnership is, we are not me.

221

When I remember this catchy phrase, I open my eyes to new perspectives. Eliminating differences is a futile waste of my precious life force. Alternatively, seeing new perspectives is invigorating and affirming.

My relationship is solid, we've been through a lot, we adore each other, and, despite all that, at times, I still feel fear. That is the predictable hell I land in sometimes. I know this familiar ache of loneliness, deeply. In the past, it was very familiar. Today, we don't go there as often, as deeply, or for as long of a stretch of time. It's no longer catastrophic.

The fabric of my existence was shot through with fear, in the past. Now, it is stitched together with faith that everything is going to be okay. More often than not, we experience relaxed joyfulness and calm abiding. Thank you, God.

My Imago Mentor Maya Kollman taught me a really mind-blowing idea: Couples would rather live in a predictable hell than have a taste of heaven and lose it.

Here's a recent example of how this shows up in our marriage. Away for business for a week, I returned home to find my paintings, paintings I created, had all been moved to another room. I didn't respond in a even-keeled fashion. Instead, I reacted with alarm.

When I am too hungry, angry, lonely or tired, I could remember HALT (don't get too hungry, angry, lonely, or tired) and take extra good care of myself. Sometimes, this isn't an option and I must get in the front door in order to do the self-care. Wired, after my travels I felt ungrounded and couldn't HALT. I scanned the environment in a hyper-vigilant fashion, looking for clues of whether I was welcome or not.

Seemingly out of the blue, I asked my husband, "Do you even want me here?" Based on this one observation: He had moved my paintings. Period. I wanted my paintings in our bedroom, he didn't.

My fear response: I concluded he didn't want me here. Ouch. He wanted neutral decor for a while and he had left me a love note to tell me this, which I had yet to discover. This familiar fear of feeling unwanted, this default place of reactivity is so very old.

If my reaction is hysterical, it is probably historical.

Am I wanted? This a default worrisome thought that sometimes gets triggered in times of stress, transition, and reconnection.

Neuroscience taught me some catchy phrases to help train my brain.

If I resist it, it persists.

If I name it, I tame it.

With this awareness, I soften to myself and share my vulnerability with my husband. Using the notion that conflict is growth trying to happen, I use the moved paintings episodic reactivity as an opportunity to heal the old wound.

I'm doing this heart healing to enjoy my own life, create a healthy environment in all my relationships, to the best of my ability. I believe that healing resentments toward self and other is vital to the health of the planet.

Willing to see things in a fresh perspective, I let go of the predictable hell and experienced a new freedom.

Where I'm from is a juicy, fertile landscape of interbeing; the essence of deep connection. I feel this most readily when I am outside. My husband and I got married at Chetzemoka Park in Port Townsend, Washington, with our couple's counselor/ licensed minister marrying us "in the cathedral of cedars and spruce." The vista of the bay, Mount Baker, friends and family was one of the most gorgeous sites burned in my memory. This was 2002. Pre-social media. Pre-capture every moment on a screen era.

As I'm sitting here, I recognize the universal need for connection, deep connection. When I dive deep into the story I tell myself, it is rich and promising. When I feed the idea that I am a lone wolf and try to go it alone, I feel terminally unique and scared. I just emerged from a lost 20 minutes. Where did it go? Social media surfing.

Where I'd like to be is in right relationship with my smart phone and social media. Though not an early adopter, in fact one of my first phones was a Jitterbug phone for elders because I wanted to keep things simple, I'm now officially hooked. It robs me of the beauty of the present moment because I think by capturing in on film it will somehow make it better. It does not necessarily do that.

One thing I can do is ask myself, how do I feel when you get on social media, while I'm on it, and when I'm done?

What matters most is being real, raw, and vulnerable, all while using discretion. Letting go of the light, bright and polite posting, the suggested etiquette of social media, I get to use social media as a tool to craft the story I tell myself and the world. For example, if I die now, is my last post how I want to be remembered? The answer, quite simply, is no. I don't want regret and remorse for one of my posts or comments to erode my serenity. Real, raw and vulnerable, coupled with honest, resilient and compassionate, now there is the secret sauce for using social media as powerful tool of deep connection.

One thing I appreciate is the ability to take the power of choice back and tune inward to ask myself if it is necessary to have my phone in my hand right now. The most precious memories of my last few decades are not on my phone: my wedding, the trip to Kanaloa, the trip to Aotearoa, the trip to North Carolina, the trip to Dosewallips. Golden precious memories reside in my mind palace and the hearth of heart, not my smart phone.

Gentle reminders: Notice bids of connection from you and toward you. When your beloved tells you about an interesting podcast he listened to on the way home from work, pay attention. Much of fertilizing the space between involves paying attention.

- Turn towards your partner, physically.
- Turn off the TV when a family member enters the house from a long day.
- Put down the phone and tend to the person standing right in front of you.
- Do not allow tech addiction to swallow you alive, because it will.
- Remember, dear reader, the preciousness of connection. There's a beautiful reality in wellness. The first part of illness is "I" and the first part of wellness is "we."
- Craft a relationship vision statement in the present tense, as if it were already happening.

Example of Relationship Vision:

We enjoy quality time together outdoors, making love, and creating an amazing life together. We have time together at least three times a week. We actively participate in making the world a better place through radical self-care, attention to the space between, volunteer efforts in the community, and philanthropic donations to public libraries and watershed organizations. We are supportive parents, children, and partners, dedicating time to each of these relationships on a weekly basis. We prepare healthy food, enjoy a healthy media diet, and mindful consumption in all areas of our lives. We tend to our bodies, minds and souls in a responsible manner, all the while recognizing our interconnectedness.

Gravity

Sometimes I question what is my higher power. Again, it is as if trying to put words to the immensity of such a power is making it small, and therefore dishonest. When I let go of the mental gymnastics that don't get me where I want to go, I know that I just want to feel support. I return to what is. Gravity.

Gravity holds the mountains steady in stoic solidity. Here where we live, we have the looming threat of eruption coupled with shifting tectonic plates and constant continental realignment brings a new dimension to the illusion of steady or solidity.

I've long told myself how steady and solid my beloved husband is. I can hear us each encouraging the other during early parenting days, "Be the rock in the river." Life is a river. Be solid like a rock in the river or let go and go with the flow. The point being is to not get lost with the energy of emotional upheaval.

Witnessing his stability has given me a recognition of my own stability.

May we grow old together knowing the security of stability as well as the power of upheaval to create new opportunities and change.

Gravity holds the rocks and allows them to move. As they tumble and crash, pointed and sharp edges erase into dust, smooth into curves. The layers of geologic time and different types of rock are evident in the shear crack of newly broken earth.

We marvel at its beauty; the layers of life compacted and beautiful, and allow the beauty of nature to reflect our own compacted layers of a beautiful life.

Gravity invites deeper depressions across the land, and the water, once fallen, greedily and speedily seeks the lowest place to rest. River cuts through gorge, and in doing so, creates beauty and flow. Scars of the earth, like the scars of the body, mind, spirit, tells stories of intensity, of resilience, of history. The lake, a place of collection, stillness, and reflection holds infinite possibilities for life.

May my heart, the *pu'u wai*, the hill of water, be a place of reflection of my deep love for the Nature and the Beloved, you.

Gravity wrestles with the wind. As wind recedes, gravity grabs the leaves to settle back down to the earth. Inhale. Exhale. *Ka makani*, the wind, invites change, invites new breath, invites the reminder of the constant of change. Fierce at times, ripping away the costumes we wear and the boxes we build for protection. At other moments, the trade winds are gentle and caressing like the most sensual touch, the lingering lover that doesn't want to leave.

Last night as I write this, on Halloween, we escorted our boys, through our friends' neighborhood. My husband dressed as a bumblebee, I as a red *'apapane*, Hawaiian honeycreeper, bird. Again, reflections. May the endangered status of the bee and the dwindling environment of the bird wake us up to positive effort toward a life worth preserving. The wind carries my prayers to the ground, littered with candy wrappers, evidence of a passing joy.

Invitations: Tenderize Your Heart on a Daily Basis

In our family, we talk to our boys regularly about the stuff some parents want to outsource to the schools and dominant culture. We talk about sex, sensuality, internet, social media, and violence. We don't let them play single shooter video games. We delayed cell phones until high school.

This all may sound rather counter-culture; it is. We discuss relationships, model intentional dialogue (see Appendix VI), and teach assertive communication. I love to tell them, "Thanks for asking for what you need." Comfortable in transparency about my recovery from addictions, they know when I go to recovery meetings. We do yoga together on occasion, we teach mindfulness meditation, and explore the importance of sleep, hydration, good food, and selfcare. And then we give them space to make their own decisions, their own mistakes, and tune-in to their own inner guidance system. There is no outsourcing in parenthood. And we cannot do it alone.

We are good enough parents.

Ask yourself, am I a good enough parent? You are not perfect. They will have their own unmet childhood needs to heal in their own relationships. Ideally, you will grow yourself out of the way by not doing for them what they can do for themselves. You will find that sweet spot in the middle of the continuum of caring, not too much (helicopter parent) and not too little (apathetic parent). The sweet spot between controlling and enabling.

Communication is an important way to tend to the space between. As a relational health coach, I explore both verbal and non-verbal communication styles with people, including, but not limited to: non-violent communication, assertiveness training, and Imago intentional dialogue.

If you are feeling anxious or upset, remember that criticism is the adult cry, conflict is growth trying to happen, and we usually protest the loss of connection with an argument.

Instead, try a bit of non-verbal communication of hugging until relaxed. Prepare to be amazed at how your heart space can settle, connection can rekindle, and negativity passes like a storm cloud in the night.

In each moment, choose *Aloha*, love, over *Pilikia*, drama, and experience the joy of positive connection!

Let go of the notion that you'll never hurt someone's feelings. You've walked on eggshells in the hopes of not offending anyone. Twisting this way and that, try as you might, you simply couldn't please everyone, all the time.

You know how slimy it feels when someone is trying to please you, yes? Naturally, the more you give yourself space to be you, not who you think others want you to be, the more you can also cut others some slack to be themselves. Again, it is both, and.

Still, despite your best intentions, conflict happens.

Some of the most important indicators a healthy relationship are the intensity of the hurt/rupture and the immediacy of the repair. Less intensity and rapid repair build resolve and resiliency in the relationship. Calm yourself down by taking a few deep breaths, and use your body as a guide for staying present in the moment. This lessens the intensity of the rupture/conflict. Deep breathing heals.

Place your hands on your heart center. Breathe in appreciation for the steady heartbeat that accompanies you, daily. Apply gentle pressure in a circular fashion. Feel the loving energy pouring in and out of you.

- Drop the stones from your heart, a qi gong movement meditation. Go to the beach, the park, your imagination, pick up a rock that is heart sized, hold it to your heart, give it your negativity, drop the stone from your heart. Repeat as needed.
- Stop doing and start being. Sometimes the most radical act is to do nothing. Surrender to the yin,

- the receiving. Our dominant culture is caught up in the yang, the doing. We need both.
- Show up to your life. Here's a quick way to define show up to your life.
- Ask yourself two questions:
- What is my first thought in the morning?
- What is my last thought at night?
- Pay attention to the story you are telling yourself about your life. If it is not the story you want to be telling yourself, don't despair. There is something you can do.
- Get curious about what tense you live in.
- My father lived in the past tense. He was always telling stories of his childhood. He was not a generally happy man and he wrestled depression demons until his last breath. My girlfriend Lydia lives in the future tense, always worried about getting fat or losing esteem or not having enough money. She's a pretty anxious gal. Depression about the past, anxiety about the future, no wonder there is so much suffering. When we get present, we recognize the river of wellbeing runs in the now.
- The eternal now is all we have, it is where magic happens.

Countless mornings begin when the touch of dread lands on my psyche and whispers sweet nothings in my ear. Worry festers soon thereafter if I don't step into my job as the Daily Tender. Daily Tender is a call to action. It is the most important job title I could possibly employ. See Appendix II for a detailed job description of Daily Tender. More important than mom, wife, daughter, coach, author. Next time someone asks me, "what do you do, Amy?" I'm going to reply, "I am a Daily Tender, I soften to my life and my experiences with vulnerability, willingness and, God-help-me, Grace."

In the past, many evenings would end with bitterness of what didn't happen or regret of what did. Nowadays, I review what went well (www) with my beloved family members and invite acceptance and gratitude to guide me into slumber. I gently put my head to the pillow, book-ending my day with gratitude. I start the morning with a smile before my feet touch the floor and I end the day with a smile and tell myself, "I'm a good enough mother, good enough wife, etc." sometimes it is as simple as, "I'm enough." I also whisper to my husband, "I love you and I need you." Expressing a need, out loud and in person, has been one of the single most challenging accomplishments in my life, why it even felt harder to accomplish than earning a Master's Degree in Contemplative Psychology.

These simple acts tenderize my heart on a daily basis. Weaving a web of support around me and actively participating in supporting others, I thrive as a compassion activist and relational health coach.

Think of how much more powerful you are when you are tender. The arrows of life's challenges can't pierce you, rather they bounce off, benign. When we embrace the world with our soft front, and sustain our structural support with our strong back, we are powerful beyond measure. This image of a vulnerable heart, a tender chest, with a lung tree voluptuously taking in bountiful oxygen emerges. This tenderness merges with the image of a super strong spine. We can enjoy holistic heart health being both soft and strong.

The eleventh distinction of an extraordinary life is generosity. I invite you to imagine bringing your best self to the table at any moment possible. Imagine others are doing their best, too. Generosity of spirit is a perspective-shifting miracle-worker. Carl Jung said, "The most terrifying thing in life is to accept oneself completely." Acceptance is the key of a generous attitude.

Chapter Twelve:
Consciousness

consciousness-ordinary definition:
the fact of awareness by the mind of itself and the world

consciousness-extraordinary definition:
entering portals and creating rituals

Beyond living and dreaming there is something more important: waking up.
~Antonio Machado

Stroker

"Hut."

"Ho."

These are the utterances of the crew of the canoe, when they are switching sides, with the paddles digging deep and snapping back. Bending forward at the waist, bracing with my feet, pulling back alongside the *wa'a*, the outrigger canoe, setting the pace for the entire canoe. This is the *kuleana*, responsibility, of the stroker.

Sitting in seat one, as the stroker, I get the best view in the world. The full moon setting in the pink Pacific, the sunrise peaking over Maunakea, the smiles and health pouring forth from my fellow paddlers all add to the extraordinariness of this experience. Squeezed into a tight seat, my pelvis pinched in the bow, focused on my breath, my stroke, my count, I set the pace for the crew. It's meditation in action. It is glorious.

The learning curve in my skillset as stroker was steep. Those who know me will not be surprised to hear that I was too fast at first. Too fast, then too tight, then too loose. Holding the paddle too tight. Then too loose, sloppily making the transition from one side to the next, missing the first count. I refused, however, to become overly apologetic, which I realize is often a seemingly polite form of self-aggression. I let myself be gently informed by what is going on. I focused. I breathed. I shouted out my favorite line from Yogi Bhajan, "Keep up and you will be kept up." And, I add with sincerity, "don't forget to breathe!"

Diversity is a good thing, especially when there is a common purpose. We have *choke* diversity, which is another way of saying we have plenty of diversity. The canoe club I belong to meets at 6 a.m., three times a week. It is the *kūpuna*, or elders. Perhaps I'm an honorary member, as oftentimes I'm one of the youngest of the crew. Much of the time I'm in seat one, the seat of the stroker.

Those of us in the canoe club have some things in common and a lot of differences. Our common purposes of staying upright, avoiding the *huli* (flip over), and enjoying the natural great beauty as we are moving toward a common destination. Diversity thrives on common purpose. These bond us as *'ohana*, family. And as in any *'ohana*, we have our share of differences.

Those differences help make us stronger. Already mentioned the age factor, and you might guess that some want to go faster than others. Some want to talk story, chit chat, while others crave silence and a meditative experience. Some want to race and win, while others would rather look for dolphins, whales, manta rays and turtles. We have astronomers with telescopes at the top of the sacred land of Maunakea and those who protest the telescopes on Maunakea in the same canoe. We have Democrats and Trump supporters in the same canoe. We have drinking folks and sober folks. And the beauty of it all, we share the same canoe, the same ocean, the same blood. It is an important life lesson. From this is a deep love that I call home.

I'm aware of our differences. These no longer generate tension in me or a sense of questioning my worthiness or belonging or someone else's worthiness or belonging. We all belong. I'm aware of everyone's heart. "Awareness is the home of wholeness," according to Deepak Chopra. May it be so.

Once we get to the beach, we "rest" for twenty minutes or so. Many socialize, I find it the perfect amount of time for a brief and a yummy yoga practice on the beach. Here is where the conscious (land) and the subconscious (ocean) integrate, with Kane (represented by the land) and Kanaloa (represented by the ocean) meeting here, I sense of deepening and potency of my short but powerful practice. The sunrise casts shadows and light dances. The clouds greet the day. The setting is magnificent. I pinch myself I am so blessed. Then a have a swim and possibly a wee bit of socialization if the mood strikes me.

Often the stroker, the person in seat one, the one that sets the pace for the other five paddlers, I've learned, and been humbled, that I cannot please all the people all the time, and I don't even try anymore.

Though I've been chided by a regatta paddler that sometimes it seems like I am trying to pull that canoe all by myself, I really do recognize that I cannot pull four hundred plus pounds through the ocean all by myself. I need others. And I am needed. This practice of paddling feeds my soul in a myriad of ways.

Scanning the environment for whales during whale season is another task of the stroker. It is the best seat in the canoe, in my opinion. The thrill of sighting is magnificent, the sound of the blow hole exhale is phenomenal, and the smell of the presence of great beings is powerful. Recently, I heard the inhale, oh what an amazing sound indeed! Underwater the sounds are wild, epically otherworldly, I'm not exaggerating. Listening to the whispers of the coral eating and songs of the giants are gifts in my life. So much of what we take for granted happens underneath the visible reality, below the surface of our awareness, when we meet it, our consciousness shifts. We are uplifted.

Celebrating my continued sobriety, I talked about the natural high I get out of sharing the water with whales. Late November, the whales return and the waves return. It is also the season of my sobriety birthday. The trifecta of bliss, sunrise, whales, and surfing...all while sober. We approached the breakwater after the skilled steersman of our canoe caught us a nice wave to surf, the thrill of danger, amped us all up. Then I smelt reefer from some guys in a truck as it drifted over the reef. Surfers in their trucks started their day the best way they knew how, by getting high on pot. Riding the wave of the natural high, I shouted to the other paddlers, "the smell of surrender is so much sweeter than skunk weed!" I surrender to the sweetness of this moment, right here, right now. That, Dear Reader, helps save the planet. You can't lighten up until you can settle down.

Here are some invitations to save the planet, one breath, one relationship at a time and witness the ripple effect spreading out over time and space and reach epic proportions of transformation. Establish mana enhancing agreements with yourself, each other and something greater than ourselves. This is the SOS of our time; source our resilience, activate compassion, and be of service to heal the relational space in front of us.

Review your mana enhancing agreements today. If you don't have any, there's an opportunity to being, right now. It's never too late to drop the stones of resentment from your heart and begin again.

If I could only share three things with the world:

- Recover from addictions that rob your soul of the beauty of the present moment. This includes substances such as alcohol and sugar, as well as technology and distraction.
- Heal your relationship with Self, Other, & Spirit, this is the S.O.S. of our time. Heal one, heal them all. Our interconnectedness is staggering.
- Contemplate grace daily through yoga and meditation outside! Connect with a higher power daily, Natural Great Beauty is the ultimate Source.
- Ask yourself now, what if the slate were wiped clean and you had the opportunity to share only 3 things with your beloveds, your family, your world, what would that be?

I feel compelled to share with you a *mele* that to me embodies the beauty of the language, the landscape and the beauty of Hawai'i.

This *mele* that follows places the learner within the cardinal center of potential using Hawai'i Island's sacred geography as a metaphor. In the Hawaiian language, the right hand is called *'ākau*, which also means north; the left hand is termed *hema*, which is the south. Stepping into this orientation then positions the rising sun at the back of the person and the setting sun at the front, or face of the person. Maunakea is the head, and as Maunakea is sacred so is the head of the native person. Maunaloa is the womb from which all magma rises from the core of the earth; hence Maunaloa is the primal base, as Maunakea is the celestial reach. Hualalai muli kuahiwi (Hualalai is the youngest of mountains) speaks to profound germination. Lei o Hilo ka ua pē i ka uahi (Hilo's lei is that of rain scented with smoke) speaks to the crux of our life founded on water and fire!

Hawai'i Lifeways—Lei o Kilo Ka Ua Pē i ka Uahi

The Lei of Hilo is the Rain Scented with Smoke

Ha'eha'e ku'u hi'ikua

I bear the sun of Ha'eha'e on my back

Pu'u ohau ku'u hi'ialo

I caress the sun of Pu'uohau at my chest

A pō maila ia ao ē, pai a ka hulu kōnane

And when night alights, it's the feathery glow of moonlight that sustains me entirely!

Ki'ina 'Ūpolu e ka 'akau

My right hand reaches for 'Ūpolu

Hēkau ē ka hema iā Kālae

My left hand anchored at Kālae

Lele kawa me he lele wai pipi'o lua Hi'ilawe

Jumping in feet first like the water fall, Hi'ilawe in profound arch

Na ka hau o Maunakea ku'u ni'o

The snow of Maunakea sets my zenith

Na ke ahi o Maunaloa ku'u mole

The fire of Maunaloa establishes my nadir

Hualalai muli kuahiwi ē 'iewe nei

Ka moana nui pāmamao o ka moku

Hualalai conceiving in the womb the journeys upon further shores

Inā kāua nauane, nauane

Let's make a move and make a stir

Ke ala e 'imia nei i ka pono e kau ala

For the path seeking profound experiences avails itself

Inā ho'i kāua nauane, nauane

Let's indeed make our move

A pāpahi i ka hāliko 'apapane lei lehua

Until we are worthy of wearing the lei of scarlet lehua

Lei o Hilo ka ua pē i ka uahi

The lei of Hilo is that of rain drenched in volcanic promise

He ola, he ola, he Hāloa iwihilo ē,

A life, a life this is, a life breathing right through to the core!

Composed by Dr. Taupōuri Tangarō, September 2006

One thing I appreciate is the way people in Hawai'i greet each other, hugs, kisses, sharing breath, and touching foreheads in a respectful moment that embodies the connection. The aloha spirit is alive and well and shows in the energetic exchange with each other, the creatures and features of the landscape and the *'aumakua,* the ancestral spirits. How we greet the day, ourselves and each other matters. You matter. Your relationships matter.

As I'm sitting here I'm experiencing a shift in my consciousness. I just moved my bed, my desk, cleaned the stagnant chi and cleared out the roach traps. I scooped up the gecko poop and made the space fresh again. I allowed space for grace to enter and work in my life in a way that is indeed miraculous.

Where I'm from we let the calendar be our portal to new experiences. It's Monday Moan Day, time to return to work. It's Twofer Tuesday where the rock station played two songs by the same artist. It's Wednesday Hump Day, half way to the weekend, the destination, the goal in every week. It's Thirsty Thursday, two-for-one drinks at the bar to get ready for the weekend. Loverboy piped in the back ground, all about working for the weekend. It's Finally Friday, with a bigger rush hour traffic scene and everybody talking about the weekend plans. We did not live in the moment. You know what? When the weekend finally rolled around, we got loaded and didn't even experience the moment. Sunday had a weird vibe to it, the ticking stopwatch of the TV show 60 Minutes in the background triggered an anxious state in my system. I felt so much anxiety based on the dominant culture and Hallmark calendar expectations of me and my mental state. What if I enjoy Monday morning and the fresh start on the week? What if I don't drink on Thursdays? What if I don't want to get loaded on St. Paddy's Day?

Now, I do it differently. In a flow state, this is what a week might look like for me. Monday is Money day. Ideally, my sweetie and I talk about our finances and activate our next goal. A needed area of healing in my life presently is my financial reality. If God is everything or God is nothing, I turn this, too, over to my higher power. I pay bills. I enter receipts. (As I type all this it is a good reminder, maybe part of me still rejects Monday vibes.) Tuesday is writing and client day. Wednesday is we-day, the day to connect with friends. Thursday is writing and client and a longer yoga practice day, sometimes on the beach. Friday is coconut day, fresh coconut water delivered by our friend. Aloha Friday is paddling day. Friday nights we get together with friends. Saturday is soccer day, recovery meetings, and family. Sunday is chore day and media free day. I write daily.

Where I'd like to be is disciplined and spacious in my schedule. Time is the great equalizer, we all have the same amount of it.

One thing I can do to get me there is list and focus on my three MITs, most important things, in any given day. Then I gently put my mind in a twenty-minute corral to harness my thoughts and energy and calmly get shit done. I'm unstoppable.

One thing I appreciate is the portal of intention. This intention shows up with chanting, with mindset, with purpose. It guides me daily, moment by moment, breath by breath.

Chanting is sharing breath, exchanging energy and making transitions sacred. The idea of asking permission before entering the forest, the day is a profoundly simple and meaningful acknowledgement of the transitions of the day.

You know I love sunrise. I bet you do, too. Why not greet this with a chant?

E ALA Ē

E ala ē, ka lā i ka hikina
I ka moana, ka moana hōhonu
Pi'i ka lewa, ka lewa nu'u
I ka hikina, aia ka lā, e ala ē!

Awaken/Arise, the sun in the east
From the ocean, the deep ocean
Climbing to heaven, the highest heaven
In the East, there is the sun, rise up!
~Pualani Kanahele, Edith Kanaka'ole Foundation

For example, when I first walk outside, I say, "Good morning, morning." I say thank you to the rain, hello to the rainbows, I pet the plants as I walk on my way. This is when I'm in the moment and present with all that is around me. Up until now, I have been focused on the next activity and tended to miss what was around me. Paying attention to transitions, paying attention to the natural world, creates space for grace to enter my heart.

Love Tastes Like...

Love tastes like juicy, tender flesh of a mango. My friend George grows the perfect mangos. They are a sensory delight. After a morning of paddling our canoes on the ocean, swimming with the whales, and greeting the sunrise over Maunakea, we are fresh for our day. The endorphins are kicking through the brain and the cascading over the entire nervous system like a water waterfall of wonder. George beckons me over to his van.

He plunks a hefty ripe mango in my right hand. The weight of it is perfect, substantial, hearty without being heavy, kind of like me. My left hand pets the smooth textural roundness. My eyes feast on the colors of red, yellow, green gold with freckles of dark sparkly sunlight cast in time. My nose smells the exquisite sweetness that it is oh so classy, rich and fragrant with whiffs of delicate care and prime conditions for maturing to this perfect state of ripeness. The tastes; well, the taste will wait for later, when my husband gets off work and we enter the ocean for sunset, juice dripping down his beard, a linger-longer-kiss waiting in the wings.

This, Dear Reader, this is what love tastes like.

A Tiny Speck on a Blue Dot

Sitting on a rock on a rock in the middle of the ocean, over two thousand miles from another majorly inhabited land mass of equal or bigger size, nestled between two flowering trees, I hear birdsong. My spirit soars. I smell the sweat of my armpits coupled with the deep earth of this crevice on the side of Kohala mountain. Here, I am home. And still, I feel lonely, at times. And still, I seek solace and reassurance, at times. I have an uncanny ability to feel like I don't fit in, it could be in my family, in my marriage, in my class, anywhere. Anywhere and everywhere I have felt the warm wash of doubt engulf me and take my breath away. This existential loneliness ebbs and flows.

Anywhere and everywhere I have felt the warm wash of doubt engulf me and take my breath away. Running away to paradise doesn't antidote it, for some it amplifies it and they get "rock fevered" and return swiftly to the mainland. Others don't feel they belong at all. I notice my fleeting moments that are far less frequent than they ever were before and I say hi and ask if we can have a cup of tea together. Always say yes to a cup of tea, particularly if it is with an aspect of yourself that demands your attention and needs a little reassurance.

Where I'm from, I was told to keep busy (by my mom), but don't move so fast (by my dad). During a boyfriend break-up, the messages around me consisted of belittling the dude, "what a jerk;" ignoring the feelings, "you'll be better off without him'" and distracting the mind, "keep yourself busy." Drown yourself in work, the time passes more quickly that way. Time has a big puffy role in my life. Time is *IT*. It heals all wounds, It is grumpy on Monday mornings when it is time to go to work, It dances on Wednesdays, hump day, and It parties it up on weekends. It fed me the lie that some moments are better than others, some people are better than others, some feelings are better than others.

As I'm sitting here, I'm looking for the middle way, the sweet spot of integration, the inner landscape of calm abiding in the eternal now, the present moment of infinite possibilities. Integrating my mind with contemplative practices gives me energy when I need energy and rest when I need rest, none of which is contingent upon substances like caffeinated energy drinks or alcohol to enhance these states.

Where I'd like to be is in a place of mental integration steeped in a sense of enough time, understanding time is the great equalizer, we all have the same amount of it on any given day. I'm no longer willing to look busy to feel important, this is an employee mindset that doesn't work for me anymore. I am the CEO of my life. I can integrate between what neuroscientist Dan Siegel calls the banks of rigidity and chaos, and dive into the river of wellbeing, the river of integration.

What matters most is the grace of the transitions, from my right hemisphere to my left, from my sleep to my awakened state, from my job as life coach to my role as parent. How I move in those transitions is what stiches together the fat quarters of my life, the minutes of my day, the thoughts in my mind. You see, I finally got the message, how I do one thing is how I do everything. If I allow space for grace in my day, my schedule, my mind, my life flows.

One thing I can do to integrate my mind is to maintain a daily yoga practice. Period. You see, the benefits of yoga are enumerable.

One thing I appreciate is how much the internet, that which I used to resist, is actually quite instrumental in my daily yoga practice. I start to integrate it into my being, my knowing, my morning routine. Occasionally, I will tune into my paid course at Kundalini Yoga University through Spirit Voyage, sign up for a 14-day yoga challenge with amazing Yoga with Adriene, or listen to Snatam Kaur to augment my *pranayama* breathing practices. By stepping into command central of my own nervous system, I'm empowered. I cannot blame any more, I can take ownership. Stepping into the planetary nervous system, the internet, I can take advantage of the opportunities of the vast and rich teachings offered. But like anything, too much of a good thing is too much, I have to limit the time on the computer.

The twelfth distinction of an extraordinary life is consciousness. I do believe we can shift our consciousness through our actions and our connections. I invite you, Dear Reader, to aim high, dive deep, and live an extraordinary life. Support is here to guide you.

Whales

I sometimes wonder if...

the mama whale dives too deep and has to hustle to the surface for air.

The last ten yards perhaps a nervous flight toward relief. This is called scratching, diving too deep and gasping for air. I do it in my life all the time. I wonder if mama whale does. I tend to doubt it.

I sometimes wonder if...

the hunger of those many months in Hawai'i is even something the humpbacks notice. No feeding, just birthing and breeding. It takes one thing off the to-do list. What can I take off my to-do list, at least seasonally?

I sometimes wonder if...

the whales detect the changes in the weather patterns. The water temperature rises, certainly they know that, or are they like the frogs in the water of a pot starting to boil, that subtle shifts are undetected. Did they see the intense lightning storm on Sunday? Of course they did. Do they sense more cars snaking down the hill of Kawaihae Road? Do they know there is no out there out there?

I sometimes wonder if...

the whales live longer in certain parts of the world more than other? Is there a Blue Zones (an area defined by longevity and quality of life) in the deep blue? If they know some places are healthier, do they spend more time there?

I sometimes wonder if...

the song of the whales expresses emotion—if the last stanza or two changes each year and if all the whales, the males, find the same song by the end of the season, what are they singing about? If human men are like that, why, pray tell, are you listening to Donald Trump? Either as a supporter or as an opponent, either way, you are still listening. Has he changed your tune?

I sometimes wonder if...

the breaching, the splashing, the flipper slapping is an expression of emotion. We anthropomorophosize the joy and pure delight, just like people project on to others the grace and beauty of the charmed life. What about the tremendous amount of energy it takes to propel upwards and outwards on a regular basis. Do you feel like this in the morning getting out of bed? Let the whale inspire you, imagine that the whale enjoys it, and lunge out of bed with vim and vigor and express, "GOOD MORNING, MORNING" with the utmost vibrant conviction. It will rock your world. And your partners. And your kids. And your pets. And your plants. And...

I sometimes wonder if...

the ever-present presence of gravity is something the whales wrestle with or if gliding effortlessly in existence of all that is is that status quo. The fishing line that tangles brings a halt, the brave rescuer untethers the free spirit of this magnanimous creature. The big eye looks back, knowing appreciation and communicating it as such. Be the rescuer, start with yourself, untether from that which drags you down, and look your rescuer, yourself, or *perhaps Ke Akua Nui*, Source of all Creation, and say, *Mahalo nui loa*, great big thanks.

Sometimes I need to hang out with things that are greater than me to remember at my core, a great power exists. I jump in the water with dolphins, my nervous system relaxed. In fact, our guide told us to release the vagal nerve, release the pinch. I hopped off the boat, into the deep blue ocean. The pilot whales appeared before me. A whole tribe of them. A pod, I guess. Right then, before I could freak out, one of them pooped, literally released the pinch. Whale poop, and you know what, Dear Reader, it was beautiful. Amazing. With whales, I release the pinch as they teach me. Additionally, I connect with my ancestors and the landscape around me.

Mo'okū'auhau

The invitation is to write your own genealogical chant, your personal continuum of where and who you come from. To know where one is from, and to understand the genealogy as a means of maintaining balance between past and present, also sets a course for the future. Traditionally, the three portals of connection, the three *piko,* navel points, were these: The belly button connects to the mother. The top of the head connects to the ancestors. The genitals connect to the descendants.

The *mo'okū'auhau* serves as identification of purpose and belonging. I am hungry to claim my sense of purpose and belonging and to anchor my relatives with me in this point in and on this time and space continuum. Please note this is in no ways an exhaustive ancestry research project. This is what I have been told, what I feel, what I sense, in this moment. This *mo'oku'auhau* is mine and mine alone. No one else has one like it. Whoa. This just struck me as my unique fingerprint on the planet, my unique DNA to be here now. Having earned my seat, I'm claiming it.

Pick either maternal or paternal lineage. Pick the child you are focusing on, I chose my mother and tracked back. Identify your great grandmother on one side of the family and go from there. If you cannot remember, or don't have access to the information, borrow mine.

Get familiar with where you live. Specific land features and creatures. You have energetic exchange with all of this, whether you are aware of it or not, why not be aware? Source sources you. Name your mountain, your fresh water, the place where you live now. This lesson is vital is naming your center of the universe, grounding yourself in the moment, and recognizing you are never alone. This is how. Connect in with them.

There are 40,000 deities in this indigenous culture of Hawai'i. That's 80,000 eyes watching out for you. Give that there's a lot of chaos and upheaval in the world, this is incredibly good news. We need a lot of help. We can recognize the chaos and upheaval are part of the creation process and don't swept away by it all. When we ask for deep guidance to restore order and peace, we become part of the solution rather than perpetuating the problem.

Whether this cosmology resonates with your or not, recognize your intricate connection to the landscape around you. Knowing where you are and where you are from is part of the journey of integrating back to wholeness, and to living an extraordinary heart-centric life.

Part of integrating one's life narrative is naming the ancestors and landscape features and creatures that create the world you live in to this day, and the world you came from originally.

Here is My *Mo'okū'auhau*

Mo'o, here, is the same as *mo'o* in *mo'olelo*. The *mo'okū'auhau* is your personal continuum, or genealogical chant. Using the format of the below *ko'ihonua*, or cosmology, create your own *Mele Mo'okū'auhau* or genealogical chant. Here is mine.

'O Wilahemena Hawerrot no Manomano Loko Erie 'Ohaio
Noho iā Thomas Keenan no Manomano Loko Erie 'Ohaio
Hānau 'o Dorothy Elizabeth Keenan, he wahine

'O Dorothy Elizabeth Keenan no Manomano Loko Erie 'Ohaio
Noho iā William Russell Joyce no Kai Kū 'Ono, Loke 'Ailana
Hānau 'o Elizabeth Ann Joyce, he wahine

'O Elizabeth Ann Joyce no Manomano Loko Erie 'Ohaio
Noho iā Herman Daniel Williams no Chesapeake kapa kai,
Hānau 'o Amy Elizabeth Williams, he wahine

'O Lanikepu ko'u ahupua'a ma ka moku 'o Kohala
'O Lanikepu ko'u pu'u, 'o Kohala ko'u mauna
'O Lanikepu ka wai, 'o Pacific ke kai
'O ka wao kanaka ku'u 'āina e noho nei. OLA!

Mo'okū'auhau

'O _____ no _____

Noho iā _____ no _____

Hānau 'o _____, he _____ (for each offspring)

'O _____ no _____

Noho iā _____ no_____

Hānau 'o _____, he _____

'O _____ no _____

Noho iā _____ no _____

Hānau 'o _____, he _____ (you)

'O _____ ko'u ahupua'a ma ka moku 'o _____

(the region and district you are currently living)

'O _____ ko'u pu'u/mauna (your hill your mountain)

'O _____ ka wai / ke kai (your fresh water/your ocean)

'O ka wao _____ ku'u 'āina e noho nei. OLA!

(the plane you live in on this great land. LIFE!)

Exercises

One-minute breath—

- 20 second inhale,
- 20 second hold at the peak of inhalation,
- 20 second exhale.

This breath takes time and practice to get. I find reclining posture to facilitate this the best. This works wonders in terms of working your brain hemispheres in an integrated fashion.

Exercises: The Lung Trees

Place one hand on your beloved's heart and the other on your belly. Have your partner do the same. Invite a soft gaze into your eyes, you know what I mean, let your eyes smile. Be fully present in this moment with your partner. Turn off devices. Share with your partner three breaths fully and deeply into your lung trees, your belly, even your toes, while watching your hand rise as your partner breaths deeply also.

In Closing—what we did

First, we re-established trust with ourselves. We focused on ourselves. Re repaired our broken-heartedness. We reactivated a faith that works and cultivated core compassion. We threw ourselves wholeheartedly into service. We led with generosity and grace.

We paid attention to the command central back home, we recognized mental hygiene is just as important as dental hygiene.

Through yoga, breathing and meditation, key contemplative practices, we are not victim to the ups and downs life.

My heart is as wide as the sky, as vast as the sea, and as stoic as the mountain. In my heart center I can hold all of life's experiences and not abandon myself. From this loving space of equanimity, generosity and compassion, I can, indeed, be source for a transformed world. You can, too.

Expect to be amazed at the support that comes; or rather, your awareness of the support. Go outdoors and hug a tree. We often say, get to nature, for that level of healing and connection. I'm fascinated, but not surprised, to learn that in 'ōlelo Hawai'i, there is no word for "nature." It's like asking a fish what water is, or me what God is. It just is. Everywhere. God is everything or God is nothing. You notice it when it is not there. Wake up to that fact, now. Together, we can.

Name your mountain or land features and creatures that define the place you call home, the place you identify with. This is equally as important as naming your relatives. Perhaps even more.

My big promise is that in softening, we strengthen. When we tenderize our hearts on a daily basis, we create a homecoming for ourselves that is best described as calm abiding. How I can make the biggest difference for you is to share my own experience, strength, and vision for the world

I love. The more you tighten in your suit of outrage, the more you, yourself, become a target. The more you grip the greed, the hate, the scarcity by holding jealousy, judgement and self-pity, the more you are caught in the problem, vs. living in the solution.

By choosing a positive story to tell myself and you about my life, I'm exercising free will. It is not make-believe, it is my truth. I have more blessings in my life than I can say grace over, and I face my ample challenges with my full aliveness. I love deeply and I feel the sorrow of the world. It is all *both, and.* I no longer see things as *either, or.*

If I did, I wouldn't have hosted a foreign exchange student from a country that my president told me to be afraid of. I wouldn't have moved to a place where I am the minority and my previous landlord in Washington told me I wouldn't be welcome in Hawai'i. I wouldn't have sold my house in a wonderful community if I believed that was the only wonderful, wholesome, and amazing community that ever existed. I wouldn't have agreed to make this leap of faith with my in-laws if I fed the old story that I have heard repeatedly, "I could never live with my in-laws."

I've been called a Renaissance woman. What does that mean in modern terms? It means I am a social pioneer. I let go of my right to hate, to judge, and to condemn. I open up to taking really good care of myself and trusting this is more important than cleaning the garage when I'm exhausted. I open to setting my daily challenge; to look for the inherent worth and dignity in every human being. Some days it is so hard to find. My own fears and insecurities get in the way of seeing with love.

There is no out there out there.

I am the center of the universe, as are you. May we have the courage to look out at others and trust that what we see is reflection of us, of our creation. We are co-creators of each other. Hate begets hate. Violence begets violence. Stealing myself against the other didn't get me where I wanted to go.

No longer homeless to myself, I inhabit myself fully and challenge myself regularly. I feel the things that are stretchy, and I stretch anyways. I house-sit quite a bit, I enjoy travel, I am fairly adaptable and flexible. I thrive if I have quiet and cool and dark at night and access to trees and outdoors during the dawn; I can feel at home anywhere. But the old behaviors of spinning out and tightening up to fit in or make other people okay so that I am okay, that fueled my homelessness.

In the dark corners of the Realm of Resilience, the dump of unwanted thoughts stinks. Here, the guilt-ridden little girl of capitalist Craigslist culture tells me I should be working, earning, consuming and complaining. I heard on the radio this morning that the latest research shows that we can only focus for a few hours at a time. How am I spending my few hours of focus today? Writing for you, Dear Reader. Interviewing thought leaders of relational health on my online shows, Power in Partnership (PIP) and A League of Extraordinary Couples. Posting video recordings called PIP Clips, quick tips to enhance your relationships on social media. Coaching clients how to enjoy healthy relationships and holistic heart health so that they can be a powerful positive presence on this planet.

How to come home to myself is a matter of courage and kindness. I'm like Oprah—I consider my religion to be gratitude, and with this attitude, all things are possible.

Presently, I live with my in-laws in this tropical paradise. Whatever challenges erupt, I feel called to ramp up my spiritual connection with a power greater than myself. I call on the retinue of angels who have my back. I whisper to the ancestors of blood and of place, as I have been *hinai*'ed here, adopted, by this place. I chant permission to enter the ocean and I cleanse myself of worry.

What I have to offer is a slice of my subjective reality. I realize I know only a little. The suggestions I make in my writing are just that, suggestions. Please take what you can use and leave the rest.

May you be a stand for transformation in the World.

On a practical level, as you travel the planet, take only photos, leave only footprints, and maybe cover them up to. Don't take the lava or the stones or the shells. Pick up trash. Don't use single use plastic. Carry a metal straw, a spoon, a fork. Take your own cup with you to refill water and tea and coffee. Hydrate wildly. Participate in upriver clean up. Protect our watersheds, (literally and figuratively).

Be gentle with yourself when you fall short, because you will, momentarily; you're human. Inspire others by bringing your best self forward. The space between us in the playground of the child, even if you have no children, the child is your soul. Let's not be noxious and let's not create more toxins.

Let's be the beauty we see in the river. Let our eyes, like the lakes, by the windows of the world. Let's appreciate the thunder but know it is the gentle rain that cultivates the garden, not the booming crack and flash.

Be the silence breakers and speak the truth. We are stewards of our soul, this takes care of the land. We are survivors of hope and fear and healing artists processing life. Conserve the natural resources by purifying your thoughts, your blood, your own internal waterways. Listen to the symphony of the coral, and the parrot fish eating the coral. Listen to the waves crashing, and the cries of children losing the sand castle. Listen to your exhale, right now.

You matter. Your relationships matter.

Thank you for growing conscious connection to yourself, your beloved, and each other.

Benediction

May you know the love within you and around you.
May that love be reflected in your thought, word and deed.
May you soften your gaze to the succulent strength within;
and feel your reach expand.
May you vote for a better world through your diet,
your media diet, your communication,
and your presence on this precious planet.
May you be a powerful point of light; we need you.
You matter. Your relationships matter.

~Amy Elizabeth Gordon, Waimea, 2019

Appendix I

Resistance

I reviewed the classic text, *The War of Art* by Steven Pressfield. Many of my mentors kept suggesting this book, and so, once I quit resisting reading it because I didn't like the word "War" in the title, I read it. I recommend that you read it, too.

I found his ideas deeply resonant, as a creative, resistance is well-known to me. My relationship with resistance shows up fully in each and every idea he presents, which he refers to as Resitance's Greatest Hits. This is how these hits show up in my life presently.

1. *I am writing this book and painting without destroying my work.*
2. *I am launching my coaching business, gig called life, for abundant profit, so the hungry philanthropist in me can feast and feed others.*
3. *I am eating healthy, local, organic food, hydrating wildly, sleeping sufficiently, and lovingly moving my body, daily. I am surrendering, daily.*
4. *I am meditating, praying, and connecting to Source, daily.*
5. *I am spending time in plank pose, strengthening my yogic core, daily.*
6. *I am recovering from alcoholism and working a program of recovery, daily.*
7. *I am learning something new, daily. As a graduate level student who is a lifelong student of life, this whets my appetite for the mystery of life.*
8. *I am living with my in-laws, which requires daily courage and recognizing and atoning some unworthy patterns of thought and conduct in myself. It pulls my best self forth.*

9. *I am living with my family so that we can share resources, share challenges, share joys and be a powerful presence of light in the world. My husband and I intend to share profit from gig called life coaching with watershed alliance and public libraries; our aim is to participate in upriver cleanup (literally & figuratively) and advancement of knowledge.*

10. *I am committing to the heart in all of the above activities and much more. I paddle regularly on the Pacific. I wake pre-dawn, I wrestle with Resistance, and I show up. I help others and they help me. This is the way my life works best. I got married, despite thinking I would stay single. I had children, despite not knowing how to parent. We hosted a foreign exchange student from a vastly different country and culture than ours. We stayed married, despite all the questioning.*

11. *I am taking a principled stand in the face of adversity presently by speaking clearly on the side of unconditional love. I believe that shame, blame and criticism of ourselves or others is not going to ultimately get us where we want to go. And this unconditional love is vast, deep, and impenetrable. This stand includes taking a stand for the men of our society who are taking their own lives at an alarming rate. I take a stand to squelch the epidemic of blame, which is often the shadowy side of empowerment, and get to deeper causes and conditions, to stand as source for a transformed world.*

I know each of these acts which Pressfield lists in his book, acts of taking the higher road over staying in my comfort zone, firsthand. Resistance pushes me forth, grooms me to be greater, and cannot dim my light. I write this in real time as I'm making my manuscript print worthy, so the publisher will pass my content evaluation. I get to let go of so much reliance on shame, blame or criticism at an even deeper level. I get to face the resistance inherent in publishing a memoir, say, oh, what the f*ck, and go for it anyway.

Appendix II

Daily Tender Job Description by Amy Elizabeth Gordon MA

Daily Tender is a simple position of ultimate and radical self-care. Here's a quick list of the duties, responsibilities and privileges of this enlightened role.

- Smile upon awakening.
- Give thanks for this moment.
- Stretch and massage. Make love, alone or with beloved.
- Make the bed.
- Relieve self of what is no longer needed by tapping into Source.
- Brush teeth.
- Dry skin brush and cold shower -- most mornings.
- Practice Yoga, daily.
- Breathe, consciously, while the hot water in the tea kettle boils.
- Meditate.
- Consume yummy food and lots of love and hugs.
- Tidy the kitchen.
- Chore day Sunday.
- Assemble hydration station every morning for tea, coffee, water.
- Water garden (literally and figuratively).
- Express thanks. Often.
- Chant. Buddhist prayers, yoga prayers, Hawai'i prayers.
- Sweep the floor, removing the dust of yesterday.

- Exercise outdoors.
- Exhibit discipline around tech. Adopt fairly strict media diet.
- Write, create, make a mess.
- Switch from the mentality of performance driven living of Do, Be, Have, to a new emphasis on ways of being with: Be, Do, Have.
- Keep appointments with people. Be timely.
- Coach and be coached.
- Invest in wellbeing.
- Cherish time with family.
- Stop when triggered, drop what I'm doing, and breathe.
- Deeply breathe.
- Clean up my side of the street and set right wrongs I've made.
- Allow space for grace to enter in a way that is indeed miraculous.
- Express thanks. Yes, again.
- Read inspiring words.
- Play. Dance. Laugh: pepper these throughout the day.
- Connect with friends on Wednesday, We-day, if not more often.
- Surrender to what is.

Appendix III

'ōlelo Hawai'i—The Hawaiian Language

Proverbs or sayings in *'ōlelo Hawai'i* are rich with multiple meanings. Aloha has multiple meanings. I'm only in the beginning stages of my comprehension of all that is, I have a beginner's mind in learning the language. And the more I know, the more mysterious it all gets.

The language of my soul is poetic and lyrical, expressed in dreams and moments of clarity. Flowery and expressive, the language of Hawai'i is fascinating, poetic and lyrical, it speaks to my soul. When I show up at sunrise for paddling the six-person outrigger canoe I share, we greet one another with *Aloha Kakahiaka Kākou*, Good morning to us all, my fellow paddlers, the sunrise, the waves, the creatures seen and unseen, above and below.

The word "Hawaiian" is a term from missionary times. The correct term is *'ōlelo Hawai'i*, "The language of Hawai'i." In the Hawaiian language, there are only twelve letters in the alphabet; the five vowels and *h, k,l,m,n,,p,w*. The vowels are pronounced as they would be in Spanish: *a* as in water, *e* in they, *i* in blink, *o* in float, and *u* in cruise or hula. Oftentimes the *w* is softened to a *v* sound. The *kahakō*, or macron over a letter (*ā*) gives it a longer stress. The *'okina*, or glottal stop, indicates a stopping sound where the voice pauses between letters, as in the English "uh-oh." Syllables always end with a vowel. Go ahead, pronounce!

A dictionary opens up opportunities to break Hawaiian words into smaller words, diacrons, and to consider multiple definitions. I enjoy this process. It keeps things fresh. An example: A-Bay is what I have called the spot where I have been practicing yoga on the beach for over three years. Now I can easily pronounce it, *Anaeho'omalu* Bay (peaceful shelter for the mullet fish). I love saying it, it dances off my tongue. Each vowel is pronounced. A(short a)-ny(like by)-ho(like go)-o-ma(like your mama)-lu(loo).

I invite you to look up the definitions and meanings of the italicized words in the text. Break up the words into little chunks, explore what definitions emerge for. I've been blown away by learning what I can of this beautiful, poetic language of *'ōlelo Hawai'i*.

There is no specific Hawaiian word for "nature." My guess is that people steeped in something don't need to identify it as separate from them. There are names for each wind, each hill, each crater. Each place has recognition. And check this out—Four words for "we." To me this reflects the value of the collective.

Kāua, We: you and me

Māua, We: me and someone else

Kākou, We: you and me and someone else

Mākou, We: me and other peoples, but not you.

Appendix IV

The Don'ts & Dos of Evolution by Bruce Lipton

I have long wanted to change the world and depleted some of my life energy fighting for good causes. Everything is energy. Some people I want to be around, others, not so much. Learning from Bruce Lipton helped me recalibrate my efforts and I hope they can help you, too.

Quotes from this brilliant man:
Because You Are an Energy Field…

1. Don't try to change other people; if you go in to change negative energy with your positive energy, it's called *destructive interference.*

   Do: Focus on yourself and finding like-minded people to create a community in which all your energies are enhanced.

2. Don't try to change the system; if you charge in with your wonderful energy to try to change it, your energy will be canceled.

   Do: Put your energy into constructing a new system; if you build a better system, people in the old one will gravitate to the new one.

3. Don't spend your life protesting.

    Do: Find out who's protesting with you; that's *constructive interference*, when energies come together and multiply each other.

4. Don't become frightened or angry or burned out.

    Do: Create the best and healthiest and happiest experience for yourself—and share it with the community.

Bruce H. Lipton PhD, cell biologist and lecturer, is an internationally recognized leader in bridging science and spirit. He was on the faculty of the University of Wisconsin's School of Medicine and later performed groundbreaking stem cell research at Stanford Medical School. His pioneering research on cloned human stem cells presaged today's revolutionary new field of Epigenetics. He received the prestigious Goi Peace Award (Japan) in 2009 in honor of his scientific contribution to world harmony. He is the best-selling author of *The Biology of Belief* and *The Honeymoon Effect*, and is the coauthor with Steve Bhaerman of Spontaneous Evolution. www.brucelipton.com

Appendix V

Practices to Cultivate C.O.R.E. Compassion by Amy Elizabeth Gordon MA

Clear your Mind

- make the bed
- meditate daily
- memorize a mantra

Open your Heart

- smile upon awakening
- move the body
- adopt an attitude of gratitude

Reactivate your Spirit

- breathe deeply
- create something now
- spend time outdoors

Energize your Life

- receive what comes
- let go of what goes
- don't chase after anything...

Appendix VI

Invitation to Enter Portals of Deep Connection

Using Imago Intentional Dialogue is a portal to healing the planet. This is upriver cleanup. It teaches us to talk without judgement and listen without interruption, not planning what you want to say, or questioning what is said. Learning the art of dialogue has granted me a skill of immense value. I can promote safety in the space between. I can allow your reality to be your reality, without attempting to alter it.

The intentional dialogue uses the skill of deep listening, basically emptying yourself of yourself to fully receive what the sender is sending. You, when you are in the role of the receiver, are crossing the bridge to the island of the sender. This is a precious gift to receive.

As the sender, you welcome the receiver to your world. You respectfully send digestible chunks of information that you wish to convey. You gain more clarity into the neighborhoods of your own mind through this process.

The receiver reflects what sender shares, we call it mirroring. The receiver asks, "Am I getting you? Is there more? This is like pulling nectar out of a flower, the sweet sustenance of communication. This is in stark contrast to the gruff "Are you done?" "Don't interrupt me," "You don't know what you're talking about," "Are you outta your mind?" kind of interactions that lead to the chronic negativity of dissatisfying relations.

If the receiver misses something, the sender shares, "you got most of it, what I really want you to hear is..." which magically keeps the bridge stable, safe and intact.

Imagine for a moment if the sender shared, "No, you didn't get me at all, you never get me, why can't you listen to me..."

this is the toxic spill into the space between that pollutes the environment of the planet.

Unhealthy relationships contribute to most of the afflictions that our society faces. Domestic abuse, crime, addictions, heart disease...not to mention the effect on the children. Children with school issues, both behavioral and comprehensive, stem from consequences and concerns from bad relations at home. Teen pregnancy, crime, addictions...so many issues of our society have a taproot in toxic soil of the home front. Throwing money at downriver cleanup is trying to treat the symptoms of a dis-ease that reaches farther back.

Children who have parents who communicate lovingly are basically growing up in good soil. We need good soil to grow healthy things, agreed? Let us focus not so much on the crop, "I want to grow a star student who wins football scholarship and becomes a successful lawyer," rather let us focus on the soil, the nutritive goodness that promotes the wellbeing of the child and allows space for grace to enter and inform and delight the wonder of the child's mind and feed the child's soul.

Imagine a healthy field, water it daily. Detox the space of harsh additives. Don't use the big guns of toxic weed killers sprayed on random weekends to deal with problems. Lovingly tend to the garden daily, at least four times a day. These four transitions in an average day are way more powerful than the weekend warrior approach to relationships.

How you greet each other in the morning, upon departure for the day, returning from the day's activities, and returning to slumber? Plant good seeds of intention. Water the seeds of compassion, honestly, self-care, and love. Fertilize with love infusions, intentional dialogue, and sleep hygiene. Cultivate that which you want to grow and pull out the weeds of negativity. Feast and feed others from this harvest of love.

Imago intentional dialogue tends to that space between, the relationship, the relational field in a way that promotes healthy connection, and eliminates shame, blame and criticism.

From here, I believe all things are possible. Build a culture of appreciation at home and in your intimate relations and watch the ripple effect into our wonderful world.

M.O.V.E. Dialogue

Sit together, knees touching, facing each other, and share a timed dialogue with each other. Decide who will go first by who has the next birthday. That person gets to decide on the role of sender or receiver. Take turns being the sender and the receiver. Use the M.O.V.E. acronym to help you track the steps of the dialogue. Mirror, Over and Over, Validate, Empathize. Practice. Practice. Practice. This is building safety and containment in your relationship. It works!

M.O.V.E. These are the prompts for the Receiver to use in the dialogue.

Mirror

"Let me see if I'm getting you, what I hear you saying is..."
"Am I getting you?"

Over and Over

"Is there more?"

Validate

"You make sense to me, given what I know about you and what makes sense is..."

Empathize

"I imagine you might be feeling..."

"Is this how you are feeling?"
"Are there any other feelings you might be having?"

Use these sentences stems when you are the Sender throughout the dialogue.

As I'm sitting here I'm experiencing...
(identify feelings, thoughts, body sensations)
Where I'd like to be at the end of the day is....
(clearly identify wishes)
One thing I can do to get me there is...
(clearly take ownership for your life)
One thing I appreciate about you is...
(build a culture of appreciation)

Writing Prompts

Couples, do this Annual review, details to follow, either at the start of the calendar year or on your anniversary. Siblings, do this with each other. Anyone you are in intimate relationship with, take stock. Take inventory of what's working and what you can improve upon, in a gentle atmosphere of curiosity and guidance. No shame, No blame. No criticism. Ask where you are on a scale of 0-10 and inquire what you can do to get your relationship to a 10, today!

Share with each other. This is a powerful indicator of whether you are hitting the mark of your extraordinary life. Think of it as your North Star, or better yet, your *Hokule'a*, the star of gladness. This is the star the celestial navigators used to find Hawai'i in the middle of the vast Pacific. The vast unconscious holds our sovereign realities. Find it. Be the source of a transformed world.

Annual Review

How did I add to your life in this last year?
How would you like me to add to your life in the next year?

What helped you to feel loved and safe in this last year?
What would help you to feel loved and safe in the next year?

What precious memories do you have this last year?
What precious memories would you like to create in the next year?

How did you see me grow this last year?
In what ways would you like me to grow in the next year?

What did you learn from me in this last year?
What would you like us to learn in the next year?

Recommendations: Books and Influencers

Alicia Muñoz, *No More Fighting: 20 Minutes a Week to a Stronger Relationship*

Tommy Rosen, *Recovery 2.0*

Kristen Noel, B*est Self Magazine*

Mark Hyman, *Broken Brain Series, Ted Talks*

Snatam Kaur, *Kundalini Yoga University*

Harville Hendrix and Helen Lakely Hunt, *Getting the Love You Want*

John O'Donohue, *To Bless the Space Between Us*

Adriene, *Yoga with Adriene, YouTube*

Barbara Marx Hubbard, *a social pioneer*

Ash Ghandahari, *HeartCore Leadership training*

Shanda Sumpter, *HeartCore Business*

Michael Strasner, *Mastering Leadership, and all the coaches in this heart-centered work. Michael respectfully gave me permission to use his idea of "distinctions."*

Joanna Macy, *The Work that Reconnects, who told me many years ago in an Active Hope community workshop, "The book will write itself."*

Brene Brown, *The Gifts of Imperfection, who gives me chills every time I hear her speak, even when I first met her a decade ago and asked her what platform she suggested for my blog, she said Wordpress or SquareSpace, I listened. To practical instruction and divine inspiration.*

Kekuhi Keali'ikanaka'oleohaililani, *Trainer, Hālau 'Ōhi'a, my kumu who changed my life in more ways than I can mention.*

Dr. Christiane Northrup, *The Wisdom of Menopause, who changed how I see my body, live in my body and care for my body.*

Kate Northrup & Mike Watts, *who showed my husband and I how beautiful it is to work together as a couple.*

Barbara Montgomery Dossey, RN, PhD, FAAN, *Florence Nightingale: Mystic, Visionary, Healer; Holistic Nursing: A Handbook for Practice; Nurse Coaching, Integrative Approaches for Health and Wellbeing.*

Larry Dossey, MD, *One Mind: How Our Individual Mind Is Part of a Greater Consciousness and Why It Matters.*

Bruce Lipton, *The Biology of Belief*

David R. Hawkins, M.D., *Power vs. Force*

Rick Hanson, PhD, *Just One Thing*

Dan Siegel, MD, *Mindsight*

Many neuroscientists and Buddhist practitioners have helped me to understand my mind better, therefore it is not such a scary neighborhood to dwell.

Thank you to the speakers I have had on my two online shows, *Power in Partnership* and *A League of Extraordinary Couples.*

Tame Iti, *of the Tūhoe Iwi in Aotearoa. He reminds that I am more than a recovering alcoholic; I don't need to hit my head against the wall to protest wrongdoing. Art saves lives.*

Michelle Obama, *Becoming. I will borrow a few of your closing lines in their entirety, "I'm an ordinary person who found herself on an extraordinary journey. In sharing my story, I hope to help create space for other stories and other voices, to widen the pathway for who belongs and why. There's power in allowing yourself to be known and heard, in owning your unique story, in using your authentic voice."*

About the Author

Cutting through chaos of dominant culture, opening minds riddled with lack, rekindling souls starving for connection, Amy Elizabeth is a master facilitator, **social pioneer,** and conscious evolutionary leader.

A lifelong student, Amy Elizabeth is continually learning both personally and professionally. She has spent several decades advocating for big compassion, healthy relationships, and holistic wellbeing. Her professional training includes M.A. in Contemplative Psychotherapy from Naropa University, Nationally Certified Addictions Counselor, Certified Imago International Relationship Therapist, and HeartCore Leadership Training.

A dedicated woman of integrity, Amy Elizabeth sees her roles as wife, mother, daughter, relational health coach, compassion activist, yogini, paddler, hula dancer, and fellow human being as an ever-expanding opportunity to heal the planet, one relationship at a time. This is her first published book. More information at www.amyelizabethgordon.com or email her at authoramye@gmail.com

In addition, Amy Elizabeth is a resident of Hawai'i and a founding member of Hālau 'Ōhi'a Hawai'i Stewardship Training. Bridging indigenous lifeways and modern technology in a fruitful foundation for the future, Hālau 'Ōhi'a focuses on **establishing and deepening familial relationships to the world around us, and** aims to enhance the ways we engage with our *'āina* (landscape) community and *kanaka* (human) community.